Zombie Sc
Survival Guide

Zombie Scrum Survival Guide

A Journey to Recovery

Christiaan Verwijs
Johannes Schartau
Barry Overeem

Addison-Wesley

Boston • Columbus • New York • San Francisco • Amsterdam • Cape Town
Dubai • London • Madrid • Milan • Munich • Paris • Montreal • Toronto • Delhi • Mexico City
São Paulo • Sydney • Hong Kong • Seoul • Singapore • Taipei • Tokyo

For information about buying this title in bulk quantities, or for special sales opportunities (which may include electronic versions; custom cover designs; and content particular to your business, training goals, marketing focus, or branding interests), please contact our corporate sales department at corpsales@pearsoned.com or (800) 382-3419.

For government sales inquiries, please contact governmentsales@pearsoned.com.

For questions about sales outside the U.S., please contact intlcs@pearson.com.

Visit us on the Web: informit.com/aw

Library of Congress Control Number: 2020944524

Cover and interior illustrations by Thea Schukken

ISBN-13: 978-0-13-652326-0
ISBN-10: 0-13-652326-9

Zombie Scrum Survival Guide is dedicated to all the nameless victims and unsung heroes in the ongoing struggle against Zombie Scrum. We are here to support you.

Contents

Foreword by Dave West

Scrum is cited by analysts and the press as the most widely used agile framework, with potentially millions of people applying it every day. To prove its impact, just wear a T-shirt with *Scrum* written on it and walk through an airport. People will stop you and ask you questions about Scrum and if you can help them do *x* or *y*. But there are many people using Scrum and not getting the most out of it. They are, as Christiaan, Johannes, and Barry describe, acting like zombies, mindlessly using the Scrum artifacts, events, and roles but not really getting the benefits from it.

But there is hope! The Zombie Scrum infection can be cured, with focus and perseverance. Christiaan, Johannes, and Barry have written this excellent *survival guide* to help teams and organizations improve their use of Scrum to achieve better results. It is a perfect complement to the other titles in The Professional Scrum Series, all of which focus on helping to improve the ability of Scrum Teams to deliver value in a complex and sometimes chaotic world.

Professional Scrum, the antithesis of Zombie Scrum, consists of two elements. First is Scrum, which is of course the framework as described in the Scrum Guide, but also the foundations that framework is based upon. Those foundations are empirical process; empowered, self-managed teams; and a focus on continuous improvement. Surrounding the framework and its ideas are four additional elements:

- **Discipline.** To be effective with Scrum requires discipline. You have to deliver to gain learning; you have to do the mechanics of Scrum; you have to challenge your preconceived ideas about your skills, role, and understanding of the problem; and you have to work in a transparent and structured way. Discipline is hard and may at times seem unfair as your work exposes problem after problem and your efforts seem in vain.
- **Behaviors.** The Scrum values were introduced to the Scrum Guide in 2016 in response to the need for a supporting culture for Scrum to be successful. The Scrum values describe five simple ideas that when practiced encourage an agile culture. Courage, focus, commitment, respect, and openness describe behaviors that both Scrum Teams and the organizations they work within should exhibit.
- **Value.** Scrum Teams work on problems that deliver value to stakeholders when they are solved. Teams work for a customer who rewards them for that work. But the relationship is complex because the problems are complex; the customer might not know what they want, or the economics of the solution might also be unclear, or the quality and safety of the solution may also be unknown. The job of a professional Scrum Team is, to the best of their ability, to do the right thing for all these parties by delivering a solution that best meets their customers' needs within the constraints that have been placed on them. That requires transparency, respect for each other and for customers, and a healthy curiosity to uncover the truth.
- **Active Community Membership.** Scrum is a team sport where the team is small. That means that the team is often the underdog trying to solve problems that it barely has the skills and experience to solve. To be effective professional Scrum Teams must work with other members of their community to learn new skills and share experiences. Helping to scale the agility of the community is not completely altruistic, because the helper often learns valuable things that they can bring back to help their own team. Professional Scrum encourages people to form professional networks in which ideas and experiences that help teams can be exchanged.

Professional Scrum and Zombie Scrum are two mortal enemies in eternal locked combat. If you relax your guard for a moment, Zombie Scrum comes back. In this book Christiaan, Johannes, and Barry describe a guide for how to stay on your guard, providing practical tips for both identifying when you have become a zombie and how to stop this happening. Their humorous and very visual material is a must-have for any Zombie Scrum hunter.

Good luck in fighting Zombie Scrum!

—Dave West
CEO, Scrum.org

Foreword by Henri Lipmanowicz

Scrum is an excellent framework, but—there's always a *but*, isn't there?!—its users and practitioners are, like everyone, imperfect, diverse, and unpredictable. They will show up as they are, quiet or talkative, hesitant or interrupting, reckless or cautious, linear or creative, bossy or timid. And all, Scrum Masters included, bring reflexive habits of what they do routinely while working in a group. In other words, all the people ingredients that can make ordinary meetings dysfunctional are present in Scrum Events. This is why Scrum practitioners must be prepared to fortify the framework with suitable techniques to ensure that every event delivers its full potential, regardless of the personalities in the room. In short, every Scrum Event must be facilitated well enough to be productive, engaging, rewarding, and enjoyable.

Liberating Structures are ideal fortifiers of Scrum because they perfectly complement it. First, they are easy to use, flexible, efficient, and effective. Second and most important, Liberating Structures ensure that every participant is actively engaged and contributes. This makes the Scrum Events both productive and rewarding for all.

As Scrum Teams learn how to use a few Liberating Structures, they acquire tools that are universally and routinely useful in all manner of situations at work or outside work. For example, a simple "1-2-4-All" or "Impromptu Networking" can engage groups in deeper thinking during a Sprint Review, Sprint Planning, or Sprint Retrospective. "Min Specs" or "Ecocycle Planning" can help Product Owners work with stakeholders to order the Product Backlog. And structures like "Conversation Cafe," "Troika Consulting," and "Wise Crowds" can be used to navigate complex challenges and concerns and build trust. Throughout this book, you'll notice many examples of how Scrum Teams can use Liberating Structures to overcome Zombie Scrum.

Barry, Christiaan, and Johannes have done a magnificent job of accumulating successful experiences and sharing their inspiring stories in this very practical book. They don't shy away from telling it like it is, which is why their proposals are always useful, as they are grounded in reality.

—Henri Lipmanowicz
Cofounder, Liberating Structures

Acknowledgments

Although this book has only three authors listed on the title page, it was made possible by a significantly larger group. We want to start by thanking Dave West, Kurt Bittner, and Sabrina Love from Scrum.org for their support, encouragement, and trust in this book about Zombie Scrum. Kurt Bittner, in particular, deserves a deep bow for his repeated reviews of our initially long-winded chapters. Like a Product Owner, he helped us focus on what mattered most and say “no” (even when it hurt) to the rest.

We also want to thank the team from Pearson, Haze Humbert, Tracy Brown, Sheri Replin, Menka Mehta, Christopher Keane, Vaishnavi Venkatesan, and Julie Nahil, for their time and effort. And for the trust they put in us when we suggested writing, reviewing, and editing the book in a more incremental fashion than what is customary in the publishing world. Another group that deserves a deep bow are the Scrum Masters who reviewed this book and supported us with their thorough feedback: Ton Sweep, Thomas Vitzky, Saskia Vermeer-Ooms, Tom Suter, Christian Hofstetter, Chris Davies, Graeme Robinson, Tábata P. Renteria, Sjors de Valk, Carsten Grønbjerg Lützen, Yury Zaryaninov, and Simon Flossman. This book is much, much better because of you.

One person who made this book come alive in particular is Thea Schukken. She created all the beautiful, clever, and funny illustrations in this book and adds a much-needed visual perspective. And then there are all the reviewers in the community who helped us with their feedback and suggestions when we posted tidbits of it on our blogs.

Our work and thinking stand on the shoulders of giants. First of all, there are Ken Schwaber and Jeff Sutherland, the creators of the Scrum Framework. Their work changed our lives and those of many others. The same goes for Keith McCandless and Henri Lipmanowicz, who collected and invented Liberating Structures as a way to unleash and include everyone in groups of any size. Others who shaped and guided our work are Gunther Verheyen, Gareth Morgan, Thomas Friedman, and many Professional Scrum Trainers and stewards of Scrum.org.

Other shoulders we've stood on are those of our partners, Gerdien, Fiona, and Lisanne, as well as our families. They supported us throughout as we had to withdraw yet another evening into our home offices to write this book.

But the most important acknowledgment is to all the Scrum Masters, Product Owners, and Development Teams out there who are working hard to deliver value to their stakeholders—in particular those who are carrying on despite severe Zombie Scrum. We are indebted to your persistence. This book is here for you.

Register your copy of the *Zombie Scrum Survival Guide* on the InformIT website for convenient access to updates and corrections as they become available. To start the registration process, go to informit.com/register and log in or create an account. Enter the product ISBN (9780136523260) and click Submit. Look on the Registered Products tab for an Access Bonus Content link next to this product, and follow that link to access any available bonus materials. If you would like to be notified of exclusive offers on new editions and updates, please check the box to receive email from us.

About the Authors

Christiaan Verwijs is one of the two founders of The Liberators, together with Barry Overeem. The mission of The Liberators is to unleash organizational superpowers with Scrum and Liberating Structures. Somewhere in a dusty drawer, he has degrees in organizational psychology and business information technology. He has over twenty years of experience as a developer, Scrum Master, and trainer and steward for Scrum.org, in both small and large organizations. In those years he has seen his share of severe Zombie Scrum, as well as how many of those teams found the road to recovery. Christiaan loves to write (posts and code), read, and play games. There's also a weird fascination with LEGO and squeezing as much of it as possible into his home office. You can follow his writing online at medium.com/the-liberators.

Johannes Schartau is a consultant, trainer, and coach for agile product development and organizational improvement. His interests in ethnology (with a focus on Amazonian shamanism), psychology, technology, integral thinking, complexity science, and stand-up comedy finally coalesced when he was introduced to Scrum in 2010. Since then he has dedicated himself to exploring organizations from all possible angles together with the people working in them. His mission is to bring life and meaning back to the workplace by spreading Healthy Agile and Liberating Structures around the world. Aside from his work, he is passionate about cast iron (both in the gym and the kitchen), mixed martial arts, and humor. Being a proud husband and the father of two wicked boys gives his life meaning and beauty.

Barry Overeem is the other founder of The Liberators. In line with the mission of The Liberators, Barry liberates organizations from outdated modes of working and learning, using Scrum and Liberating Structures as sources of inspiration. Although becoming a journalist and teacher was his original plan, he ended up with a degree in business administration. He spent the first half of his twenty-plus-year professional journey being an application manager and IT project manager. In 2010, working in software development environments, he started his first experiments with Scrum. In the past ten years, Barry has worked with a wide variety of teams and organizations. Some got stuck with Zombie Scrum; others managed to recover. In 2015, he joined Scrum.org as a trainer and, together with Christiaan, created the Professional Scrum Master II class. When not fighting Zombie Scrum, he enjoys reading and writing, walking long distances, and spending time with his kids, Melandri, Guinessa, and Fayenne.

About the Illustrator

Thea Schukken is the founder of the company Beeld in Werking. As a visual facilitator, she transforms complex information into simple and attractive illustrations, animations, and infographics. She combines her drawing skills with more than twenty-five years of experience in IT and management. For this book, Thea translated our story into simple, powerful visuals that underscore our message of how to recognize and recover from Zombie Scrum.

Thea Schukken, the founder of Beeld in Werking, created over fifty illustrations for *Zombie Scrum Survival Guide*.

1 Getting Started

There's us and the dead. We survive this by pulling together, not apart.

—Rick Grimes, AMC's *The Walking Dead*

In This Chapter

- Start recognizing that something may be off with how Scrum is used in your team.
- Explore the purpose of this book.
- Discover for whom this book is perfectly suited.

Congratulations on joining the Zombie Scrum Resistance! Your membership comes with all kinds of perks and benefits. In your hands, you are holding the *Zombie Scrum Survival Guide*. All new members get one. This guide contains our collective experiences. It will equip you with everything needed in your ongoing struggle against Zombie Scrum.

You may have picked up this book because something feels off with how your team or organization is working with Scrum. Or you casually walked into the office this morning and noticed a number of zombies staring at you (Figure 1.1). Whatever the case, we expect you to be reading this guide while trapped in a challenging situation. Maybe you are hiding out in the broom closet, beneath a pile of Sprint Goal templates, or behind a flip chart with the results of last month's Retrospective. Although no one will find you there for a while, we still know that time is of the essence for you. So let us not mince words and get right into it.

Figure 1.1 Just another day at the office?

Do You Recognize This?

You've been working as the Scrum Master for team Power Rangers for a year now. When you started with Scrum, all seemed well. You liked the idea of building small, incremental versions of your product. The team seemed to like it too. It made sense.

But somewhere along the way, something went wrong, although you're unsure where. What you are sure of is that this isn't working. Just consider how the events in Scrum are going, for example. Daily Scrums always take too long, with people going on and on about that one thing they've been working on. And because everyone's working on their own things anyway, nobody pays attention. The Sprint Retrospective that promised "continuous improvement" results in the same minor improvements that never really get addressed every single time (like "fix the router," "better coffee," and "I don't like Timmy").

Initially this surprised you—you expected people to get the hang of the format that the team always uses. But now you've just accepted that nothing really comes out of this time spent in a boring, smelly meeting room. Except for stickies with words on them that inevitably end up in your drawer as a reminder to do something with it in the future.

And let's not get started about the Sprint Review. That awkward moment at the end of a Sprint where the message is basically that "We're almost done." But with only the Development Team—and sometimes the Product Owner—attending, it doesn't really matter anyway. There's always another Sprint to finish the work. Even the Product Owner stopped caring.

Welcome to the world of "Zombie Scrum," a heartbreaking condition where people are simply going through the motions, imitating real Scrum, but without being alive or engaged. Over time, you've learned to accept that this is apparently what Scrum is for this organization. And if nobody cares about it, why should you? But still, you have this nagging feeling that things can be better. Then you found this book.

How Bad Is It, Really?

We are continuously monitoring the spread and prevalence of Zombie Scrum with our online Symptoms Checker at **survey.zombiescrum.org**. Of the Scrum Teams that have participated at the time of writing:*

- 77% don't actively collaborate with customers or have a clear vision of what they need.
- 69% don't work in an environment where they can self-organize around shared goals.
- 67% don't manage to deliver working and high-quality software every Sprint.
- 62% don't work in an environment where they can improve over time.
- 42% feel that Scrum isn't very effective for them.

* The percentages represent teams that scored a 6 or lower on a 10-point scale. Each topic was measured with 10 to 30 questions. The results represent 1,764 teams that participated in the self-reported survey at **survey.zombiescrum.org** between June 2019 and May 2020.

Purpose of This Book

There are many excellent books on Scrum out there that you should definitely read. What makes this a book worth reading? In our work with Scrum Teams, we noticed a strong pattern: most begin with great enthusiasm, only to find themselves stuck in complacency, merely going through the motions after a while. Curiously, few people in the community seemed to talk about this or were willing to admit openly that it wasn't working for them. So we decided to test our assumptions, capture some zombies (see Figure 1.2), and gather data. Was it just us or was this actually a widespread phenomenon? It turned out the problem was worse than we thought.

Figure 1.2 Thankfully, capturing zombies to talk to wasn't hard.

The *Zombie Scrum Survival Guide* is a book about practical strategies to start recovering from Zombie Scrum. While writing this book, we kept three principles in mind:

- We don't assume that management is supportive, that all team members are enthusiastic about the change, nor that the entire organization is involved. Instead, we work from a position where, according to our research, most Scrum Teams find themselves: stuck in an environment where it is difficult to make even minor changes.

- We want to help you understand why Zombie Scrum is happening on a fundamental level while also equipping you with practical tools to start improving.
- We want to help you build communities of people, both within and outside your organization, to start resolving the hard challenges that you face.

DO YOU NEED THIS BOOK?

This book is for everyone who works with Scrum and feels that it just isn't working. You may be part of a Scrum Team yourself or work very closely with them. It may not even be called "Scrum" where you work, even though it has all the characteristics.

Perhaps you can easily point out what isn't working. Or something just feels off and Scrum is not doing what you hoped it would do. It doesn't matter if you are a Scrum Master, Product Owner, a member of a Development Team, an Agile Coach, or someone in a management position.

Wherever you are and whatever you do, this book is for you if you recognize at least one thing from the checklist shown in Table 1.1 in the Scrum Team(s) you work with.

Table 1.1 Checklist for Diagnosing Zombie Scrum

Do You Recognize the Following?	Yup!
At the end of the Sprint, there is no working product to inspect together.	
Sprint Retrospectives tend to be boring and repetitive.	
People in your team mostly work on their own items during a Sprint.	
The Product Owner has little to no say over what goes on the Product Backlog and in what order.	
The Sprint Review is rarely attended by the stakeholders of your product.	

Do You Recognize the Following?	Yup!
When a Sprint did not go well, nobody in the team feels bad about it.	
In your organization, "business" and "IT" are considered separate things.	
There is no fun and excitement in your Scrum Teams.	
The Daily Scrum is merely a status update with the Scrum Master as the chairperson.	
The most important item from the recent Sprint Retrospective was to get better coffee for the cafeteria.	
Management focuses entirely on how much work Scrum Teams can do.	

Check Your Scrum Team

Zombie Scrum can be hard to spot, which makes it all the more devious. Diagnose your team for free with our Zombie Scrum Symptoms Checker at **survey.zombiescrum.org**.

How This Book Is Organized

You probably don't have time to read this book in one go if you find yourself surrounded by hungry zombies. You need to act now! So the next chapter is a **First Aid Kit**. It will help you get moving as quickly as possible to get out of harm's way.

When you've overcome the initial shock, it's time to delve deeper into this book and find helpful strategies to recover. With so much to say and so many experiments to offer, we organized this book into five parts. Each part focuses on one area where Zombie Scrum can manifest. You can skip straight to what matters most and visit other parts later:

- **Part I: (Zombie) Scrum.** We set the stage by exploring what Zombie Scrum looks like. What are the symptoms and causes? And how is it spreading? We will then help you understand the underlying purpose of the Scrum

Framework, and how it is all about navigating complex problems and reducing risk.

- **Part II: Build What Stakeholders Need.** Scrum Teams exist to deliver value to stakeholders. But teams that suffer from Zombie Scrum are so distant from stakeholders, and so unaware of their needs, that they have no idea what value means.
- **Part III: Ship It Fast.** Shipping fast allows Scrum Teams to learn what their stakeholders need and reduce the risks of building the wrong things. In organizations with Zombie Scrum, this is so challenging that teams are effectively unable to learn.
- **Part IV: Improve Continuously.** Many tough impediments will emerge when Scrum Teams try to build what customers need and start shipping faster. But that only works if those impediments are resolved, even when it is done one step at a time. This rarely happens in Zombie Scrum and teams remain stuck where they started.
- **Part V: Self-Organize.** When Scrum Teams have autonomy and control over how to do their work, it makes it much easier for them to improve continuously and overcome all those tough impediments that get in their way. Unfortunately, organizations with Zombie Scrum limit the ability of teams to self-manage to such an extent that everyone effectively remains stuck.

Each part follows a similar structure. We start with a case taken from our personal experience. You may recognize some or all of it. This may be a painful realization, but we want to prepare you for the worst.

After the case, we present the results of our research. We describe the most common symptoms of Zombie Scrum for the part that you are reading. Based on our research, you learn how to reliably identify Zombie Scrum in this area and understand what may be causing it. This is important because it helps you understand how Zombie Scrum manifests itself and makes it easier to explain what is happening and get others to join our mission.

After presenting our research on symptoms and causes, we offer a variety of experiments that you can try immediately to start recovering. All experiments are based on direct, real-life experience. Some are simple and straightforward. Others require more effort and energy. But results are guaranteed for all of them. While it is unlikely that this cures Zombie Scrum right away, these experiments will improve the situation you are in. Most experiments can be easily modified for virtual use with remote teams; others will require more creativity. See **zombiescrum.org** for more information and more experiments.

Our last chapter helps you get started on **The Road to Recovery**. No matter how bad things are, there is always hope. Every infection of Zombie Scrum can be treated and cured.

No Time to Lose: Off You Go!

We're in this nightmare together, and the time to do something about it was many years ago. We are losing people to Zombie Scrum faster than we are recruiting them to join the Zombie Scrum Resistance (Figure 1.3).

Figure 1.3 Join the Zombie Scrum Resistance.

This Survival Guide equips you with a host of valuable experiments to use in your fight against Zombie Scrum. We won't waste time explaining all the details of how Zombie Scrum has spread across the globe. Instead, we want you to be ready for the fight against it and make a difference within your team immediately.

> *"Always remember, recruit: Your mind is your sharpest weapon! It gets even better when you enlist the help and support of others. The Zombie Scrum Resistance is there for you. You are not alone in this struggle!"*

2 First Aid Kit

Alive or dead, the truth won't rest. Rise up while you can.

—Mira Grant, *Feed*

Yes, this is happening. You've discovered Zombie Scrum in your team or organization. With this First Aid Kit, you can guide your initial response and start fighting Zombie Scrum.

Table 2.1 First Aid Kit for Fighting Zombie Scrum

	**1. Take Responsibility** You haven't caused this situation, but nothing will change unless people like you step up. Don't blame or hide behind others. Model responsible behavior and investigate how you may be, inadvertently, contributing to Zombie Scrum yourself.
	**2. Assess the Situation** Find out as much as you can about what is going on. What problems do you see? How do they manifest? Do you have data to back up what you're saying? Why should others care? If you can't answer these questions, you will fight alone.

3. Create Awareness

Make others—both inside and outside your team—aware of what is happening. They may not have realized it yet. Create urgency and show what is lost to your team and the organization because of the problems caused by Zombie Scrum.

4. Find Other Survivors

Once you have created awareness, you will find others in your organization who have started to see the problem too. Form groups and build networks to increase your reach and strengthen your ability to recover.

5. Start Small

Instead of immediately going for the "Big Ones," start with the small and incremental changes that you have control over. Recovering from Zombie Scrum is complex work, so use short feedback cycles to quickly adapt to the situation as it unfolds.

6. Stay Positive

Complaints, cynicism, and sarcasm don't help anyone. They may even contribute to teams sliding further into Zombie Scrum. Instead, highlight what is working well, where improvements are taking place, and what is possible when you work together. Use humor to lighten the mood, but not to sugarcoat the truth.

7. Celebrate

You won't recover from Zombie Scrum overnight. It may take a while before you start noticing improvements. This is perfectly okay. No matter how small they are, celebrate successes together when they happen, to offset the eventual setbacks you will also face.

8. Find Help

Look for help outside of your own organization. Join or start a regional Scrum Meetup. Reach out to Scrum Masters who inspire you. Or join workshops or classes with people who face similar challenges.

Download the rest of the Zombie Scrum First Aid Kit from **zombiescrum.org/firstaidkit.** It contains helpful materials for some of the experiments in this book, as well as other useful exercises. You can also order a physical copy there.

I

(Zombie) Scrum

3 A Primer on Zombie Scrum

Zombies can't believe the energy we waste on nonfood pursuits.

—Patton Oswalt,
Zombie Spaceship Wasteland

In This Chapter

- Understand the symptoms and causes of Zombie Scrum.
- Diagnose your team with our Zombie Scrum Checker.
- Sigh with relief to discover it's possible to recover from Zombie Scrum.

"All right, recruit: We trust you have gotten yourself into a more or less safe environment with the help of the First Aid Kit. Take a deep breath. The chance of you getting mauled by these zombies is now a bit less than 100%! That is some serious progress. We understand that you're itching to get back out there and find a cure. For now we need you to sit tight though! We need to make sure you will be able to spot Zombie Scrum infections within seconds. This knowledge can save lives. And kittens!"

An Experience from the Field

A couple of years ago we did work for a large financial institution. They had the seemingly perfect transformation plan to roll out fifty-plus Scrum Teams in one year. Every week, a couple of new Scrum Teams were launched. Everyone buzzed with excitement. "Scrum of Scrums" started. Big Room Planning sessions were organized. Release Trains were planned. At the end of the year, the transformation plan was completed, and it was time for a big party. The agile transformation was a success!

However, the only metrics they used to track "success" were how busy people were, such as the number of Story Points completed per Sprint and whether all the items from the Sprint Backlog were finished. Teams were actively compared on these metrics and encouraged to get more work done. Instead of going after larger organizational impediments, teams were asked to focus on what they could improve within their team. People felt misled, manipulated, and controlled. Although their metrics showed that they were very busy, everyone felt something was off. . . .

Two years after the agile transformation had kicked off, they started to explore different kinds of metrics in an effort to identify what was wrong. Instead of focusing on how much work was being done, they started tracking metrics that more directly measured agility. From tracking and comparing Story Points, they shifted to measuring the time that elapsed between the start of working on an item from the Product Backlog to its delivery (cycle time), how happy customers were with what was being delivered (customer satisfaction), how happy teams were (team morale), how much money was being returned from what was being invested in development, the quality of what was being delivered (e.g., total defects), and how much time teams spent on innovation (innovation rate).

When the first results came in, everyone was shocked. Their cycle time had increased, customer satisfaction had gone down, teams were unhappy, the return on investment was very low, the number of defects seemed to go through the roof, and as a result, there wasn't any time for innovation anymore.

What was going on? They had implemented everything they thought was part of the Scrum Framework. All the artifacts, roles, and events were in place. They had even added some extra practices like Scrum of Scrums, Story Points and Big Room Planning. Why wasn't Scrum delivering on its promise?

The State of Scrum

There is no doubt about it: Scrum is wildly popular. It has been adopted by many organizations from all over the world. The two official organizations that spread the Scrum Framework far and wide together— Scrum.org and Scrum Alliance—have hundreds of trainers worldwide. More than a million people have been certified. Countless books and comic books and articles on Scrum have been written and every country has one or more user groups. You can even find songs about Scrum on YouTube!

Following the promise of agility, Scrum has become the agile framework of choice for many organizations. The fact that many organizations and teams are trying Scrum is certainly a reason for celebration. On the other hand, although many think they're doing Scrum, they're still only touching the surface of what is possible. Like the organization described the case, most are stuck in painful mediocrity, struggling to find their way out.

Organizations and teams often think they're doing Scrum when everyone is certified, when the roles, events, and artifacts are in place, and when an army of well-paid (external) coaches and trainers is available to support the implementation (see Figure 3.1). Who can blame them for this kind of "Checklist Scrum" when so little time is spent on actually understanding the purpose of Scrum and its underlying principles and values?

Figure 3.1 The agile transformation process

The changes that the Scrum Framework brings remain superficial when there is no useful and valuable increment at the end of every Sprint—that is, when there is no new version of the product ready to release to stakeholders. Unfortunately, and for reasons we'll explore in this book, work is often organized in such a way that it is very difficult for Scrum Teams to release at the end of every Sprint. So instead of solving these deeper problems, Scrum Teams give up and concede that "it doesn't work here." Or worse, the Scrum Framework is blamed for exposing just how little focus organizations have on stakeholder value and being (more) responsive.

Just as trying to eat healthier by adding a salad to your existing diet of burgers and beer isn't much help, adding a good idea on top of an otherwise broken system isn't going to result in magical improvements. Instead, discipline, courage, and determination are necessary to start changing the system that is getting in the way. And that doesn't happen nearly as often as it should.

This kind of superficial Scrum easily devolves into what we've come to call Zombie Scrum. There's a lot of it out there (see "How Bad Is It, Really?" in Chapter 1).

Zombie Scrum

The thumbnail description of Zombie Scrum is that it looks like Scrum, but without the beating heart. It is a bit like a zombie shuffling towards you on a foggy night. All seems well from a distance: Two legs, check! Two arms, check! A head, check! But on closer inspection, it's obvious you need to run for your life. Something has clearly gone wrong!

The same goes for Zombie Scrum. From a distance, all seems well as Scrum Teams go through the motions of the Scrum Framework. Sprint Planning takes place at the start of the Sprint, the Daily Scrum once every twenty-four hours, a Sprint Review and Sprint Retrospective at the end of the Sprint. And there's even a Definition of Done! With the Scrum Guide as a checklist, you'd say that the team is doing "Scrum by the book." But instead of supporting how people do their work, Scrum feels like a chore. There's no beating heart and not much of a working brain either.

Through years of research inside and outside our lab, we've found that Zombie Scrum manifests in four key areas:

Symptom 1: Zombie Scrum Teams Don't Know the Needs of Their Stakeholders

Different from movie zombies who attack human beings to devour their flesh, teams affected by Zombie Scrum prefer to hide away from people and keep to their familiar surroundings (see Figure 3.2). They care neither what's upstream nor what's downstream in the value chain. It's safer to just hide behind screens and be busy with design, analysis, or writing code. Zombie Scrum Teams see themselves as a cog in the wheel, unable or unwilling to change anything to have a real impact. Sadly, this metaphor is usually quite accurate.

Their work, as well as the system it takes place in, is often designed to keep them far away from the people that actually use or pay for the product. In traditional organizations, developers only write code, just as managers manage, designers design, and analysts analyze. When they are done, they hand off the work to someone else and work on the next item without knowing what happened to the previous one. This old-fashioned silo-thinking goes against the idea of cross-functional teams that have the necessary skills and behaviors to create valuable products with stakeholders.

The result is that teams churn out a stream of product features with questionable value. The features may not be what the stakeholders actually needed. Or they're nice to have but don't really help the users be much more effective. This creates what is probably the biggest waste in product development: mediocre products that don't offer much value.

Figure 3.2 Zombie Scrum Teams are shy like that.

Symptom 2: Zombie Scrum Teams Don't Ship Fast

Teams that suffer from Zombie Scrum struggle to deliver anything of value at the end of a Sprint. Often, there isn't even a working increment. If there is, it takes months before it can be released to stakeholders. Even though Scrum Teams go through the motions of Scrum, there is little to inspect and adapt (see Figure 3.3).

This is most apparent during the Sprint Review. Stakeholders don't have the opportunity to take the keyboard and mouse to use the product and validate what was created. Instead, the team turns on the projector for a fancy presentation, shows screenshots, or simply talks about what was on the Sprint Backlog. If the product is inspected at all, it is either very technical or annotated with comments like "We have to finish this next Sprint" or "Whoops, that isn't working yet." A more subtle indicator is the lack of interaction during the Sprint Review. There are no opinions expressed, suggestions raised, or new ideas discussed. Stakeholders are rarely present. And the Product Owner seems to be OK with everything. Instead of inspecting a new version of the product, the Sprint Review is mostly ticking off boxes from the specifications. It's all boring, brainless, and without much of a heart. And nobody seems to mind.

These crucial conversations to determine the value of the product and the direction in which development is headed are only possible when people can inspect and talk about something tangible. A potentially releasable version of a product that stakeholders can actually interact with is an incredible conversation piece and answers many more questions than precise documentation. The right questions and comments arise only when people get the chance to try the product directly, without having to rely on their imagination and assumptions about what should be.

This symptom also manifests in how teams define when something is "done." For teams that suffer from Zombie Scrum, something is already done when it works on their machines, when the code compiles, and when it doesn't break when you look at it. All the other work that is needed to deliver something of quality—such as testing, security checks, performance scans, and deployments—happens elsewhere anyways. Or it doesn't happen at all.

Scrum is pointless when teams are unable to deliver a useful and valuable increment of their product at the end of a Sprint. It's like pretending to be in a real car when instead you're in one of those spring-mounted playground cars. You can make loud and impressive engine noises and flash your expensive race glasses all you want, but it won't get you anywhere.

Figure 3.3 Sorry, no working product. But a presentation with make-believe will do.

Symptom 3: Zombie Scrum Teams Don't Improve (Continuously)

Like a zombie that doesn't complain when an arm falls off, Zombie Scrum Teams show no response to a failed Sprint, or even a successful one. When other teams curse or rejoice, they simply keep their empty stare of numb resignation. Team morale is low. Items from the Sprint Backlog are carried over to the next Sprint without question. Because why not? There's always a next Sprint, and the iterations are artificial anyway! Figure 3.4 tells that story.

Because items on the Sprint Backlog are not tied to any specific Sprint Goal, they can be completed whenever the team feels like it, as team members continue their aimless trudge through a barren wasteland of product development. No signposts, no direction, no alignment, and some tumbleweeds blowing over the road. Walking at a snail's pace into the sunset without showing any emotions or any drive to improve.

And can you blame the team? The Product Owner is hardly present during the Sprint Review or Sprint Planning. The only thing that matters is how much work they get done, not how useful and valuable that work actually is to stakeholders. There is no time to reflect on what is lost because of this situation. Teams are highly unstable, as members are continuously moved around to where their specialized skills are needed the most. And there's no actual Scrum Master present to help the team grow. Some of the bottlenecks may be real, while others may be imagined. The bottom line is that nothing improves. If there is any desire to improve in the first place, it is quickly squashed by the harsh reality of life in a Zombie Scrum system. And so the team struggles on, losing a limb here and there, and groaning like there's no tomorrow.

Figure 3.4 "If it ain't broke, don't fix it." Even when the wheels are coming off, the engine is sputtering, and you can't hear each other over the noise.

Symptom 4: Zombie Scrum Teams Don't Self-Organize to Overcome Impediments

Scrum Teams that operate in environments with Zombie Scrum can't flexibly work with the people they need for creating an amazing product (see Figure 3.5). They can't choose their own tools. They can't even make crucial decisions about their own product. They have to ask for permission for nearly everything, and their requests are often denied. This lack of autonomy results in a very understandable lack of ownership. Why would you care about the success of a product when you're not actually involved in shaping it?

But every now and again the occasional Zombie Scrum Team gets lucky. Their manager reads something about "agile" and decides to give them more space. She declares the team autonomous overnight. The problem is that self-organization doesn't happen just because a team is given permission to forge their own path. They have to develop the skills to navigate this autonomy, to align their work with the broader organization and be supported in doing so. Without that support, failure is inevitable. And the manager will likely take control again, even more rigidly than before, since she now has further proof that this "agile thing" doesn't work!

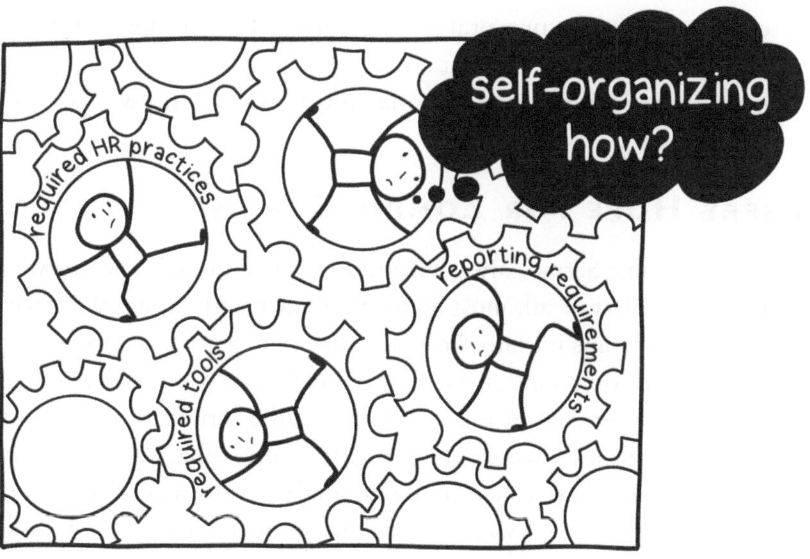

Figure 3.5 Like cogs in the machine. A very rigid machine.

It's All Connected

As we mentioned earlier, the four symptoms are closely connected. When Sprints rarely result in working versions of the product, the team can't benefit from the short feedback loop the Scrum Framework offers. This lack of feedback from stakeholders means that vital opportunities for validating critical assumptions about the product and its use are lost. Without the beating heart of this short feedback loop, it is no wonder that Sprints feel like artificial timeboxes. In these environments, there is no urge to make the best of each Sprint. Nor will teams feel bummed out when the Sprint doesn't achieve its goal. And even though the team may be aware that this isn't how things are supposed to be in Scrum, nothing is done to change it, because people feel like they're stuck in a system without any power to change it.

Isn't This Just Cargo Cult Scrum or Dark Scrum?

A simple search on the web yields many other metaphors to describe bad Scrum, such as "Cargo Cult Scrum," "Mechanical Scrum," and "Dark Scrum." Aside from the fact that we just love zombies and use any excuse to work them into our writing, we also feel that "Zombie Scrum" emphasizes the lack of motivation, the missing drive to improve, and the slow pace that characterizes this unnatural type of Scrum. Plus, a funny, over-the-top metaphor gives plenty of opportunities for serious fun. After an initial laugh, a more critical closer inspection may offer insights into ways to improve.

Is There Hope for Zombie Scrum?

Once Zombie Scrum, always Zombie Scrum? Luckily the answer is a resounding "No." First of all, most teams that start with Scrum will face some or all of the symptoms initially. Provided that they learn from their mistakes and find ways to overcome them, there is nothing wrong with making mistakes. Working empirically, using a framework like Scrum, is often at odds with how organizations are used to operating. It's impossible to change everything at once, so you'll have to learn how to apply Scrum successfully in the same incremental way that you deliver your product. This may take a long time and a lot of learning.

Second, we know from experience that you can recover from Zombie Scrum even when your team has been stuck in it for a long time. Sure, recovering will be painful, challenging, and time-consuming, but it's definitely possible to fully recover. Why else would we have invested time in writing a book that's packed with experiments to prevent and fix Zombie Scrum?

Nonetheless, we have to face the painful truth: Zombie Scrum has spread on a global scale and threatens the existence of many large and small organizations. The number of new teams that are suffering from Zombie Scrum is rapidly increasing. Entire departments are becoming zombified on a weekly basis. Many organizations panic once they've recognized the seriousness of this infection. Often, after the first panic settles in, the phase of denial starts. You'll hear statements such as these:

- "That's just the way things work here."
- "This is a one-of-a-kind organization. We're too unique to do Scrum by the book."
- "We don't have time for all these Scrum ceremonies."
- "Our developers just want to code. Doing 'real' Scrum will only make them less productive."
- "If we increase the maturity of our employees to level 5, Scrum will work just fine."

The purpose of this book is to offer tangible experiments that help you fight Zombie Scrum. This approach does require you to be brave, bold, and ferocious. And we are fully convinced that you and your team can do this! Remember, you're not in this alone. You're part of a global movement that fights Zombie Scrum together!

Experiment: Diagnose Your Team Together

Throughout this book, you'll find many experiments and interventions that you can do with your team. They are all designed to help create transparency around what is happening, to allow inspection and encourage adaptation. Every experiment follows a similar pattern. We start with the purpose. Then we explain the steps and give direction on what to watch out for.

This first experiment is all about creating transparency and starting a conversation around Zombie Scrum (see Figure 3.6). This is a critical first step towards recovery and to confront the truth that work is needed. This experiment helps you progress on the first three steps of the First Aid Kit (Chapter 2): take responsibility, assess the situation, and create awareness.

This experiment is based on the Liberating Structure "What, So What, Now What?"[1] It is a good way to build confidence, celebrate small successes, and build the muscle to get through the hard stuff.

Skill/Impact Ratio

Skill	★☆☆☆☆	No skill is required for filling in a survey and inspecting the results together with your team.
Impact on survival	★★★★★	This experiment creates transparency around what is going on in your team (and around it) in terms of Zombie Scrum. It's a crucial first step on your way to recovery.

Figure 3.6 Team diagnoses in progress

1. Lipmanowicz, H., and K. McCandless. 2014. *The Surprising Power of Liberating Structures: Simple Rules to Unleash a Culture of Innovation*. Liberating Structures Press. ASN: 978-0615975306.

Steps

The following steps help you do this experiment:

1. Go to **survey.zombiescrum.org** and fill out the extensive free survey for your Scrum Team. Invite others from your team to join your "sample" as instructed. To protect others' privacy and avoid abuse of the survey, scores from individual members are only shown to each survey taker.
2. When you've completed the survey, you'll receive a detailed report (see Figure 3.7). The report will be updated every time someone joins the sample. In the report, you'll find results for the four symptoms of Zombie Scrum, as well as a more detailed breakdown. The report also gives feedback and recommendations based on the results.
3. When everyone has participated, schedule a one-hour workshop to inspect the results together. We recommend doing this with only the Scrum Team: the Product Owner, the Scrum Master, and the Development Team.
4. Prepare for the workshop. You can print the report and hand out copies, put prints on the walls, or simply put up the profile on a screen.
5. Start the workshop by reiterating the purpose clearly and emphasizing what will happen with the outcomes (and what won't). Make sure to emphasize that improvement is always a gradual, incremental, and often messy process and that this workshop is a step in that process.
6. Invite everyone to inspect the results silently and note down observations. Ask: "What do you notice in the results?" Encourage people to stick to the facts, and avoid jumping to conclusions, for the first round. After a few minutes, ask people to share their observations in pairs for another couple of minutes and notice similarities and differences. If you have eight or more people, ask pairs to join another pair and take a few minutes to share observations and notice patterns. Ask the small groups to share their most important insights with the whole group, and capture them in a way that remains visible to everyone present.
7. Following the pattern outlined in the previous step, repeat twice more with different questions. For round two, ask people "So, what does this mean for our work as a team?" For round three, ask people "Where do we

have the freedom and autonomy to improve as a team? What are small, first steps we can commit to?" Make sure to keep capturing the most salient outcomes.

8. Put the most important actionable improvement on the Sprint Backlog for the next Sprint. Involve others as needed to keep making progress.

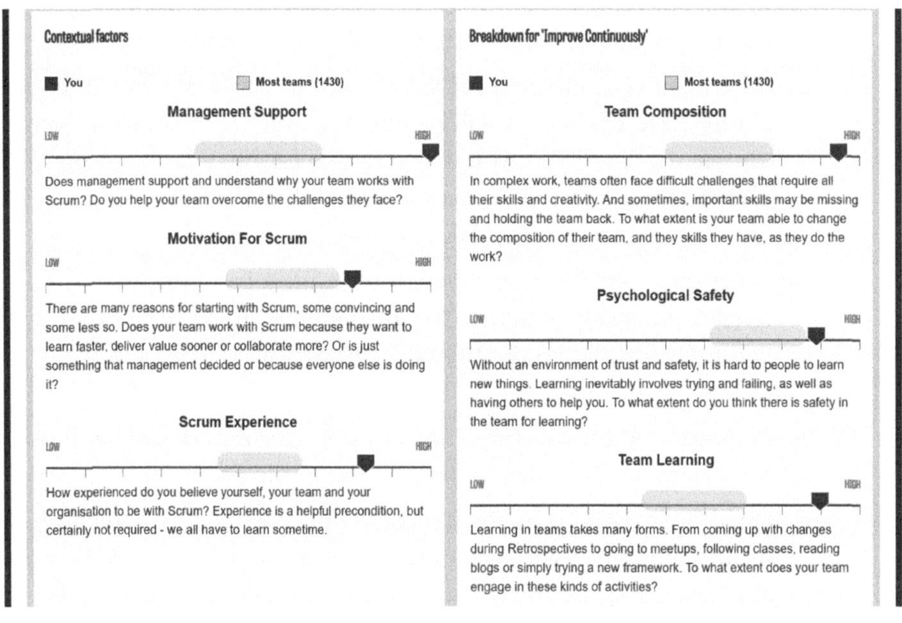

Figure 3.7 Part of the report you'll receive after completing the Zombie Scrum Survey

Our Findings

- It can be tempting to identify dozens of potential improvements and end up doing nothing at all. Instead, keep a strong focus on improving one thing first before moving onto something else. If that improvement is too big to commit to doing it in a single Sprint, make it smaller.
- When you ask people to participate in this survey, you're asking them to trust you with their honest answers. Be deeply respectful of that. Don't spread reports to people outside of the team or forward them to

management unless you have clear and unambiguous approval from everyone involved.

- Don't use the report to compare teams. Doing so will erode trust much faster than you can rebuild it.

Now What?

In this chapter, we explored how Zombie Scrum is something that looks like Scrum from a distance. It has all the mechanical parts: the roles, events, and artifacts. But there is no beating heart. There are no frequent releases. Stakeholders are hardly involved. People don't feel like they own what they are doing. And there's generally no drive to do something about the situation. Unfortunately, this state of affairs is remarkably common, according to the data we've collected.

Thankfully there's a way out. Even though recovering from Zombie Scrum may feel like having to pull yourself up by your bootstraps, we've seen many teams and organizations do so. The remainder of this book is here to help you better understand what causes Zombie Scrum and to start improving with your team.

4 The Purpose of Scrum

Often, a school is your best bet—perhaps not for education but certainly for protection from an undead attack.

—Max Brooks,
The Zombie Survival Guide

In This Chapter

- Discover how Zombie Scrum compares to Scrum as it is intended.
- Understand the underlying purpose of the Scrum Framework, and how Scrum is all about navigating complex problems and reducing risk.

In our frantic search for an antidote to Zombie Scrum, we looked on the other side of stickies, behind whiteboards, and under our beds. We studied the symptoms and tried tracing them back to their origin. In a nutshell, when talking about the causes of Zombie Scrum, the discussion usually ends with the questions "What are the reasons people have for using the Scrum Framework in the first place? What are they hoping to get out of it?" One persistent theme is that Zombie Scrum thrives in environments where people respond to these questions with an empty stare.

Recovering from Zombie Scrum starts with understanding the purpose of the Scrum Framework. When you understand that zombies are driven by an appetite for fresh brains, you can make the entirely sensible decision to keep as far away from them as you can. But avoiding Zombie Scrum doesn't end with understanding the purpose of the Scrum Framework. From there follows the hard work of removing the impediments that get in the way of delivering value to stakeholders sooner. When you don't know what you're aiming for, it's hard to effectively cure Zombie Scrum. Understanding the purpose also makes clear how the various experiments and interventions in this book are connected.

In this chapter, we explore the purpose of the Scrum Framework and how its elements work together to make that possible. For a more thorough refresher of the entire Scrum Framework, you can refer to **zombiescrum.org/scrumframework**.

"Time to hit the books, recruit! Our calculations show that you have a 0% chance of being successful when you don't know what you're dealing with. Cramming this information into your brain will help keep you from becoming a zombie snack."

It's All about Complex Adaptive Problems

What reasons do people have for adopting Scrum? The Scrum Framework is part of something called agile software development. And that's often where the confusion starts. In our work, we like to ask people to find synonyms for the word *agile*. When you use a thesaurus, you find alternatives like *flexible*, *adaptive*, and *nimble*. These are fantastic qualities to have in environments of increased uncertainty. Scrum is designed to help you learn quickly and make adjustments based on that learning.

But does Scrum work everywhere and every time? The definition that the official Scrum Guide offers already sends us in the right direction:

> **Scrum (n):** A framework within which people can address complex adaptive problems, while productively and creatively delivering products of the highest possible value.[1]

The key to understanding the purpose of Scrum lies in the words "complex adaptive problems." This tiny and hard-to-miss sentence in the Scrum Guide is a rabbit hole into a different approach to a specific class of problems. Let's break this down a bit further.

Problems

What do we mean when we talk about "problems"? It might seem trivial to even ask this question, but understanding what a problem is and isn't, is a good start to discover the purpose of the Scrum Framework.

The English word *problem* originates from Ancient Greek, where it means "hindrance" or "obstacle." Problems are those obstacles that prevent us from doing or knowing something that we need. In a very real sense, they are puzzles we need to solve in order to move forward. Just like with puzzle games, some take only a bit of effort and have a well-defined successful outcome; others require more effort and don't have a clear successful outcome.

Within the context of product development, there are many different puzzles on a variety of levels. Some problems may be about solving a certain bug, fixing a typo, or replacing an image; other problems involve finding a way to address the needs of a group of users or coming up with a scalable architecture. Most of these problems essentially break down into many smaller problems that we need to solve.

1. Sutherland, J. K., and K. Schwaber. 2017. *The Scrum Guide*. Retrieved on May 26, 2020, from **https://www.scrumguides.org**.

Complex, Adaptive Problems

Problems vary in their degree of complexity. This results from the number of variables—or puzzle pieces—involved and the degree to which you know what a successful outcome looks like. Just like a jigsaw puzzle, at some point, it becomes too difficult to look at all the pieces at once to see the big picture. In order to make progress, you need to shift from purely analyzing the problem to moving pieces around on the table to see how they fit.

"Complex" means that a solution to a problem cannot be found by simply analyzing and thinking about it. There are too many factors involved and the way the pieces interact is not something you can predict up front. In product development, many variables affect our success. Although some are obvious, most are not. In our work with teams, we often ask people to brainstorm the variables that they think influence their success in implementing the solution that they have in mind. Within minutes, people generate huge lists. For example:

- The understanding of what a user needs for a particular feature
- The differences in communication styles and skills
- The mandate and support within the organization
- The skill level of the team(s)
- A clear goal and/or vision to guide decision-making
- The quality, size, and knowledge of the existing code base
- The relationship with suppliers of required components

Unlike a jigsaw puzzle, these "puzzle pieces" are abstract and hard to define. And they interact in unpredictable and unexpected ways that can only be understood in hindsight. To complicate things further, many problems in product development don't have a clear and obvious solution, and they involve many people and perspectives that change continuously. This is what makes them "complex *and* adaptive." While doing the work with others, your understanding of the problem and the solution will change in unpredictable and unexpected ways, sometimes gradually and other times very rapidly. So you'll have to develop (new) skills and find better ways to work together.

One example of this was the development of a product to manage incidents on the Dutch railways and involved one of the authors in a supporting role. Contrary to what the customer was used to, the product was developed incrementally over a period of several years by six co-located and cross-functional Scrum Teams. One major source of complexity was how this product had to interact reliably with dozens of old and new subsystems to retrieve, synchronize, and update real-time information about what was happening on and around the tracks. In some cases, lives literally depended on the accuracy of the information. Technical complexity aside, the product was used by partners ranging from logistical companies, emergency services, passenger rail services, and other utility providers. Even seemingly straightforward items from the Product Backlog often turned out to be much harder to solve than expected as performance issues surfaced, compatibility with older systems and hardware caused problems, and the teams struggled with the political realities of having many stakeholders. Not only was the development of the product as a whole a complex and adaptive problem, so was each item on the Product Backlog. But thanks to an empirical approach, the teams were able to incrementally deliver a successful product that is still in use today and has cut response time to incidents by 60 percent.

Complexity, Uncertainty, and Risk

A key attribute of complex problems is that they are inherently uncertain and unpredictable. Because both the problem and the solution require active exploration with stakeholders, and because there is no unambiguous definition of success, what is going to happen next becomes increasingly unclear as you look further into the future. Just like the weather, you will have a pretty good idea about what is going to happen tomorrow, a general sense of what will happen next week, and no clue at all about what is going to happen one month down the road. This uncertainty inherently means there are risks. The risk of going in the wrong direction, the risk of spending time and money on the wrong things, and the risk of getting lost altogether.

A knee-jerk strategy to reduce this risk is to further analyze and overthink the problem before implementing a solution. For simple problems, this approach can work. But for complex problems, more analysis is as pointless as trying to solve a 10,000-piece jigsaw puzzle by looking at the pieces and trying to fit them together only in your head.

Yet this is how many organizations approach complex problems. They create task forces to think about solutions, spend more time in the design stage or require more detailed plans. Instead of actually moving jigsaw pieces around to see how they fit, they engage in increasingly ritualistic ways to exorcise complexity. But none of these rituals actually reduces risk because the simple truth remains that complex problems are inherently uncontrollable and uncertain.

Thankfully, there is an excellent way to actually reduce the risk of complex, adaptive problems. This is where Empirical Process Control Theory and the Scrum Framework come into view.

Empiricism and Process Control Theory

We are surrounded by complex problems. Even seemingly straightforward problems turn out to be complex on closer inspection. One way to find an answer to these problems is through reasoning or using intuition. You can also rely on previous experiences. But how reliable is experience when you've never done something before or when the variables change all the time?

Chemical engineers have long wrestled with complex challenges too. As it turns out, even seemingly straightforward chemical processes are complex on closer inspection. How do you keep the temperature of a liquid constant? How do you heat crude oil for transport without reducing its quality? So many variables influence these processes that it requires a different approach to control them. This topic is what has come to be known as Empirical Process Control Theory.[2] Instead of trying to identify all possible variables and their interactions in comprehensive models, important key variables are constantly monitored with sensors. When their values exceed certain

2. Ogunnaike, B. A., and W. H. Ray. 1994. *Process Dynamics, Modeling, and Control.* New York: Oxford University Press.

thresholds, other variables are modified to adjust the system back to the desired state. More heat can be applied, air can be vented, water can be added or removed. Here, knowledge to drive decisions does not come from models or assumptions. Instead, it comes from a short feedback loop where adjustments are made as needed based on frequent measurements.

This way of developing knowledge from experience is called "Empiricism." Developed as early back as ancient Greek times, it is the foundation of modern science. It contrasts with rationalism, where analysis and logical reasoning are used to arrive at knowledge. In empiricism, nothing is assumed to be true until it has been verified through observation.

Although Empirical Process Control was developed in part to control complex chemical processes in industrial plants, its principles can be applied to complex problems in other domains all the same. The Scrum Framework is one example of such an application.

Empiricism and the Scrum Framework

The Scrum Framework was developed by Ken Schwaber and Jeff Sutherland in the 1990s and first formalized in 1995 to address the inherent complexity of product and software development.[3] More recently, the Scrum Framework is being applied to complex problems in a variety of domains, such as marketing, organizational change, and scientific research. The Scrum Framework is built on three pillars that allow empirical process control (see Figure 4.1):

- **Transparency.** You gather data—such as metrics, feedback, and other experiences—to find out what is going on.
- **Inspection.** You inspect the progress with everyone involved and decide what that means for your ambitions.
- **Adaptation.** You make changes that you hope will bring you closer to your ambitions.

3. Sutherland, J. V., D. Patel, C. Casanave, G. Hollowell, and J. Miller, eds. 1997. *Business Object Design and Implementation: OOPSLA '95 Workshop Proceedings*. The University of Michigan. ISBN: 978-3540760962.

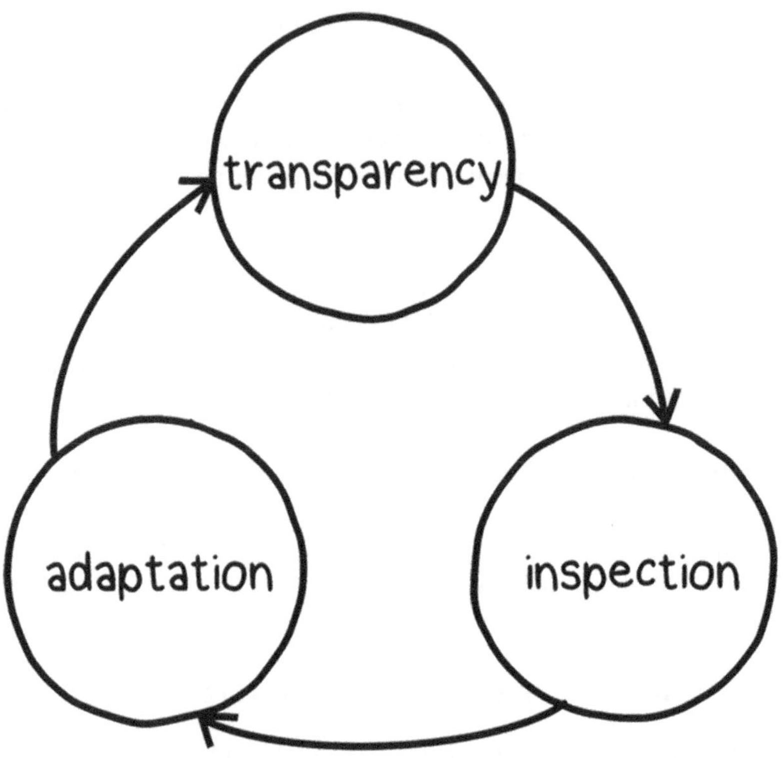

Figure 4.1 The short cycles of creating transparency, inspecting the outcomes, and adapting what else is needed

This cycle repeats as often as necessary to catch deviations, unexpected discoveries, and potential opportunities that emerge as the work is done. The process happens not once a year or when the project is completed, but continuously on a daily, weekly, or monthly basis. Rather than basing our decisions on risky assumptions about potential futures that will probably never unfold, we're instead making decisions based on the signals we've detected up to this point. This is empiricism. And you'll discover later in this chapter that everything in the Scrum Framework is designed around these pillars.

What the Scrum Framework Makes Possible

The empirical approach that the Scrum Framework offers becomes tremendously useful when you accept that you don't know everything and can't control every variable. Because of that, your understanding of what is needed changes. You have to accept that mistakes and new insights will emerge that you never considered initially. Instead of making a precise plan up front and then sticking to it no matter what, you have to treat ideas as assumptions or hypotheses that you validate with the Scrum Framework.

The Scrum Framework allows you to learn whether you're off track and need to make adjustments much sooner than when you're simply following a plan. Instead of going all in on one solution, you're now able to tackle the biggest problem you're facing first.

This is especially important when you operate in an uncertain, changing environment. Reasonable assumptions you have at the beginning of your work may fly out the window as you're developing your product. Instead of catastrophic failure at the end of a long project, an empirical approach reduces unexpected changes to minor speed bumps that require you to correct course a bit.

If anything, the Scrum Framework helps to reduce the risk of the inherent unpredictability and uncertainty of complex, adaptive problems. It allows you to continuously verify that you're still moving towards solving the problem you set out to solve. Even better is that you now have a process that actively encourages the discovery of better ideas and includes them in shaping your next steps. Now uncertainty becomes an asset because of all the underlying possibilities within it.

Scrum: An Evolving Set of Minimal Boundaries to Work Empirically

When you read the Scrum Guide, or our description of the Scrum Framework,[4] you may notice that the Scrum Framework leaves many things open. For example, how do you define Sprint Goals? How do you create cross-functional teams? What are practices that help Product Owners or

4. Download the PDF from https://zombiescrum.org/scrumframework.

Scrum Masters be successful? Coming to the Scrum Framework with a fresh eye may be a frustrating experience, as people looking for a complete methodology understandably wonder, "But how do I do this?"

The Scrum Framework is incomplete on purpose. It is best understood as a minimal set of boundaries for working empirically. It describes only what you need to do, not how to do it. The Scrum Guide makes no mention of specific practices such as test-driven development, story points, or user stories. Every team, product, and organization is different. This complexity means that there is no silver bullet or one-size-fits-all solution. Instead, the Scrum Framework encourages teams to discover their own local solutions and ways of doing things within each team's boundaries. There are many potential sources for learning what might work, from simply trying different things to getting inspiration from blog posts, podcasts, and meetups.

The Scrum Framework isn't static either. It has changed over time. Since its first formal description in 1995, the collective insights and experiences of teams working with Scrum have resulted in many small and large adaptations. A general trend is that the Scrum Framework is increasingly applied in domains outside product and software development. This is reflected in the removal of specific practices—such as burndown charts—from the framework. Wording has changed to emphasize the intention over the implementation. Newer versions increasingly emphasize the importance of Sprint Goals and values to drive decision-making in complex environments. The Scrum Framework itself is subject to its own process of transparency, inspection, and adaptation.

Zombie Scrum and the Efficiency Mindset

Where does Zombie Scrum connect to all this? One clear theme we've found is that people use the Scrum Framework for the wrong reasons. When you ask people in a Zombie Scrum organization what they are hoping to get out of Scrum, you'll hear things like "more speed," "more brains," "more output," and "more efficiency." That's very different from the actual meaning of the word *agile*. It's also very different from what the Scrum Framework is designed for. Where does this contradiction come from?

The traditional way of managing organizations and product development is designed to achieve the opposite of agility. This mental model is often called the *efficiency mindset*. A full history of the efficiency mindset is beyond the scope of this book, but Gareth Morgan's work offers a good introduction.[5] Suffice to say that its aim is to reduce uncertainty as much as possible, increase predictability, and drive efficiency. This mindset usually manifests in detailed plans for upcoming work, the standardization of work through protocols and procedures, a high degree of task specialization, and measuring efficiency (such as units of work per day, resource utilization, or number of errors). This mindset can certainly work in environments where work is fairly repetitive and simple, such as assembly lines or certain administrative work. But it certainly doesn't work in environments where people deal with complex, adaptive problems that are inherently unpredictable and uncertain.

And yet this mental model is so ingrained that it's effectively invisible. It completely shapes the way we design organizations, structure interactions, and build our culture. When you look at the Scrum Framework from this perspective, it makes sense that people try to understand the framework in terms of how it impacts efficiency, speed, and output—only to be disappointed when it doesn't seem to do that.

In a very broad sense, the Scrum Framework is more concerned with being effective than being efficient. Where efficiency is about getting as much work done as possible (the output), effectiveness is about the value and usefulness of that work (the outcome). Although it is entirely possible that efficiency improves with the Scrum Framework, it is neither a promise nor a goal in itself.

In environments where Zombie Scrum is going on, the efficiency mindset is so strong that people see only the structural elements of the Scrum Framework: the roles, events, and artifacts. They don't see nor appreciate the value of the

5. Morgan, G. 2006. *Images of Organization*. Sage Publications. ISBN: 1412939798.

empirical process underneath (see Figure 4.2). And that is why Zombie Scrum only looks like Scrum, but without the beating heart of empiricism.

Figure 4.2 Looking at the wrong things? Zombie Scrum goes hand in hand with a strong focus on performance and how much work is done. But are customers happy? Is value delivered?

What about Simple Problems?

When the Scrum Framework is designed for complex and adaptive problems, what does that mean for situations where you are dealing with simpler problems? What if you're in doubt about whether or not you're confronting a complex problem in the first place?

First, the people doing the work often have the best chance of detecting complexity. What may seem incredibly straightforward for a stakeholder may be very hard for developers. One of the authors once encountered a stakeholder who boldly stated that building a web shop involved nothing more than putting a USB stick into a laptop. Obviously, this stakeholder benefited from this belief, as he hoped it would keep the price of development down. But we all have examples of situations where someone who is not doing the work claims that "it can't be that difficult." If anything, complexity should be judged by the people doing the work.

Nevertheless, even the people doing the work can easily fool themselves. Complex problems are deceptive in that their complexity is often not obvious at first glance. It's only when you start solving them that you discover there is a lot more beneath the surface. Most developers know what this is like: they start with a seemingly small change, only to discover that this small change affects many other components, and cascades into unexpected issues. What started out as a seemingly simple problem turned out to be a complex one instead.

A third consideration is that complexity doesn't have to spring from technical matters alone. Although changing the text on a button on a website may be easy, complexity also emerges when many groups of stakeholders have to be involved. As the number of people in the mix increases, complexity tends to increase along with it.

Finally there is the question of scale. Even the most complex problem can be broken down into small tasks that are in themselves straightforward and simple. In a sense, this is exactly what we're doing in the Scrum Framework: a large problem is decomposed into a series of smaller problems that each fits into a Sprint. Those smaller problems are in turn broken down into even smaller problems that are represented by the items on the Sprint Backlog. Sometimes all we see are the simpler tasks on the Sprint Backlog. Using this to conclude that the problem isn't complex ignores the bigger picture.

When we take these considerations into account, we firmly believe that the majority of the problems we face in the modern workplace are complex and benefit from empiricism in one form or another. The few exceptions generally involve work that consists of repetitive tasks where each can be successfully completed without coordination with others. When in doubt, you're better off to assume complexity and rely on an empirical approach such as Scrum, Kanban, DevOps, or Extreme Programming. If the problem really turns out to be simple, you will quickly notice that an empirical approach doesn't yield new insights or useful adaptations. In this case, the decision that an empirical approach is not useful is made empirically too. And it helps to avoid the risk of assuming that something is simple, only to discover that it isn't and having to rethink your entire approach and the expectations you've created.

More detailed analyses on how to distinguish simple from complex problems, as well as recommended approaches, can be found in work by Ralph Stacey[6] and Cynthia Kurtz and Dave Snowden.[7]

Now What?

Zombie Scrum happens when teams lose focus on, or don't understand, the purpose of the Scrum Framework. That is why we used this chapter to explain how the Scrum Framework exists to help teams navigate the inherent risk of complex problems. It is not a detailed methodology that you can execute without thinking. Instead, the Scrum Framework offers a minimal set of boundaries that allow teams to work empirically on complex problems of any kind. In its simplest form, it encourages teams to work collaboratively in small steps to solve complex problems together with those who have a stake in the problem. Every step is used to learn about what else is needed, to validate assumptions, and to make decisions about the next steps.

It is true that the Scrum Framework is easy to learn. But it is hard to master. Every journey with the Scrum Framework starts somewhere. Whatever your starting point is, the best way to learn how to work with Scrum is to do it. The iterative and incremental nature of the Scrum Framework is a great vehicle for learning and improvement when you keep its purpose in mind. Although the journey may be hard, even seemingly impossible at times, improvement will happen over time. And thankfully there is a huge and passionate community of people working with Scrum around the globe, ready to help you. And there's this book, of course. In the coming chapters, we explore the symptoms and causes of Zombie Scrum in more detail and offer practical experiments to recover.

6. Stacey, R. 1996. *Complexity and Creativity in Organizations*. ISBN: 978-1881052890.
7. Kurtz, C., and D. J. Snowden. 2003. "The New Dynamics of Strategy: Sense-making in a Complex and Complicated World." *IBM Systems Journal* 42, no. 3.

II
Build What Stakeholders Need

5 Symptoms and Causes

With sunglasses, a hat, and half a pack of Band-Aids, Roger could pass as a human.

—Nadia Higgins,
Zombie Camp

In This Chapter

- Explore the common symptoms of Zombie Scrum related to not building what the stakeholders need.
- Explore the causes and reasons for not involving stakeholders, with the purpose of understanding why this is happening.
- Understand what the involvement of stakeholders should look like in healthy Scrum Teams, and why close collaboration with stakeholders is a prerequisite for success.

An Experience from the Field

Janet works as a software developer for an insurance company. Her team adopted Scrum about six months ago. During Sprint Planning, the Product Owner explains what the Development Team needs to do next. It is very important that the team finishes the work in the two-week Sprint timebox. Failing to do so would derail the plan, as the Product Owner has planned all the Sprints well into the next year.

Every Sprint, Janet works on the items that she is being assigned during Sprint Planning. She fights through the boredom of each Daily Scrum. During the Sprint Review, the Development Team shows the Product Owner what they have achieved. The Product Owner ticks boxes. Then the next Sprint starts. The team feels good that they deliver everything the Product Owner asks of them. Yet Janet can't help but think, "Maybe there is more out there we're overlooking."

So during a team meeting last fall, she remarked that the user interface of the product looked outdated and complicated. Janet would frankly hate to use it herself if she had to. She wondered out loud if the users were okay with it and suggested to maybe involve them more in development. The Product Owner reprimanded her for making assumptions. As a Product Owner, he was responsible for relaying the many feature requests from sales, support, and management to the Development Team. There was really no need to talk with users. Plus, support never relayed any complaints about the interface. He reminded her that they were working for a professional insurance company and not a hip start-up. That was the moment when Janet stopped asking questions about users and simply did what was asked of her.

This case illustrates a pattern that many Zombie Scrum Teams will be familiar with. Instead of collaborating closely with actual stakeholders—such as users and customers—Development Teams deliver what the Product Owner ordered. Product Owners, in turn, simply translate the requirements that were handed to them by sales or marketing. Scrum Teams mostly don't know what happens with their work after a Sprint ends, let alone how their work impacts the users. In this chapter we explore one of the most significant symptoms of Zombie Scrum: not building what stakeholders need.

How Bad Is It, Really?

- We are continuously monitoring the spread of Zombie Scrum around the world with our online Symptoms Checker at **survey.zombiescrum.org**. Of the Scrum Teams that have participated at the time of writing:*
- 65% have little interaction with other departments during the Sprint (e.g., legal, marketing, sales).
- 65% have a Product Owner who rarely rejects work or says "No."
- 63% never or rarely remove items from the Product Backlog.
- 62% don't see frequent interaction between the Development Team and stakeholders during the Sprint.
- 62% have a Product Owner who is the only member of the team who interacts with stakeholders.
- 60% have a Product Owner who doesn't have the mandate to decide how to spend the budget.
- 59% have Sprint Reviews that are attended only by the Scrum Team (no stakeholders).
- 53% have a Product Owner who doesn't or rarely involves stakeholders in ordering or updating the Product Backlog.

* The percentages represent teams that scored a 6 or lower on a 10-point scale. Each topic was measured with 10 to 30 questions. The results represent 1,764 teams that participated in the self-reported survey at **survey.zombiescrum.org** between June 2019 and May 2020.

Why Bother Involving Stakeholders?

Organizations can continue to exist only if they offer something valuable to their environment. It doesn't matter if they're commercial enterprises, non-profits, or governmental agencies. This sounds obvious, right? But somehow, we forget what this means in our day-to-day work. Why is it that in many organizations—large or small—the people who are actually working on a product (designers, developers, managers, testers, and so on) rarely really talk to actual stakeholders? Hidden behind layers of "organizational fat" (sales, marketing, account managers, project managers), the stakeholder has become an abstraction.

WHO ARE THE STAKEHOLDERS, ACTUALLY?

It sounds obvious that you should include your stakeholders. But who are they? Are we talking about users? Customers? Internal or external customers? Product Managers? While some organizations work exclusively for external customers, many also have people inside the organization who should be included in deciding what is valuable. And in other organizations, such as NGOs and governmental agencies, the term "customer" is not familiar to staffers.

For this reason, the Scrum Guide purposefully talks about "stakeholders" to mean everyone who has a stake in the product. Particularly in Zombie Scrum, we see many examples where the vagueness of "stakeholders" is leveraged into making teams believe that talking only to internal stakeholders, domain experts, or intermediaries is exactly what Scrum intends. The people paying for or using the product are not involved.

And that is a huge issue. In product development, we want to balance the perspectives of users and customers with a business perspective. Focusing on only one of them is going to lead to trouble. Yet in virtually all the Zombie Scrum Teams we have worked with, the interests of the customers and the users were woefully underrepresented. This imbalance easily leads to many of the symptoms we see in this book.

This part of the book is about including the right people at the right time. These are the people who have something to gain when the product delivers and something to lose if it doesn't. Including them is the best way to reduce the risk of building the wrong product.

Although it is easy to include many people in product development and simply call them "stakeholders," it is far more difficult to find the people who have an actual stake in your product. We find the following questions helpful to discover who they are:

- Is this person using, or going to use, the product on a regular basis?
- Is this person investing significantly in the development of the product?
- Is this person deeply invested in solving a challenge that your product addresses?

You will notice that these questions are about value. A stakeholder is someone who helps you decide what is valuable to work on next because it's important to them to get a return on their investment of time or money. Everyone else is your "audience." This likely includes domain experts, intermediaries, and other people who are interested in your product but have no personal stake in it. You can happily invite them for the ride, but you want to focus on your stakeholders. Naturally, this perspective emphasizes the involvement of the people using your product (users) and the people paying for it (customers). These groups often overlap.

Recovering from Zombie Scrum starts with finding the right stakeholders and continuously refining who is part of that group and who isn't.

Validating Assumptions about Value

As we explored in Chapter 4, product development is complex work. Inherent to this work is that teams make many assumptions about the needs of stakeholders and how best to fulfill them, or about what is valuable. Each assumption comes with the risk of being wrong. So instead of validating these assumptions at the very end of development, and risk losing a lot of time and money when they turn out to be wrong, we reduce this risk by validating assumptions early and often. This approach means answering questions such as the following:

- Do people understand how to use this new feature?
- Does the feature actually solve the problem it is intended to solve?
- Does the description for this field make sense?
- Does this change improve the conversion rate?
- When we implement this feature, does it indeed reduce the time it takes to perform a certain task?

The Scrum Framework lays down the bare essentials for a process that promotes collaborative discovery to validate these assumptions. By frequently delivering incremental versions of a product, developers and stakeholders can have important conversations about what is valuable and how to build it. "Does the feature, implemented this way, help you solve the problem?", "What can we do to make this feature more valuable?" and "What new, valuable ideas pop up when you see this?" are the kind of things you want developers and stakeholders to be talking about.

Inspecting the Increment for your product that comes out of a Sprint is where a feedback loop for your product closes. This is the moment when a Scrum Team examines how the results align with the intentions. Inspecting a working Increment allows all the people present to look at the same thing, understand it in the same way, and speak the same language. Without this step, the conversation is bound to stay theoretical and superficial, and delivering a product the stakeholders actually need becomes much harder.

Why Are We Not Involving Stakeholders?

If it is so important to involve stakeholders, why isn't it happening as much as it should in organizations that suffer from Zombie Scrum? There are many reasons for this shortcoming, and we'll explore the ones we see most often next. When you are aware of the causes, it is easier to select the right interventions and experiments. Understanding also builds empathy with Zombie Scrum and how it often emerges despite everyone's best intentions.

"Okay, junior! Now we're finally getting into the meat . . . sorry, the core of Zombie Scrum. Delivering value and involving stakeholders are really the bones . . . sorry, the heart . . . what's wrong with me today? Well, these are important things. We'll get you all set up for spotting the symptoms of the missing stakeholder so that you can try out several experiments safely. Break a leg! Or rather good luck and don't get bitten!"

We Don't Really Understand the Purpose of Our Product

Scrum Teams that operate in environments with Zombie Scrum rarely have a clear answer as to what makes their product valuable. They don't know how it helps their stakeholders, nor how to make it more appealing. They also don't know how the product helps their organization achieve its mission.

Without understanding the purpose of a product, how can Scrum Teams separate the *important* work from all the *potential* work that comes their way? Instead, they focus on the technical part of what is needed to build the product rather than understand why that work actually matters. Much like zombies that stumble around without a sense of direction, many Zombie Scrum Teams work hard on getting nowhere in particular.

Signs to look for:

- When asked to complete the sentence "This product exists in order to . . . ," nobody—including the Product Owner—offers a meaningful response.
- When you pick any item from your team's task board, nobody on the team can clearly explain why that item matters to stakeholders and what need it addresses, other than "they told us to."
- In the environments where the teams work, no artifacts relate to the vision or purpose of the product. Or the product is never even mentioned.
- The Product Owner rarely or never says "No" to items that are suggested for the Product Backlog. The Product Backlog is very long and continues growing.
- Sprint Goals are either missing entirely or they don't say anything about why a Sprint is valuable for stakeholders.
- When asked, a Product Owner is unable to tell the story of how the items on the Product Backlog are ordered in terms of "First we deliver value by doing this . . . followed by . . . so that we can do . . . ."

The role of the Product Owner exists to continuously make decisions about the product based on feedback from stakeholders and what is happening in the environment. Many different options—ideas, suggestions, and opportunities—will present themselves. Product Owners should find themselves asking questions like these:

- Does it fit with the product's purpose or vision?
- Does it fit with the mission of our organization?

- Does it align with the needs of most stakeholders?
- Is it complete enough to work, but not too complicated to clutter up the product?

When a Product Owner tries to balance budget and time against the value generated by each option, many of these questions need to be answered with a resounding "No." These are hard decisions and can be disappointing for those who suggested the options. How can Product Owners and their Scrum Teams make these difficult decisions without a clear understanding of the purpose of their product?

A product's purpose or vision doesn't have to be fancy or incredibly inventive, but it should explain which needs of the stakeholders it primarily aims to address at this moment in time. A product strategy then describes in what order those needs will be addressed and what work is necessary to make that happen. Obviously, both are continuously tuned and refined as new insights emerge while developing the product. But they act as a yardstick to make decisions about what should end up in the product and what doesn't.

Without a purpose or a strategy, Scrum Teams end up with Gung-ho development, where anything goes. All the work becomes equally (un)important. You end up with a huge—and growing—Product Backlog. And worse, you'll waste a lot of time and money on a bloated, overcomplicated product that is shunned by stakeholders in favor of more elegant alternatives.

Try these experiments to improve with your team (see Chapter 6):

- Express Desired Outcomes, Not Work to Be Done
- Start a Stakeholder Treasure Hunt
- Limit the Maximum Length of Your Product Backlog
- Map Your Product Backlog on an Ecocycle
- Decorate the Team Room with the Product Purpose

We Make Assumptions about What Stakeholders Need

One of the authors once coached a medium-size company where the CEO proudly boasted that he knew better what the stakeholders needed than they did. For him, involving stakeholders wasn't important. Which was ironic, considering that the company was losing its market share to competitors that offered more innovative solutions.

We hear this sentiment a lot in organizations with Zombie Scrum. "We know what people want. So we will ship it and they will love it."

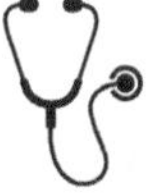

Signs to look for:

- Teams don't invest time in exploring ways, tools, and techniques to validate what they are doing with stakeholders.
- Sprints are never intended to test a hypothesis about what might help stakeholders (or add more value).
- Whenever stakeholders are involved during the Sprint or Sprint Reviews, it is only to inform them about what was done. They are not invited to actually use the product.
- Despite initial praise and high hopes for a new feature, it fizzles and fails to take off after releasing it.

Statements like these are often made by Product Owners who have zero contact with their stakeholders. Instead, they rely on their own intuitions and assumptions. But this attitude ignores the complexities of product development by making three faulty assumptions:

- That you fully understand what kinds of problems your stakeholder is trying to solve with the product
- That what you once identified as helpful hasn't changed
- That involving stakeholders can't help you be even more successful than you already are

The degree to which a product is effective can only be determined by stakeholders. You only know if they're willing to pay for it when they put money on the table. Or invest the time to use your product. The Scrum Framework is designed to help you validate these assumptions as you go. And not taking advantage of that is fraught with risk.

The Sprint Review is a good example of where this belief manifests. When Product Owners or entire Scrum Teams make themselves believe that they know exactly what their stakeholders want, there is no need to involve them. And when stakeholders do show up, it is only to inform them of what happened, without any actual validation of how useful that work was.

No matter what organization you work for, or what your context is, there is no excuse for not validating if the time and money you're spending are actually worth the effort. Do it together and do it often. Remove or change everything that prevents this practice or makes it difficult.

Try these experiments to improve with your team (see Chapter 6):

- Invite Stakeholders to a "Feedback Party"
- Give the Stakeholder a Desk Close to the Scrum Team
- Guerrilla Testing
- Go on a User Safari
- Start a Stakeholder Treasure Hunt

We Create Distance between Developers and Stakeholders

If we had a penny for every Zombie Scrum Team we worked with that had no contact with actual users, we would have bought the Brain X-Tractor 3000 a long time ago (and not just last week when it was practically too late). For these teams, the stakeholder is usually the person who hands them their requirements. These people are often the former Project Manager, Business Analyst, head of department, or someone in a parent company. When you go further up the chain, however, you often find that the person who was labeled as a stakeholder is four or five steps removed from anyone actually using the product themselves. They don't own the real problem that is being solved and are just one link in an absurdly long chain of requirements being passed down in a game of telephone (see Figure 5.1).

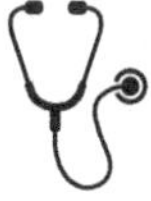

Signs to look for:

- There is a lot of talk of "internal stakeholders" and what they need, but rarely talk of actual product users ("real" stakeholders).
- Sprint Reviews are never attended by people who use the product to address a challenge they face. Instead, Sprint Reviews are attended by people from within the organization who have a stake in the product, such as product managers, people from sales and marketing, or the CEO.
- When you ask someone on the Development Team to name one person who's really using or going to use the product, all you get is an empty stare.

This chain has its advantages. It makes sense in an organization where work is organized along functional roles, as it clearly defines which functional role is responsible for certain kinds of risks. It is also rather predictable and standardized in how, when, and by whom communication takes place. But there are significant downsides, especially when dealing with work where the problem isn't clear and there is no out-of-the-box solution available. Here you have to figure both out along the way. And to make that sort of "shared discovery" possible, there needs to be frequent collaboration between the people owning the problem and the ones solving it.

If this chain is enforced by organizations, as is often the case, it actively discourages this kind of collaboration. It's likely that everyone in the chain has more work to do for other projects and other stakeholders. So continuously relaying feedback, ideas, and messages between stakeholders and developers causes too much overhead. Instead, feedback ends up being grouped into monthly or quarterly meetings. Or it is discouraged altogether. As a result, the functional "silos" that form in these organizations create distance between the people using the products and the people developing them. If any kind of Sprint Review takes place, it ends up attended by people who cannot provide meaningful feedback on how they experience the use of the product. Maybe boxes are ticked and documents are updated. But no insight into the usability of the product is generated and there is no conversation about the way forward. After several Sprints, something of questionable value is delivered. The team feels confident about their performance, however, because the person they call their stakeholder is happy that things are going according to their plan.

Figure 5.1 The "Game of Telephone" that breaks down communication in traditional organizations where there are many "hops" between the people using the product and the people developing it

Try these experiments to improve with your team (see Chapter 6):

- Give the Stakeholder a Desk Close to the Scrum Team
- Create Transparency with the Stakeholder Distance Metric
- Go on a User Safari
- Guerrilla Testing

We See Business and IT As Separate Things

One important cause for Zombie Scrum lies in the line that many organizations draw between "Business" and "IT." Usually the "IT people" includes everyone with knowledge of software and hardware, such as testers, developers, support employees, architects, and IT managers. The "Business people," on the other hand, are the people doing sales, marketing, or management (see Figure 5.2). They generally act as "internal stakeholders" of needs that serve the actual, external stakeholders.

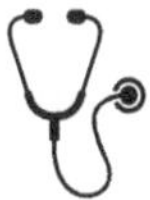

Signs to look for:

- People talk about "Business" and "IT" as separate departments or separate perspectives.
- There is a lot of negative gossip. People complain about how "IT never gets anything done" or "Business always wants things done yesterday."
- The "IT people" work in different departments or even different buildings from the "Business people."

Following their functional roles and the subset of risks they are responsible for, "Business" and "IT" often "collaborate" by means of contracts and documents. During tough negotiations about costs and requirements, the actual stakeholders are forgotten. Distinct rifts form within the organization and you start hearing things like, "If you want to get anything done, don't talk to IT" and "Business keeps changing their mind."

Figure 5.2 Business and IT as two, somehow separate, parts of the same company

One outcome of this separation of "IT" and "Business" is that it encourages a Scrum Team to focus on the needs of "internal stakeholders" over the customers of an organization and the users of the product, and "Business" comes to believe that they are the customers of the product instead, purchasing it on behalf of the real customers. Another outcome is a deep mutual distrust between "Business" and "IT" that drives even tougher negotiations and more extensive contractual agreements. Because the whole circus takes so long, important business opportunities are not exploited because people stop making the effort.

"Software is eating the world," said Marc Andreessen in 2011,[1] when he observed that more and more organizations, regardless of their sector and industry, depend on software to perform their primary processes and remain competitive. That makes the distinction between "IT" and "Business" just as meaningless as arguing over whether you need your brain or your intelligence to solve puzzles; you need both. Unfortunately, organizations with Zombie Scrum cling to this meaningless distinction and let it actively get in the way of delivering value to their actual stakeholders.

1. Andreessen, M. 2011. "Why Software Is Eating the World." *Wall Street Journal,* August 20. Retrieved on May 27, 2020, from **https://www.wsj.com/articles/SB10001424053111903480904576512250915629460.**

Try these experiments to improve with your team (see Chapter 6):

- Give the Stakeholder a Desk Close to the Scrum Team
- Create Transparency with the Stakeholder Distance Metric
- Go on a User Safari
- Start a Stakeholder Treasure Hunt

We Don't Allow Product Owners to Actually Own the Product

In organizations with Zombie Scrum, Product Owners simply translate requirements into items for the Product Backlog, without much of a say in what goes on it or in what order. They fulfill their roles as "Order Takers" with no actual ownership or mandate (see Figure 5.3). Whenever a decision needs to be made about the ordering or what goes on the Product Backlog, either they don't make a decision at all or they have to defer to someone higher up in the organizational hierarchy.

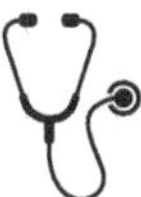

Signs to look for:

- During the Sprint Review, the Product Owner gathers sticky notes with feedback. But other people decide if these ideas are actually going to happen or not.
- When the Development Team considers the product ready to release, the Product Owner needs to ask the entire chain of command for permission, making it impossible to release multiple times during the Sprint.
- When asked, the Product Owner has no idea how much actual value was generated by the outcome of a Sprint.

This lack of autonomy is curious, because the Scrum Guide states that "the Product Owner is responsible for maximizing the value of the product resulting from work of the Development Team."[2] When Product Owners don't take an active role in deciding what goes on the Product Backlog and in what order, it will be nearly impossible for them to maximize value. Instead, the focus shifts to getting as much work done as possible. Unfortunately, much of that work will be of questionable value compared to the money and effort that was poured into doing it.

Figure 5.3 When Product Owners act as "Order Takers," they mindlessly transfer requests from stakeholders to the Development Team.

When Product Owners fulfill their role as intended, they become "Order Makers" instead. They have to if they want to filter the many needs and requests of many potential stakeholders into a useful and valuable product. With the inherent limitations on budget and time, Product Owners have to work closely with stakeholders to decide what is important and what isn't. Without mandate, they won't be able to make these decisions at all, or it will simply take too long to navigate the organizational hierarchy and internal policies. When they are "Order Makers," Product Owners truly maximize the work *not* done.

2. Sutherland, J. K., and K. Schwaber. 2017. *The Scrum Guide*. Retrieved on May 26, 2020, from **https://www.scrumguides.org**.

Try these experiments to improve with your team (see Chapter 6):

- Limit the Maximum Length of Your Product Backlog
- Map Your Product Backlog on an Ecocycle

We Measure Output over Value

Up to this point, one underlying root cause of Zombie Scrum is that it focuses on getting as much work done (output) rather than judging the value of that work to stakeholders (outcome). This symptom also shows in, and is often amplified by, how Scrum Teams report their work.

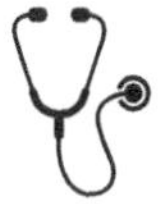

Signs to look for:

- Scrum Teams report metrics that capture how much work is being done, such as velocity, the number of items completed, or the number of bugs fixed.
- None of the metrics used by Scrum Teams captures the value of that work. For example, how quality or performance improves or how the work is appreciated by stakeholders.
- Scrum Teams are actively compared by others on their output and (implicitly or explicitly) told to work harder.

This focus on measuring output makes sense when you consider the guiding philosophy behind how work is organized. When organizations design work along functional roles, they often want to measure how that work is done by those roles. How many leads are generated by sales? How many projects are delivered on time by project management? And how many support calls are handled by support? For Scrum Teams, this translates into how much work they can get done in a certain amount of time.

The purpose of this reporting is to improve the efficiency of the entire organization by tuning the efficiency of individual components (people, teams, departments). The assumption here is that the efficiency of the entire system improves when individual components become more efficient. And although that might apply to environments where work is predictable and follows recipes, such as assembly lines and manufacturing processes, it doesn't work for complex environments where the degree of collaboration needed to deliver value is much higher.

In complex environments, focusing on the efficiency of individual units—people or teams—actually reduces the overall output because it tries to keep each unit as busy as possible. And that undermines collaboration within the organization and with stakeholders. In Chapter 9, we share more helpful metrics.

Try these experiments to improve with your team (see Chapter 6):

- Decorate the Team Room with the Product Purpose
- Limit the Length of the Product Backlog
- Express Desired Outcomes, Not Work to Be Done

We Believe That Developers Should Only Write Code

In Zombie Scrum, developers are generally encouraged to focus on writing code while other people work with stakeholders. Or developers promote this belief themselves by stating that they're "only here to code" and anything else is considered a waste of time (see Figure 5.4).

Signs to look for:

- Developers don't attend Scrum Events or other gatherings because it takes time away from writing code.
- Developers are assumed to lack the social skills needed to talk to stakeholders.
- Job descriptions for developers only mention technical skills and don't mention anything about creating valuable products together with stakeholders.

This attitude where the work is disconnected from those it serves makes sense in organizations where work is organized along functional roles. Developers are recruited entirely on their ability to write code. Being capable of working with stakeholders is not a job requirement. And yet, that is exactly the kind of collaboration you need when you do something as complex as developing products.

Figure 5.4 The "I'm only here to code" attitude is a great way to avoid dealing with the frustrations of real stakeholders.

The "I'm only here to code" attitude is a mental enabler of Zombie Scrum. It encourages people to reject ownership of anything outside their immediate functional responsibility. It also paints a stereotype of developers and other roles as being incapable of talking with stakeholders.

Agile software development shifts a developer's responsibility from being someone who writes code to someone who works with stakeholders to solve complex problems. The same goes for every other specialization, such as UI/UX expert, systems architect, database admin, and so forth. Instead of focusing on individual role responsibilities, the team as a whole becomes responsible for the product.

Try these experiments to improve with your team (see Chapter 6):

- Go on a User Safari
- Invite Stakeholders to a "Feedback Party"
- Give the Stakeholder a Desk Close to the Scrum Team

We Have Stakeholders Who Don't Want to Be Involved

Scrum Teams sometimes avoid involving stakeholders because they don't want to bother them. A driving assumption here is that asking questions is seen as unprofessional and inexperienced or is a waste of stakeholders' valuable time. Stakeholders sometimes use a similar argument: "You are the professionals, go and figure it out."

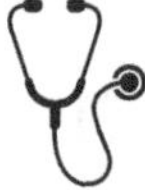

Signs to look for:

- Stakeholders consistently don't make time available to attend Sprint Reviews.
- After the initial briefing of requirements, customers openly question why their involvement is necessary during development.
- When a member of the Development Team asks for clarification or has questions about a feature, the stakeholders point them to the specification documents.

One of the authors once attended a kickoff where a key stakeholder—the customer paying for development—noted that he didn't need to be involved during the development of his tailor-made product. He felt that he had sufficiently briefed the Product Owner and was expecting great results. The Scrum Team cleverly responded by asking questions like "What makes you certain that your stakeholders will be happy with the product as you've described it?", "How certain are you that the solution we have in mind now is also the best one?" and "Would you exclude new, valuable ideas that emerge during development?" As an experiment, the stakeholder agreed to join the first three Sprint Reviews. Although the initial two Sprint Reviews resulted in no spectacular changes, the third Sprint Review yielded an entirely new feature that was pushed to the top of the Product Backlog. And it convinced the stakeholder that there was huge value in being involved.

What helped this Scrum Team convince the stakeholder was their ability to deliver a done and releasable Increment to production every Sprint. Because value was delivered every Sprint, the stakeholder shifted from being present to oblige the Scrum Team to being present because it helped him get more value out of his investments. Each Sprint Review presented him with an opportunity to add new ideas, make corrections with the team, and stay up to date with what was being released and when. Over the coming Sprints, more and more stakeholders—including many users—started attending the Sprint Reviews for the same reason.

Unfortunately, teams that suffer from Zombie Scrum often don't have much to show by the end of a Sprint. Even when they have a "Done" Increment, it still takes months for their work to reach production. With such a delay, who can blame stakeholders for not seeing the need to be present? All sense of immediacy is lost as they have to wait a long time for their influence to show in what is released. It's easy to understand why they'd rather wait with their feedback until a release is imminent, or even afterward.

The complexities of product development lie in the ambiguity of both the problem and the solution. As the example notes, this reality requires that Scrum Teams better explain what is to be gained from a collaborative approach. In turn, this approach only works when Scrum Teams are able to ship (and respond) fast to feedback from stakeholders. If it is very difficult for stakeholders to find the time to join, pragmatic solutions may be called for, such as organizing the Sprint Review at the stakeholders' location or involving them through teleconferencing.

Try these experiments to improve with your team (see Chapter 6):

- Give the Stakeholder a Desk Close to the Scrum Team
- Express Desired Outcomes, Not Work to Be Done
- Start a Stakeholder Treasure Hunt
- Guerrilla Testing

HEALTHY SCRUM

As we've seen in this chapter, Scrum Teams that operate in environments with Zombie Scrum don't know their stakeholders nor what is valuable to them. This distance is created when organizations design work along functional roles, and when they focus on the efficiency of how work is done by those roles. In contrast, healthy Scrum Teams are more concerned with how effective their work is—that is, how much value it delivers to their stakeholders and the organization they work for. They can't do this without close and frequent collaboration with actual stakeholders.

WHO SHOULD GET TO KNOW THE STAKEHOLDERS?

In a traditional organizational structure, the stakeholder contacts are probably the product manager or people from sales. When these organizations switch to the Scrum Framework, they often make the Product Owner responsible for connecting with stakeholders. But that is a missed opportunity for collaborative discovery.

Getting to know the stakeholders is something the entire Scrum Team should be involved in. Although a Product Owner will naturally spend more time with groups of stakeholders to determine what is needed in the product, and in what order, the conversations should naturally involve the entire Development Team as well.

We like to explain that the Product Owner is the person who is continuously on a journey to identify what is valuable and important to stakeholders. But instead of translating these value judgments into detailed specifications for the Development Team, the Product Owner creates a Product Backlog that is essentially a list of conversations that should take place somewhere down the road between the Development Team, the Product Owner, and relevant stakeholders. These conversations should take place soon for items near the top of the Product Backlog, and later for others.

Whatever the case, each conversation results in some kind of refinement of the work that is needed. This can result in changes to the Product Backlog or its ordering. Information can also be captured as a workflow drawn out on a whiteboard, a list of notes on a piece of paper, a more detailed description in a tool, or a good recollection from the minds of those present. But the point is that the best products are created when developers and stakeholders work together. Everything that gets in the way of this dynamic should be removed. The purpose is not specification, but conversation.

This approach makes the Product Owner more of a facilitator of the interactions between the Development Team and the stakeholders. No Product Owner, no matter how good or clever they are, can comprehend the playing field on their own. Instead, they can use the intelligence of the entire Scrum Team to clarify what is needed, how to get it done, and in what order.

When to Involve Stakeholders

When should Scrum Teams involve their stakeholders? Healthy Scrum Teams involve them in different ways and at different moments.

Involve Stakeholders during the Creation of the Product Purpose

In this chapter, we explained how a lack of vision and purpose makes it difficult to deliver valuable outcomes to stakeholders. It makes sense to start by clarifying the purpose. And this is an excellent opportunity for Product Owners to bring together the perspectives of stakeholders and the people building the product to create clarity. This effort can take the shape of a workshop, a summit, or an online session. And although "clarifying the purpose" might seem complicated, it essentially boils down to completing the statements "This product exists in order to . . ." and "This product does not exist in order to . . . ."

Considering the complexity of product development, it is only natural that the understanding of a product's purpose changes over time as work proceeds and new opportunities take shape. So tune the purpose periodically.

Involve Stakeholders during the Product Development Kickoff

Inviting stakeholders to the kickoff of development is a great way to get a strong value focus ingrained from the start. The goal here is to create the foundation for collaboration between the people developing the product and the people using it, paying for it, or relying on it. So instead of starting up a PowerPoint deck of dozens of sheets, focus on facilitating a highly interactive session. Let people get to know each other, using a variety of introductory games. Focus on what people expect from the product and each other.

Involve Stakeholders during the Sprint Review

The most obvious moment to invite stakeholders is during the Sprint Review. It's up to the Product Owner to decide who, or which groups, can add the most value. If you have a lot of stakeholders, invite a representative sample. The goal here is actively to involve stakeholders. Don't make them sit and listen to you. Pass them the mouse and keyboard and let them use a new feature. Ask them if it works for them, what they would like to see improved, or what new ideas they have.

The purpose of a Sprint Review is not merely to demo new features and gather feedback. The Scrum Guide clearly explains the purpose in a single sentence: "A Sprint Review is held at the end of the Sprint to inspect the Increment and adapt the Product Backlog if needed."[3] This means the Sprint Review is an excellent moment to reflect on what has been built by the Development Team, and what that means for future Sprints. It is likely that feedback gathered during a Sprint Review affects what's on the Product Backlog, or the way it's ordered. Make good use of this opportunity to inspect not only the new version of the product (the "Increment") but also the Product Backlog.

Involve Stakeholders during Product Backlog Refinement

The best chefs use a practice called *mise en place*. It is the practice of putting everything in place before cooking begins. Ingredients are chopped up, meat is sliced, and sauces are mixed. All materials are arranged so that they are easily accessible. Mise en place helps cooks deal with the stress of fast-paced professional kitchens and focus on preparing delicious meals. Refinement in product development is like mise en place for cooking. It helps to prepare for upcoming work and to create focus.

3. Sutherland and Schwaber, *The Scrum Guide*.

One example of refinement is the activity of breaking down large chunks of work into smaller chunks. If we take on large chunks of work, we're likely to run into unforeseen problems. We may have forgotten about dependencies, issues in the code may emerge, and things take more time. The larger the amount of work, the higher this risk. For this reason, it is a good idea to break down large chunks into many smaller chunks.

You can do refinement during Sprint Planning. But like a cook who's trying to cut, chop, and prepare his ingredients while also cooking, you will quickly discover that this approach is stressful and exhausting. It draws energy away from the purpose of Sprint Planning: to determine a goal for the next Sprint and select the work that is necessary for that. Instead, it is better to do your mise en place and let refinement for the upcoming Sprint take place during the current Sprint. With all the ingredients ready, Sprint Planning will be much more fluent and energizing. Some teams do this in the form of time-boxed "refinement workshops," where the entire team attends; other teams use "Three Amigos sessions," where three members of the Development Team work together to refine a large feature that will be coming up soon. How you do it is entirely up to you.

Refinement is a great opportunity to involve stakeholders. When refining a certain item, you can invite relevant stakeholders to attend a refinement workshop. Or you can visit stakeholders to interview them about their needs, and then break down the work together.

Now What?

In this chapter, we explored the most common symptoms and causes for not sufficiently involving stakeholders. Without involving stakeholders, the Scrum Framework is pointless, because there is no way to actually know what is valuable.

Are you on a Scrum Team or in an organization where this is happening? Don't panic. The next chapter is loaded with practical experiments and interventions you can use to start shifting things in the right direction.

6 EXPERIMENTS

Are we all just Dark Age doctors, swearing by our leeches? We crave a greater science. We want to be proven wrong . . .

—Isaac Marion, *Warm Bodies*

In This Chapter

- Explore ten experiments to learn the needs of your stakeholders.
- Learn what impact the experiments have on surviving Zombie Scrum.
- Discover how to perform each experiment and what to look for.

This chapter presents experiments to help Scrum Teams build what their stakeholders need. Some are designed specifically to better understand the needs of your stakeholders, while others are more focused on distinguishing what is valuable and what isn't. While the experiments vary in their difficulty, each one will make the subsequent step easier.

EXPERIMENTS: GETTING TO KNOW YOUR STAKEHOLDERS

How can you help Scrum Teams develop a better understanding of what it is their stakeholders are looking for? The next section contains three simple experiments you can try to make that possible.

START A STAKEHOLDER TREASURE HUNT

Before any interaction with stakeholders can take place, Scrum Teams need to find out who these stakeholders actually are. This experiment helps Zombie Scrum Teams identify the people who care about their product by clarifying the product's purpose. This is the first step towards interacting with those stakeholders.

Effort/Impact Ratio

Effort	★★★☆☆	Going on a journey to find the real stakeholders takes time.
Impact on survival	★★★☆☆	When teams start learning who their stakeholders are, it becomes progressively easier to deliver value to them (and recover!).

Steps

Gather your team and ask the following questions to understand the purpose of your product:

- "What is the product we are building? Why does it need to exist?"
- "What would be missing if we stopped building this product?"
- "How do we justify using our precious time, money, and mental energy?"

There are many ways to engage participants in this conversation. For this particular experiment, and for many others in this book, we recommend using one or more Liberating Structures.[1] For example, you can use "1-2-4-All" and

1. Lipmanowicz, H., and K. McCandless. 2014. *The Surprising Power of Liberating Structures: Simple Rules to Unleash a Culture of Innovation*. Liberating Structures Press. ASN: 978-0615975306.

ask the participants to reflect silently on the question for one minute. Then ask them to form pairs and discuss the question for two minutes before they join another pair and discuss for another four minutes. When the time is up, ask the quartets to share their results with the large groups. You can also use other Liberating Structures, such as "Conversation Café" or "User Experience Fishbowl."

After you have successfully clarified the purpose of the product, have a look at the experiment "Decorate the Team Room with the Product Purpose" later in this chapter to put the purpose to good use. Now that you have clarity on the purpose of your product, ask these questions to hunt for your stakeholders:

- "Who actually uses our product?"
- "Who benefits from our product?"
- "Whose problem are we solving?"
- "How are we engaging these people?"

It's easy for some teams to answer these questions. Other teams don't have a clue. When the team has no clue, we recommend making your way up the chain. Ask the team:

- "Who tells us what to work on?"
- "Who tells *them* what to work on?"
- "What happens before that?"

Once you have identified your stakeholders successfully, you can try other experiments in this book to start interacting with them. "Give the Stakeholder a Desk Close to the Scrum Team" and "Invite Stakeholders to a 'Feedback Party'" from this chapter as well as "Measure Stakeholder Satisfaction" from Chapter 8 are great choices.

Our Findings

- Zombie Scrum Teams often know very little about where their requirements are coming from. It's entirely possible that asking the previous questions will earn you a lot of shrugs and confused looks. Start with the Product

Owner and see how far you get. If you can't go any further, ask around within your organization.

- Some stakeholders will receive you with open arms once you start interacting with them. Others will be just as skeptical as Zombie Scrum Teams and won't see the benefits. Find a way of showing how closer contact with the Development Team can help them!

CREATE TRANSPARENCY WITH THE STAKEHOLDER DISTANCE METRIC

One of the most important ways Scrum Masters can help organizations improve is to create transparency. This experiment is about creating transparency about the distance between developers and stakeholders (see Figure 6.1) and what happens because of that.

Effort/Impact Ratio

Effort	★★★☆☆	How much effort this requires depends on the complexity of your organization.
Impact on survival	★★★☆☆	Probably quite painful for serious Zombie Scrum, but it will hurt in the right spots.

Figure 6.1 Periodically measuring the distance from the people building the product to the people using or paying for it can reveal many impediments to agility.

Steps

The Stakeholder Distance Metric tracks the average number of people, departments, or roles you have to go through ("hops") in order to convey a question or get feedback from someone who is actually paying for the product or actively using it:

1. Take a selection of items from your Product Backlog that are representative of the kind of work that your team does.
2. Taking one item at a time, draw the chain of people, departments, and roles you have to go through—or get permission from—in order to test this item with an actual stakeholder—that is, someone who is actively using your product or is investing in it significantly.
3. For each hop, come up with a rough estimate for how many hours or days it takes to go through this hop.
4. Repeat this process a couple of times for different kinds of items. Then calculate the average number of hops and the average time the hops take. For extra effect, you can calculate how much time and money is spent waiting for the chain to complete.
5. Write the number of hops and the time they take clearly on a big board or panel that is visible to all. For an extra dramatic effect, you can periodically redraw these numbers on a prominent window or wall.
6. Have a conversation with your team about what the results of this distance are. How is it affecting your team's ability to work on the right things? How much money and time is being wasted? What is going wrong because of this distance?

Teams recovering from Zombie Scrum will slowly lose their fear of stakeholders. A good way to monitor recovery is to periodically recalculate the Stakeholder Distance Metric. You can use it to drive conversations during Sprint Retrospectives on how to decrease the distance as much as possible. Many of the experiments in this book can help you do that.

Our Findings

- Metrics don't have meaning in themselves, but they are given meaning through context and conversation. Make sure that you have this conversation with your entire team. You should never use metrics to judge, compare, or evaluate teams that you yourself do not belong to.

- Shortening the distance to the stakeholder might require you to break an existing, highly elaborate product development process. Depending on your position in the system, disrupting that process might not be possible. Nevertheless, see if you can raise awareness for the problem or circumvent the issue by still talking to users and then getting involved in discussions about requirements as early as possible.

Give the Stakeholder a Desk Close to the Scrum Team

Being distant from the stakeholder is a great excuse not to involve them. This experiment removes that excuse by bringing the stakeholder so close that there's no escaping them. It's like "Encounter Therapy," really, and it's one of the most effective ways to make progress.

Effort/Impact Ratio

Effort	★☆☆☆☆	Setting up the desk and inviting stakeholders is easy. Having the stakeholder use the desk might take more effort.
Impact on survival	★★★★★	For a tiny experiment, this is bound to have a huge impact.

Steps

To try this experiment, do the following:

1. Create a desk close to your Scrum Team where one or more stakeholders can comfortably do their own work. Candy helps!
2. Invite one or more stakeholders to make use of this desk whenever they can be available for the Scrum Team. Invite stakeholders who actively use the product or are significantly investing in it. Organize a short event to get to know each other and to clarify the purpose of this experiment.

3. If helpful, create a schedule together of when the stakeholder(s) will be there and put it somewhere clearly visible for the Scrum Team. Working arrangements also help to balance focus and interaction.
4. Observe what happens next.

When stakeholders and teams are not used to this kind of close proximity, some awkwardness is natural. Gently connect the team and the stakeholders wherever relevant if it doesn't happen on its own. Encourage the team to test assumptions with the stakeholder, such as a new design or a feature under development. Or invite them to work together on refining work for the next Sprint.

This is a great experiment to help people understand what makes product development complex. During Sprints, you're bound to run into many unforeseen issues. Having the stakeholders present allows you to resolve those problems more quickly. It also allows stakeholders to increase their appreciation of the value they add by being present.

Our Findings

- Some stakeholders assume they have little to contribute while the Scrum Team is doing their work. Having delivered their requirements, they may prefer to wait until the product is done. In that case, invite stakeholders to be present for one or two Sprints and decide afterward how useful their presence was and whether to continue being present.
- This is a great opportunity to celebrate small successes together. Keep an eye out for those moments. Simply going for lunch together is already a great help.
- You can easily flip this experiment around by giving the Development Team desks close to the stakeholders. Two of the authors of this book, in separate instances, arranged with their Scrum Teams to work on a customer site for a while. Aside from easier access to stakeholders, simply sharing the same coffee machine, celebrating the same birthdays, and having lunch together created a productive working environment.

DECORATE THE TEAM ROOM WITH THE PRODUCT PURPOSE

Zombie Scrum Teams tend to appear in environments where nothing reminds them that their purpose is something other than "complete all the work" or "write lots of code." A first step towards recovery is to change the environment to signal and clarify that purpose.

Effort/Impact Ratio

Effort	★★☆☆☆	Gathering decorations is generally not hard. Creating a clear, tangible, and compelling product purpose can take more effort.
Impact on survival	★★★★☆	This experiment triggers meaningful discussions, faster decision-making, and increased focus.

Steps

To try this experiment, do the following:

1. Considering that it is their team room, you really want to do this with your team. Let them decide how to do it, and take initiative when they don't. This is also a good opportunity to encourage the Product Owner to take the lead.
2. If no clear purpose statement is at hand for your product, you can use one of the other experiments in this chapter to begin clarifying it (such as "Start a Stakeholder Treasure Hunt"). The purpose statement doesn't have to be earth-shatteringly brilliant and can be refined over time.
3. Once you've made the product purpose visible in the team room, you can start gently using it in your day-to-day conversations with the team: "How is this item from the Product Backlog helping us work on that purpose?", "If we keep the product purpose in mind, what should we let go of?" and "Considering our product purpose, what is the next step forward?"

There are many ways to decorate the team room with the product purpose:

- Order coffee mugs that have the purpose of the product printed on them.
- Order stickers for laptops, roll-up banners, party flags, buttons, or whatever other material your team fancies that capture the purpose of the product.

- Write down the purpose statement of the product ("This product exists in order to . . .") on a banner and place it above or below the Sprint Backlog or Scrum Board.
- Create a "The User Says" wall with pictures of real users and quotes about what the product makes possible for them.
- Pick a team name or inspiring motto that captures the purpose of the product.

Our Findings

- In environments with severe Zombie Scrum, where "purpose" is just a word from a vocabulary, these kinds of experiments may understandably be frowned upon as "unnecessary" or "ridiculous." Be resilient. Even the most cynical members will start appreciating the decorations, visuals, and other artifacts.
- A good purpose statement captures why the product matters to users. What does it simplify, improve, enable, or make better for its users? How is it valuable? A statement like "This product exists to process time cards from flex workers" merely describes what it does, but not why. This statement doesn't give a lot of guidance on making user-based decisions about which features should be included. A better formulation would be: "This product exists to reduce the time flex workers have to spend on entering time cards and managers have to spend on verifying them."

Experiments: Involving Stakeholders in Product Development

Scrum without stakeholders is like a race car without a driver. It might look incredible and go really fast, but it doesn't get you anywhere in particular if there's nobody to guide it. Involving stakeholders isn't always easy. This section offers three experiments you can do to involve them in novel and creative ways.

Invite Stakeholders to a "Feedback Party"

Do stakeholders regularly miss or avoid your Sprint Review? Or do your Sprint Reviews usually take the shape of a static presentation with a silent audience? A good Sprint Review is all about gathering feedback and validating assumptions with the people present. The purpose of this experiment is to invite stakeholders to your next Sprint Review, and to use them to gather valuable feedback (see Figure 6.2). This experiment is based on the Liberating Structure "Shift & Share."[2]

Effort/Impact Ratio

Effort	★★☆☆☆	Start by inviting a few stakeholders to keep the effort low. You can invite more stakeholders to create a bigger impact, but this takes more effort.
Impact on survival	★★★★★	This experiment has the potential of creating snowball-change as the dynamic of the Sprint Review starts fulfilling its purpose.

Steps

To try this experiment, do the following:

1. Together with your Product Owner, identify which stakeholders are most likely to have ideas and feedback on the Sprint Goal that the team has been working on and the work selected for it. Invite them to the next Sprint Review. If you have to, offer cake and coffee to lure them in.
2. Before the Sprint Review, prepare together with the Scrum Team. Together, identify five to seven features or items from the Product Backlog that the team would like to get feedback on. For each feature or item, set up a station—a flip chart with some information, a laptop, tablet, or desktop—and make sure that each station has one or two members of the team present as "station owners." Provide each station with stickies or postcards to capture feedback.
3. At the start of the Sprint Review, welcome the stakeholders and make sure to reiterate why their presence is helpful. Proceed to introduce the various stations and explain that stakeholders will be "touring" the stations in short ten-minute time boxes. At each station, stakeholders have the opportunity to try and give feedback on aspects of the Increment.

2. Lipmanowicz and McCandless, *The Surprising Power of Liberating Structures.*

4. Invite the "station owners" briefly to introduce what their station is about. Everyone else then divides equally across the stations. In rounds of ten minutes, groups tour the stations in a clockwise fashion. Instead of demonstrating new features, the "station owners" invite stakeholders to take control of the laptop, tablet, or desktop and give the new features a try with only minimal guidance.
5. When the groups have visited all stations, invite everyone in the room to take a moment and silently reflect on the following question: "Based on what we've seen, what seems to be a next step for us?" After a minute, invite people to form pairs and share their ideas. Give them a few minutes, then invite the pairs to pair up again into groups of four and build on their ideas for five minutes. With the whole group, debrief and capture the most important ideas.
6. If the stakeholders have the time, you can dig deeper into next steps and their feedback. If they don't, this is a good opportunity for the Product Owner and the team to thank them for their time and extend an invitation to the next Sprint Review. With the Scrum Team, proceed by further digesting the feedback into tangible items and potential objectives for upcoming Sprints.

Our Findings

- Stick to a light-hearted, informal approach and have some fun with it. You'll notice that users may be quick to apologize for not being able to find their way around a feature or causing errors ("Sorry, I didn't mean to break it!"). Although such difficulty demonstrates a shortcoming of the product, users often feel "dumb" or "slow" if they can't figure something out. Especially when others are watching.
- If you're doing this experiment for the first time, expect things to be awkward. But persist and keep doing the Sprint Reviews like this, and you'll notice how stakeholders become increasingly engaged over time when they see how their feedback is integrated into the product.

GO ON A USER SAFARI

The purpose of this experiment is to help Scrum Teams get to know their users and what their challenges are by spending time with them. Not only does this give developers a much better understanding of the environments in which products are used and by whom, it also helps Development Teams see the purpose of their work.

Effort/Impact Ratio

Effort	★★☆☆☆	Visiting one user takes little effort. You can visit more to increase the impact, but against a higher effort.
Impact on survival	★★★★★	If you've never done this before, this experiment is likely to completely change how Development Teams understand their product and its users.

Steps

To try this experiment, do the following:

1. Working with the Product Owner, identify one or more locations where you're likely to find (many) users of the product your team is developing. For example, if your team is building a product for managing rail traffic, go visit rail operators in their control rooms.
2. Prepare the User Safari with the Scrum Team by identifying what you'd like to know from stakeholders and their environment. What are things you can observe? What questions can you ask? Also decide how you're going to record observations. Are you going to take notes? Record audio or video?
3. When you're at the location, it's best to break up into pairs to not overwhelm users. Encourage pairs to observe users as they interact with the product and gently ask some open-ended questions now and then. For extra insight, users can verbalize the steps they are taking or considering and what it is they expect will happen.
4. When you're done observing and taking notes, gather the entire Scrum Team and do a shared debrief of what you noticed. What was surprising for the team? What new ideas or improvements emerged? Capture ideas on the Product Backlog.

Here are some tips on what to ask or look for:

- Observe what sort of devices people use to view the product.
- Observe the environment that users operate in.
- Ask: "How does this feature help you in your day-to-day work?"
- Ask: "What can we do to make it easier for you to use this product?"
- Ask: "If we had to rebuild this product from the ground up, starting from scratch, what would be the first thing you'd want us to bring back?"

Our Findings

- Some users may be hesitant to let developers observe. If necessary, agree on a time box and specific work agreements up front. And always be clear about how their feedback can help make the product—and their work—easier.
- Prepare your Development Team for a scenario where users are critical of their work. Some people are better able to express criticism than others. It's helpful for Development Teams to avoid becoming disheartened or defensive, but instead explore openly where the criticism is coming from. Critical users can turn into your biggest proponents when they notice that they are being listened to.

Experience: Small Discoveries with a Lot of Feedback

Here's a tale of firsthand experience from one of this book's authors:

With four developers, we drove to a facility with a lot of planners: our users. On the site, we quickly noticed how noisy and chaotic the environment was. Telephones rang all the time, people inquired loudly about the availability of certain flex workers, and other people walked in with questions. We discovered something crucial. While on the telephone—the telephone tightly jammed between a planner's head and shoulder—the planner used our product to change the planning for a particular flex worker. Keeping the phone between the head and shoulder meant that the planner's head was tilted. Combined with the small screens that planners used, this made reading the text and navigating with the cursor difficult. Back at our office, we quickly updated the application to increase the font size and use larger buttons. It was a small change that really improved the usability of the application.

Guerrilla Testing

Finding users isn't easy. The purpose of this experiment is to perform playful user testing by getting Development Teams out of the office and close to actual and potential users.

Effort/Impact Ratio

Effort	★★★☆☆	Although the effort is relatively low, Development Teams may be a bit worried about doing this if they've never tried it before.
Impact on survival	★★★★☆	If this is the first time, this experiment is going to lead to new insights into the product and how it's being used.

Steps

To try this experiment, do the following:

1. With your Development Team, pick a discrete number of Product Backlog items or assumptions you'd like to test. This can be anything from working software to a paper prototype or a design.
2. Go to a place where you're likely to meet real users. This can be the lunchroom or a meeting point in your building if your product is for internal use. If you have external users, visit locations where you might find them. Or go to a coffee shop or the park. In some organizations, you can also find plenty of potential users in the public waiting lounge.
3. Form pairs and walk around. With a laptop in hand, ask people if they can spare a few minutes to help you improve a product. The best feedback comes from goal-based behavior. Ask a user to perform a particular action or achieve a particular goal. Write down any observations or feedback. You can even film the session if the user doesn't mind. Rinse and repeat to gather feedback from different users. It's also a great way to get a sense of who your users are and what they're looking for.

4. Periodically, gather the entire Scrum Team and do a shared debrief of what you noticed. Allow people to blow off some steam and share their excitement and discoveries. Together, explore what was surprising, what new ideas or improvements emerged, and what other things you should be looking for. Repeat with additional rounds of testing as needed.

Our Findings

- If this is the first time you're doing this, the Development Team will be understandably nervous. Working in pairs is a good way to back each other up. You can also do some role-play to practice potential interactions. Some guerrilla gear, ranging from walkie-talkies to caps, may come in handy (see Figure 6.2).
- When you do this experiment in a coffeehouse, you can offer participants free coffee in return for their time and feedback.

Figure 6.2 Take your best guerrilla gear and crawl around your users as discreetly as you can.

Experience: Researching the Users

Here's another tale of firsthand experience from one of this book's authors:

We arranged the opportunity to set up a stand at a conference that was related to our platform. This was an excellent way to do some guerrilla testing on a new workflow in our latest release. We got ourselves two monitors, a keyboard, and a mouse and set up the stand. We decorated the stand with banners and a large map, and we dressed up as "researchers," wearing lab coats and carrying clipboards. We asked each passerby if they'd like to give us feedback on our platform. Thankfully many did and sat down with us to click through the workflow. We recorded their feedback, asked what they liked and didn't like, and identified what parts of the application people often struggled with. This extended testing session not only resulted in invaluable feedback, but it also yielded a lot of people interested in our platform.

Experiments: Keeping Your Focus on What Is Valuable

Instinctively we all seem to understand the power of focus. But finding that focus, and holding onto it, is challenging. This section offers three experiments to help make this possible.

Limit the Maximum Length of Your Product Backlog

It's easy to have a huge Product Backlog. Keeping it short requires many things to be in place, including a guiding purpose and a Product Owner with a mandate and the ability to say "No" to potentially great ideas that don't fit the time and budget you have. The purpose of this experiment is to add a constraint to the length of the Product Backlog and to see what happens next.

Effort/Impact Ratio

Effort	★☆☆☆☆	The experiment itself is easy to do. What comes out of it may not be.
Impact on survival	★★★★☆	This experiment has a tendency to reveal the huge impediments that are making it hard for your Product Owner to work empirically.

Steps

To try this experiment, do the following:

1. Together with the Product Owner, define a constraint for how long the Product Backlog can be before items have to be removed. There is no single number that works best for all scenarios. But in our experience, you want a number that results in a Product Backlog that you can view in one (long) look and have a sense of what is going to happen. Generally, shorter is better. Many teams like limits between 30 and 60 items.
2. If the Product Backlog of your team is already ordered, you can jump to the next step. If not, work together with the Product Owner, the team, and stakeholders to reorder the Product Backlog with the purpose of the product in mind.
3. Invite the Product Owner to remove all the items that are beyond the constraint. Moving them elsewhere on the wall or to another list in Jira doesn't count. Actually throw them away. If teams have physical boards, we always like to bring in a trash can to do this in a very visible way. Does it hurt? Yes. Will people object or faint? Probably. But by being very clear about what is going to happen and what isn't, you create transparency for your stakeholders about what to expect.
4. Visualize the constraint on your Product Backlog. If you have a physical one, you can simply limit the space you have. Most digital tools support list constraints. Make sure to clearly show the purpose of the product next to the constraint, as this is the touchstone for each decision about what to keep and what to throw away.
5. Encourage the Product Owner to clean up the Product Backlog frequently to make the best use of the items you can put up there.

Our Findings

- This experiment can expose many impediments. It may show that your Product Owner has no say in what goes on the Product Backlog. Or it may show that your team spends too much time refining items way down the Product Backlog, making it feel wasteful to throw all those specifications away. But this experiment can also show that there is no clear guiding purpose for your product, something that helps to make decisions about what goes on the Product Backlog. Whatever the case, sticking to the constraint is a great way to keep focus on solving those impediments instead of working around them.
- Be clear, but also be respectful of the items you remove. Each of them represents a potentially great idea for the product. And when items are removed from the current Product Backlog, they may reappear if they are great enough for the product you're trying to build.

MAP YOUR PRODUCT BACKLOG ON AN ECOCYCLE

In environments where Zombie Scrum is present, you find teams stuck in an endless trudge. Sprint after Sprint, they keep working on products that themselves have become lifeless. The purpose of this experiment is to reinvigorate the Product Backlog and create space for innovation and focus.

Effort/Impact Ratio

Effort	★★★☆☆	This experiment takes time to prepare and needs to be done several times to really get into it.
Impact on survival	★★★★☆	Starting to think in terms of the Ecocycle invites people to think about innovation, value, and focus. Like a multivitamin booster, that's a lot of healthy stuff in one go!

Steps

Ecocycle Planning is part of the repertoire of Liberating Structures.[3] Its purpose is to analyze the full portfolio of activities and identify obstacles and

3. Lipmanowicz and McCandless, *The Surprising Power of Liberating Structures.*

opportunities for progress. That makes it an excellent way to periodically clean up and refocus your Product Backlog. It is based on the life cycle in nature, as shown in Figure 6.3.

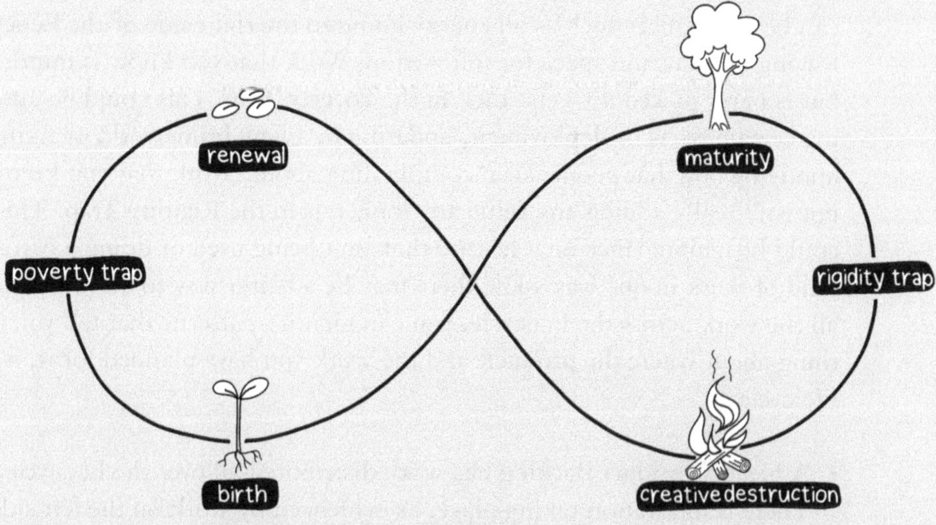

Figure 6.3 Map Your Product Backlog on an Ecocycle[4]

Within the context of Product Development, all work that happens as part of the life cycle for a product can be plotted on the Ecocycle as follows:

- **Renewal** represents ideas for future work that is completely new and innovative. It may involve ideas for exploring new technologies, new features, or new markets.
- **Birth** represents work to turn an idea from gestation into something tangible. This can involve building a prototype, testing a new design with stakeholders, or trying out the very first part of a feature.
- **Maturity** represents work on stable and mature parts of the product. This may involve support, fixing bugs, and making small, incremental tweaks to what is already there.

4. Source: Lipmanowicz and McCandless, *The Surprising Power of Liberating Structures*. Modified by Fisher Qua.

- **Creative Destruction** represents work on parts of the product that are on their way out, or work that is itself no longer valuable.

All activities flow through the Ecocycle. But they can also get stuck. Or there can be disbalances such as all energy going to the right side of the Ecocycle, leaving no time and space for innovation. Work that you know is important, but is never picked up, gets stuck in the **Poverty Trap**. This could be automating certain parts of deployment, updating to a new framework, or fixing that annoying bug that people keep complaining about. Work that you keep doing, but isn't really adding any value any longer, is in the **Rigidity Trap**. This could be maintenance on a feature that isn't being used or doing a certain kind of work in one way while there may be a better way to do it. By plotting all the work across the Ecocycle, you can identify patterns that tell you something about where the product, and the work you have planned for it, is in its life cycle:

- A healthy Product Backlog has work distributed all over the Ecocycle. There is innovation taking place, as evidenced by work on the left side of the model, and there is work to make the product more mature and robust, as evidenced by work on the right. Furthermore, teams are consciously deciding what features and work to let go of, as represented in work that is in Creative Destruction.
- Work that is in the Rigidity Trap or in Creative Destruction is a prime candidate for removal, or at least reinvention. Start there before adding new things, as the removal of work creates space for something new.
- Ecocycle Planning can be done with individual items on the Product Backlog. But you can also apply it to the features of your product. Or to your entire portfolio of products. The applications are endless. But doing it once doesn't get you far; do it often.

So how do you do this with your team? We like to do it as follows:

1. Work with the Product Owner to invite a group of stakeholders and the Development Team to participate in cleaning up the work and to refocus on what is important.

2. Introduce Ecocycle Planning. Explain the metaphor and the quadrants and give some examples to help people understand it. It's okay if people don't get it right away; you really have to experience Ecocycle Planning multiple times for people to start seeing the possibilities.
3. Invite everyone present to draw their own Ecocycle on a piece of paper or in a notebook and distribute the items where they think they are in the Ecocycle for the product. To make this easier, you can number the items on the Product Backlog and invite people to use those instead of writing the items (which is a lot of work).
4. If you have a fairly large group (more than eight to ten people), invite people to pair up and share how they distributed the items across their Ecocycles for a few minutes. Encourage them to work together to finalize the placement.
5. On a prepared larger version of the Ecocycle, perhaps even a huge one on the floor or on a wall, invite everyone to put the items where they think they are in the Ecocycle of this product.
6. Invite people to reflect on the patterns that emerge. Ask: "What does the distribution of items across the Ecocycle seem to be saying about our product, and what is important for it?" Let people do this first individually for a minute, then in pairs for a few minutes and paired up with another pair for four minutes. Encourage the groups to share the most important patterns with the whole group.
7. Invite people to form small groups and identify next steps for cleaning up the Product Backlog. Which items should be removed? What new ideas emerge that should replace existing items on the Product Backlog? Encourage teams to focus on items that are in one of the traps or items that can be creatively destroyed in other ways, as that helps clean up the Product Backlog.

Our Findings

- The way Ecocycle Planning invites us to think about products usually doesn't come natural to Zombie Scrum Teams. You really have to do this multiple times for people to understand the different quadrants and how to make sense of the patterns.

- Because this experiment gives everyone a voice, teams may sigh with relief when they discover that everyone feels the same way about where certain work is placed. Celebrate those moments: letting go of work because you discover it isn't valuable is more important than simply adding more work.
- Using Ecocycle to visualize your product shouldn't be a one-time activity. We recommend that teams create a large Ecocycle poster and put it on the wall in the team room. This encourages updating the Ecocycle continuously and will trigger useful conversations during the Scrum Events.

Express Desired Outcomes, Not Work to Be Done

The way you capture the work that needs to be done on your product has a huge impact on the team doing the work. This experiment changes the way you write your Product Backlog items (PBIs) and makes it easy to have daily conversations about outcomes and stakeholder-centricity.

Effort/Impact Ratio

Effort	★★☆☆☆	A few easy questions will get you on the right track immediately.
Impact on survival	★★★★★	This experiment has the power to change everyday language and mindsets quickly and drastically.

Steps

Despite what most people believe, you are free to use whatever format you like to describe the work on your Product Backlog. The Scrum Guide never mentions "User Story" once. No matter which format you use, don't focus on the tasks that need to be done. Focus on what you want to achieve with them and why. If it helps, mention whom you're developing this for. Here are some options to consider:

- Write your PBIs as *conversations to be had* with your stakeholder. What do you need to clarify with your stakeholder so you can start building the solution? For example: "The appearance of the option to redeem a discount code has been designed with Jimmy."

- Write your PBIs as *actual needs from actual users*. An example might be that "Tessa wants to view all orders from this week so she knows whom to invoice" or "Martin and his team want to send shipment notifications directly so they don't have to ask Pete every time."
- Write your PBIs as a final *user acceptance test*. What is it that the user is going to do that will let you know whether you've succeeded? This needs to be clear enough so that you can answer the question "Is the user able to do this?" with a simple yes or no. For example: "The user can add an item to the shopping basket." These items are perfect candidates for letting actual users try them out in a Sprint Review.
- Write your PBIs as an *outcome* or *target state*. What is the specific end state that is going to provide value? For example: "The app displays the final amount to be paid, including taxes."

So how do you do this with your team? We like to do it as follows:

1. Schedule some time together with your team to develop Product Backlog. We highly recommend inviting actual stakeholders to this workshop to help you answer questions about what is valuable and what isn't.
2. Either take a selection of items from an existing Product Backlog or perform a high-level overview of potential work if you don't already have one. A Liberating Structure such "1-2-4-All," "Min Specs," or "Impromptu Networking" is helpful here.[5]
3. For each item, use the Liberating Structure "1-2-4-All" to have the group consider these questions for each item: "Who benefits when this is done?", "What is different when this is done?", "Why is *that* important?" and "What happens if we don't do this?" Based on the answers, decide together on the best way to capture it on the Product Backlog.
4. Repeat until you have a good enough sense of the work that is coming up to continue for the coming Sprints. Resist the temptation to spend a lot of time on items that lie further into the future. The further down the Product Backlog you go, and the further into potential futures that may or may not happen, the rougher and larger the items can remain. Conserve your energy for the nearer future.

5. Lipmanowicz and McCandless, *The Surprising Power of Liberating Structures.*

Our Findings

It is easy to slip back into the pattern of describing things that need to be done instead of outcomes you would like to achieve. If you are struggling to slice your items in a way that the outcomes stay visible and testable, the experiment "Slice Your Product Backlog Items" in Chapter 8 is helpful.

Now What?

In this chapter, we explored ten experiments to start building what stakeholders need. Some are easier than others and the expected impact varies. But each experiment can be done in environments where Zombie Scrum is rife. Give them a try and see what happens.

However, in the past we also discovered that building what stakeholders need goes hand in hand with being able to ship fast to meet their needs. When it takes months for changes to reach stakeholders, there's no urgency for them to provide their feedback as early as possible. Even the most stakeholder-oriented Scrum Teams zombify when they lose this stream of feedback. In the next part, we explore what Scrum Teams can do to start shipping faster.

"Looking for more experiments, recruit? There is an extensive arsenal available at ***zombiescrum.org****. You can also help expand our arsenal by suggesting what worked well for you."*

III

Ship It Fast

7 Symptoms and Causes

Most people don't believe something can happen until it already has. That's not stupidity or weakness, that's just human nature.

—Max Brooks,
World War Z: An Oral History of the Zombie War

In This Chapter

- Discover the symptoms and observations related to not shipping fast enough for your organization's needs.
- Explore the most common causes of not shipping fast.
- Learn how healthy Scrum Teams balance shipping fast with keeping the focus.

An Experience from the Field

We recently met a team that was infected with Zombie Scrum. They told us about this very cool and innovative (online) platform they'd been working on for the past two years. It all started several years ago when the CEO woke up one night with a great idea for a new product. A Scrum Team of ace developers was formed to take on the challenge and work their way through a long Product Backlog. And so

> they did. As time passed, a lot of clever code was written, and dozens of incredible features were added. Both the company and the team appreciated the rhythm and structure that Scrum provided. They prided themselves on their strict adherence to the Scrum Framework and its prescribed roles and events.
>
> The one exception was that even though every Sprint resulted in a "potentially releasable Increment," they never actually released anything. One reason was that the Scrum Team was not sufficiently skilled in testing the delivered functionality. This was the job of the Quality Assurance (QA) department down the hall. New features could only be delivered when QA had thoroughly tested and green-lighted everything. But considering QA's substantial workload, this usually required several Sprints. Another reason was the amount of manual effort involved in deploying new versions. Because the team experienced past deployments for other products as very stressful and error-prone, they preferred to release only once for the final launch of this product. Although the team proposed to set up an automated deployment pipeline to ease this process, management decided against that approach to keep the focus on adding more features.
>
> Sixteen months later, the first version of the product was finally released to the market. Accompanied by a massive marketing campaign, the product fizzled. As it turned out, customers used the product in vastly different ways than expected. For example, the extensive API that the team had been working on for four months was used by only 2 percent of the customers. Despite initial expectations, the product failed to return on the investment.
>
> Soon after, the symptoms of Zombie Scrum began to appear. The team lost motivation; their excitement left like air rushing out of a punctured balloon. "What went wrong? We finished all the user stories in our Sprints! Wasn't Scrum supposed to prevent failures like this?" Slowly, the eyes of the developers glazed over. Despite the setback, the CEO remained steadfast and hopeful. It wasn't like there weren't any customers, just not a lot. But that would change with the next release—he promised—ten months from now.

This case illustrates how building what stakeholders need (Part II) and shipping fast (Part III) are two sides of the same coin: You can't do one well without the other. In this case, the Scrum Team built features that weren't useful to customers, but they didn't know until the product was finally released. All the money, time, and resources spent fleshing out these supposedly valuable features were wasted in the urge to "get things right the first time."

In this case, the primary source of waste was not the team slacking off, a lack of detailed specifications, or failed alignment between departments. It was a missed opportunity to launch the platform earlier and get feedback from stakeholders sooner. As it turned out, the company incorrectly believed that their platform was going to solve a problem experienced by their stakeholders. And even though some features probably did, the benefits didn't justify the price. While shipping fast doesn't guarantee success, it helps organizations find out faster whether their ideas are actually valuable, and adjust the product strategy based on feedback. This chapter is all about shipping fast, and how it is your best survival strategy when faced with complex work. We also explore the reasons—and excuses—that we encounter for not doing this.

How Bad Is It, Really?

We are continuously monitoring the spread of Zombie Scrum around the world with our online Symptoms Checker at **survey.zombiescrum.org**. Of the Scrum Teams that have participated at the time of writing:*

- 62% have to perform a significant number of manual steps in order to ship an Increment.
- 61% of the Product Owners don't or infrequently use the Sprint Review to gather feedback from stakeholders.
- 57% experience significant stress and pressure to get everything done during the final days of a Sprint.
- 52% frequently have to resolve issues in the next Sprint that could've been prevented by better testing.
- 43% don't spend time in the current Sprint to refine work for upcoming Sprints.
- 39% usually don't have an Increment that can be shipped at the end of a Sprint.
- 31% occasionally or often cancel the Sprint Review.

* The percentages represent teams that scored a 6 or lower on a 10-point scale. Each topic was measured with 10 to 30 questions. The results represent 1,764 teams that participated in the self-reported survey at **survey.zombiescrum.org** between June 2019 and May 2020.

THE BENEFITS OF SHIPPING FAST

Can you afford to burn money on features that have little to no value? Are your stakeholders' expectations of your product likely to remain the same? Do you have no competitors for your products? Can you predict, with absolute certainty, that your users or customers find value in your ideas?

Because you're reading this book, we are willing to let you feed our juicy arms to a hungry zombie if you can do any of those things. Your need to ship fast is strongly tied to the inherent risks of the complexity of developing your product. If you ask us to capture the purpose of the Scrum Framework in one sentence, it is to deliver "Done" Increments to stakeholders with a frequency that is high enough to avoid wasting money and time on something that just doesn't catch on with them. In other words, it's all about learning as quickly as possible where the risks are and how to avoid or prevent them (see Figure 7.1). What is "fast enough" depends on your environment, your product, and your organization's capabilities. But it's probably closer to one or two weeks, or even a single day, than once every few months. The more complex your work, the faster you need to learn.

COMPLEXITY IN YOUR ENVIRONMENT

Because you cannot plan success in a complex environment, and you are able to understand it only in hindsight, successfully solving complex problems requires the use of feedback loops. You need to know what's going on so you can make sense of the situation and react accordingly. The Sprint Review is only partially helpful in this regard if it is used to inspect your product and validate assumptions within the boundaries of your organization. Shipping fast allows you to inspect your product within the environment in which it's actually used. And this is what really counts; you get fast feedback on your product and learn from that feedback as quickly as possible. Was your thinking correct? How does the market react to your ideas? What do you need to adapt?

Why Scrum?

(1) In complex work more is unknown than known.

(2) The unknown is discovered by releasing "done" increments early and often.

(3) With these increments we validate assumptions.

(4) We learn what is needed and avoid the risk of spending time and money on the wrong things.

(5) As a result, we can deliver more value to our stakeholders sooner.

GO LIVE

Figure 7.1 Why bother shipping fast?

Shipping fast also allows you to respond to changes in the market more quickly. Imagine seeing an opportunity and actually being able to exploit it within a few weeks. Organizations that are burdened with long release cycles simply miss these opportunities, mired in their own ineffectiveness as competitors snatch them up. When you're able to ship fast, you can turn ideas into value within a short time frame, depending on what the business needs. That's what agility means.

Contrast this with virtually all the Zombie Scrum organizations we've seen: They shut themselves off from the outside. They become mindless machines, churning out huge piles of features in big-bang releases. The rare feedback they receive from the outside requires a lot of time to be processed and usually doesn't reach the people building the product in time. These organizations stumble along like stiff zombies, losing a limb here and there but not really noticing a difference.

Complexity in Your Product

One characteristic of complex problems is emergence. Here, seemingly straightforward activities result in a cascade of unexpected work. These are the "uh-oh" moments when developers catch on to the fact that what was assumed to be a small change turns out to be much more challenging than imagined. For example, when a stakeholder casually asks if the feature supports an obviously crucial mobile device, and the whole Scrum Team collectively facepalms because nobody ever considered that. Or when a Scrum Team works deep into the night to resolve an ever-growing list of issues that arise during the deployment of a large and complicated release.

Work on complex problems has the tendency to rapidly snowball into more work than expected. Anyone who has worked on complex problems has learned, often the hard way, that it is better to start with a small, stable system and carefully grow it over time. Instead of integration hell at the end of a long-running project, we make tiny changes and get our system back to equilibrium as quickly as possible. This process constitutes a rapid feedback loop of adding instability (in the form of development work) and returning to a stable state. That way we avoid the sometimes-catastrophic effect of delaying integration work, which makes it much easier to survive in a highly dynamic environment.

Improvements in software development tools have made it easier to simplify and automate integration, testing, and deployment. As a developer, you can check in your code and trigger an automated pipeline in which changes are built, pushed to a test environment, and, if everything goes smoothly, pushed to production. This means that you can have new working software every couple of minutes. Not every business needs to operate at such a rapid pace, but this style of working dramatically shortens the time it takes for developers to obtain feedback. It lets them know immediately when they made a mistake and reduces the complexity of working on a product.

The Bottom Line: Not Shipping Fast Is a Sign of Zombie Scrum

Organizations that suffer from Zombie Scrum struggle to ship fast. Although they work in the rhythm of Sprints, new features are delivered to customers only occasionally (e.g., as part of a yearly release cycle), without a desire to increase the pace. Excuses for not shipping faster are usually that the product is too complex, technology doesn't support it, or customers aren't asking for it. They view shipping fast as a "nice to have" but fail to see that they are missing the benefits of obtaining frequent feedback on the quality of their work. The result is a vicious cycle: the zombified use of Scrum raises barriers to shipping faster, and not shipping faster amplifies the Zombie Scrum symptoms.

Why Are We Not Shipping Fast Enough?

If shipping fast is so great, and when everyone sees the potential, then why doesn't it happen in Zombie Scrum? Next, we explore common observations and their underlying causes. When you are aware of the causes, it is easier to select the right interventions and experiments. It also builds empathy with the people caught up in a Zombie Scrum system, and how it often emerges despite everyone's best intentions.

"No need to panic, recruit. Breathe in, breathe out. Breathe in, breathe out. What are you mumbling? Did you recognize all the symptoms? Ok . . . let's panic! Just kidding. Recognizing the symptoms is a good first step. Let's see what the potential causes are. So tell me, why do you think your organization isn't shipping fast?"

We Don't Understand How Shipping Fast Reduces Risk

In environments with Zombie Scrum, people don't understand why it's important to ship fast. When you ask them, they respond with a shrug. Or with a dismissive smile, because "that can't possibly work for a product or organization as complex as ours." For them, shipping fast is only possible for small products that don't generate a lot of revenue or for huge tech companies like LinkedIn, Facebook, and Etsy. Even if they'd want to, the investment would simply be too large. It's more convenient to keep batching many updates into large, infrequent releases. Honestly, this is not very different from seeing the appeal in a healthy lifestyle but refusing to do the frequent workouts to get there.

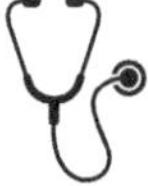

Signs to look for:

- Regardless of how much work Scrum Teams complete within a Sprint, features are batched into large quarterly or yearly releases.
- Releases are "all-hands" affairs where people clear their schedule for the evening and the next day(s) or even entire weekends to address issues caused by the release.
- "That doesn't work here" is a common response from people when you explain that every Sprint should result in a new version of the product that can be released.
- People don't have a clear answer when you ask, "What risks increase when we don't ship faster?"
- Releases are large operations and include many changes, bug fixes, and improvements. A quick look at the release notes usually tells you enough.

All these responses show that people ultimately don't understand that shipping fast is necessary to reduce the risk that comes with complex work. Ironically, the more complex the product or its environment is, the more important it is to use empiricism to reduce risks (see Figure 7.2).

Figure 7.2 "Let us take shelter first before you hit 'Release' for the yearly deployment."

For many teams, deploying a new version of their product hurts. Teams are on edge, worried about making a critical mistake. They prefer to deploy during low-traffic hours (in the middle of the night). Schedules for the days after the release are cleared to address the fallout in terms of bugs, issues, and rollbacks. It is no wonder that many teams choose to deploy as infrequently as possible.

But shipping fast is a form of organizational exercising. When Scrum Teams ship fast, they purposefully stress their processes, skills, and technologies. In response, they start to look for ways to optimize their work to deal with those frequent stressors. Scrum Teams are likely to increase their use of automation, create rapid fallback strategies, introduce techniques such as "feature toggles," and find other ways to reduce the blast radius (that is, the impact) of a new release. Just as our muscles become stronger as they recover after we slightly damage them through exercise, releasing often helps organizations build capabilities where they matter most. Although some pain is unavoidable, and just as sore muscles give rise to increased strength and endurance, each release will be easier, faster, and less risky than the one before.

Obviously, these improvements happen only when it is the Scrum Team itself doing the exercising. When people outside the Scrum Team are responsible for releasing, the Scrum Team has no incentive to improve. The Scrum Team also needs to have control over the deployment process and the tools to automate deployments. The best Scrum Teams we've worked with treated automation as part of their work on a product. They made this work transparent on their Product Backlog and refined it into smaller items as needed. Rather than treating automation as an afterthought, they used their first Sprints to create the necessary automation to deploy their product Increment to production. In subsequent Sprints, they built upon this foundation with additional automation and monitoring. All the time they would've wasted on making, and recovering from, large deployments was spent on adding more valuable features to their product.

Try these experiments to improve with your team (see Chapter 8):

- Take the First Steps to Automating Integration and Deployment
- Ship Every Sprint
- Evolve Your Definition of Done
- Make a Business Case for Continuous Delivery
- Increase Cross-Functionality with a Skill Matrix
- Ask Powerful Questions to Get Things Done

WE ARE IMPEDED BY PLAN-DRIVEN GOVERNANCE

Some organizations clearly suffer from Zombie Scrum even though the Scrum Teams are doing a great job. They create potentially releasable Increments every Sprint. The quality of the product is high. And stakeholders are being involved wherever possible. But although the engines of the Scrum Teams are burning at top speed, the entire organization isn't moving. Even though Scrum Teams are working in short Scrum cycles, everything else in the organization follows a much slower rhythm. We often see organizations create elaborate long-term project plans and yearly release schedules wrapped around the Sprints of their Scrum Teams. This is what we call *plan-driven governance*. Organizations using it completely miss the point that the purpose of the Scrum Framework is to enable inspection and adaptation.

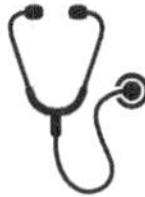

Signs to look for:

- Product budgets and product strategy are set once a year or even less frequently.
- Product Owners can only release according to an infrequent annual or biannual release schedule.
- Decisions about what goes on the Product Backlog and in what order are tightly controlled by Project Management Offices and Steering Committees.
- The goals or potential content of each individual Sprint are planned months, sometimes even years, ahead.
- Requirements and anticipated work need to be extensively documented and planned, as made apparent in lengthy Product Backlogs with a high degree of detail even for items many Sprints into the future.

Plan-driven governance leads Scrum Teams to work toward a far-distant goal that does not relate to customer satisfaction or tangible business outcomes. Their success is often measured against meeting artificial deadlines that have nothing to do with creating value for stakeholders. When conformance to a plan is rewarded instead of the flexibility to get better results, shipping fast doesn't make sense and looks like a waste of time. Even when the engines of Scrum Teams are burning at top speed, they are likely to burn out quickly as they get stuck in organizational muck. See Figure 7.3.

As we explored in Chapter 4, the Scrum Framework is based on learning from experience (or empiricism). In stark contrast, the processes and structures within organizations that engage in predictive planning are still shaped by the belief that problems can be rationally analyzed in their entirety before any actual work is done to address them (which is called rationalism). This analysis is captured in detailed product plans and associated road maps that don't allow nor encourage adaptation as insights emerge when the work is actually done. The resulting product is shipped in one large release in an attempt "to get it right the first time." This approach is not inherently wrong; it just doesn't work in complex, unpredictable environments.

Figure 7.3 "After sixty years, we can finally validate those assumptions from our Sprint Planning."

Try these experiments to improve with your team (see Chapter 8):

- Make a Business Case for Continuous Delivery
- Measure Lead and Cycle Times
- Measure Stakeholder Satisfaction
- Ship Every Sprint

We Don't Understand the Competitive Advantage of Shipping Fast

Are stakeholders happy with the speed at which value is being delivered to them in return for their investment? Are new initiatives for internal stakeholders passed over because "the IT department will take years to get it done"? Are technical concerns used to scare those rowdy people from management and sales back into their lairs whenever they come running with new opportunities?

The stakeholders are the best place to start looking for signs that teams may not be shipping fast enough. These people have a real stake in what teams do, and they pay for it with their money or time, or both. But their loyalty will only go so far. When something better comes along—another product or a competitor—they may jump ship.

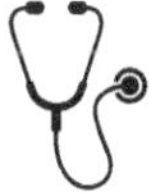

Signs to look for:

- The churn rate—the percentage of existing stakeholders that stop doing business with you—is high or increases.
- Stakeholders are generally unhappy with your responsiveness to their (changing) needs or use it as a reason to stop doing business with you.
- It takes a long time for Scrum Teams to resolve bugs that block stakeholders from using your product well.
- New initiatives are not being formed because "the IT department" needs to be involved. Everyone knows that this would take so much time that it doesn't even make sense to talk to them in the first place.
- Prototypes and new products are being developed with external companies because they are able to develop solutions quicker and cheaper.
- Most of the time, new and better tools cannot be integrated into the current infrastructure, because integration would take a very long time and the effort outweighs the benefits.

Organizations that suffer from Zombie Scrum are unable to respond quickly to the business opportunities that flow from the changing needs of stakeholders. Sometimes it's because everything IT-related is controlled by a small group of people who are unwilling to take risks or take on more work. Other times, the organization lacks the capabilities to ship fast enough. Either way, these business opportunities don't last forever, so when an organization can't respond quickly, it misses out entirely.

Experience: The False Promise of the "Castle in the Sky"

Here's a tale of firsthand experience from one of this book's authors:

I recently spent time with a Scrum Team that worked for a web agency. They'd spent the past two years working on and off on a new content management system (CMS) that would replace their existing decade-old platform. Although it had served them well in the past, the old CMS had become a bane for their customers. It worked marvelously in a ten-year-old browser, but it didn't work well in anything more recent. The performance was so bad that it zombified users on its own. The old platform lacked support for mobile devices, modern media formats, and rich text editing. But with nothing released, customers perceived the new platform as nothing but an empty promise as the team kept postponing its release in order to add more mind-blowing features. Not surprisingly, the company struggled to convince new customers to do business with them. Existing customers jumped ship to competitors as soon as they saw an opportunity. Needless to say, this team had to rethink their entire approach in order to remain in the market.

This dynamic also applies to Scrum Teams that work on internal products. One of the authors of this book worked for a company that built software for payrolling. When the company was acquired by one of the largest payrollers in the market, many of their business units started moving their product development from the shared IT department to the acquired company—much to the disappointment of the IT department. As it turned out, the acquired company used more modern technologies and was able to release biweekly, creating more opportunities for customers to inject new ideas and capitalize on market changes.

In a marketplace where technologies, practices, and needs change rapidly, shipping fast is essential to remaining competitive. As the example shows, shipping fast becomes an asset by enabling organizations to adapt to changing needs more quickly than competitors. It can be leveraged to experiment and learn faster.

Try these experiments to improve with your team (see Chapter 8):

- Make a Business Case for Continuous Delivery
- Measure Lead and Cycle Times
- Measure Stakeholder Satisfaction
- Ship Every Sprint

We Don't Remove Impediments to Shipping Fast

Even when organizations and Scrum Teams see the benefit of shipping fast, they still end up with Zombie Scrum if that knowledge does not translate into a sustained effort to remove the impediments that are getting in the way of doing so. Potential impediments are the following:

- A lot of work happens after a Scrum Team "completes" the work as part of a Sprint. For example, a QA department has to perform quality assurance in another Sprint. Or the marketing department has to write text and add pictures.
- Scrum Teams encounter delays when they depend on people outside the team to do work for them and those people are too busy.
- Completed work is batched up into large, infrequent releases.
- The skills in a Scrum Team are distributed in such a way that it causes bottlenecks.
- Scrum Teams struggle to break down their work sufficiently (for more on this, see the next section).
- Scrum Teams do not have access to the tools or technologies they need to ship faster.
- The quality of work done by the Scrum Team is too low, which causes significant rework on items in their current or next Sprint(s).

In organizations with Zombie Scrum, there is no attention to *cycle time,* the time that transpires between when work is picked up and when it is delivered to stakeholders. Cycle time tells you a lot about how comprehensive a team's

Definition of Done is, how they collaborate, and what other impediments are getting in the way of shipping fast.

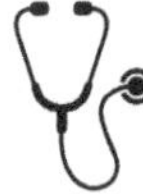

Signs to look for:

- Scrum Teams don't track their cycle time at all.
- The cycle time of Scrum Teams remains high or increases over time.
- Scrum Teams don't explore what is impacting their ability to ship fast.

When the cycle time is equal to or less than a Sprint, teams are demonstrably capable of starting work on an item and deploying it within the same Sprint (or immediately after). Low cycle time helps reduce the risks that are inherent to complex problems.

Try these experiments to improve with your team (see Chapter 8):

- Evolve Your Definition of Done
- Measure Lead and Cycle Times
- Limit Your Work in Progress
- Slice Your Product Backlog Items
- Increase Cross-Functionality with a Skill Matrix

We Work on Very Large Items during a Sprint

Shipping fast is an awesome way to reduce the risk of complex work, but it works only when what is shipped conforms to the team's Definition of Done. Releasing untested work is a great way to damage your brand, alienate customers, and take unnecessary risks.

Although releasing partially done work is a bad idea, what happens when the items on a Sprint Backlog are so large the Scrum Team can't complete them within a single Sprint? This usually means that remaining work on that item has to be carried over into the next Sprint, where the team now has even less time to work on new items. As the team keeps rolling items forward from

Sprint to Sprint, their problems compound and they increasingly feel that their Sprints are artificial time boxes in which nothing ever really gets done, let alone shipped.

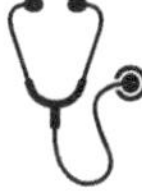

Signs to look for:

- Frequently, items on the Sprint Backlog are so large that a Scrum Team can't complete them within a single Sprint.
- Scrum Teams have only a few large items on their Sprint Backlog instead of many smaller ones.
- Scrum Teams don't spend time refining work for upcoming Sprints.

The best way for the Scrum Team to overcome this challenge is not for them to work harder, to add more people to the team, to relax their Definition of Done, or to buy larger sticky notes (see Figure 7.4), but to break down items that can't be finished in a single Sprint into smaller items that can be. It's important that teams break work down in such a way that the smaller items are still releasable in their own right. Otherwise, they won't be able to learn and receive feedback on them.

Figure 7.4 The size of your sticky notes is also a good sign that your items are too large.

Developing the skills and creativity to break down large items of work into smaller ones is one of the most important skills for Development Teams to learn. Instead of starting work on any item by writing code, a Development Team should learn to continuously challenge itself by asking: "What is the smallest possible thing we can build and deploy to learn more or increase the value of what we are delivering?"

Refinement both requires Scrum Teams to apply those skills and provides them with an opportunity to develop them. When Scrum Teams don't refine their work, or when they focus solely on writing specifications, they inevitably struggle with large items on their Sprint Backlog. Some of this refinement takes place within the Sprint, where other refinement happens before a Sprint. Either way, work flows much more smoothly through a Sprint when sufficient refinement has taken place. When we work with Scrum Teams, we try to get them to anticipate their work two or three Sprints ahead by breaking down large items. Techniques such as T-shirt sizing can help discover those XL or XXL items with relative ease, breaking them down first, then moving on to the L- and M-size items.

Try these experiments to improve with your team (see Chapter 8):

- Increase Cross-Functionality with a Skill Matrix
- Limit Your Work in Progress
- Slice Your Product Backlog Items
- Ask Powerful Questions to Get Things Done

Healthy Scrum

In Healthy Scrum, Scrum Teams work in a Sprint-based rhythm where every iteration results in a new version of the product, the Increment, that can be potentially released. At the end of a Sprint, the Increment should be in such a state that it can be deployed with the proverbial press of a button: all testing has been done and quality is assured, installation packages are ready, and support documentation has been updated. Whether or not to release it is up to the Product Owner, but if they decide to release, it can be initiated right after the Sprint Review. If the Product Owner decides not to release, the work the team has done will be released as part of a subsequent Sprint. Either way, the work the team put into getting everything release-ready wasn't wasted.

"Okay, Recruit! Still with us? Now that you know the symptoms and causes of not shipping fast, let's explore healthy Scrum. Yes, I know, the situation was bad, but it doesn't have to be like that. Let us share what shipping fast looks like. Just relax, take a seat, perhaps do five minutes of meditation and continue reading..."

Deciding to Release (or Not)

The Product Owner makes the final decision to release the Increment, informed by his or her interactions with the Development Team and stakeholders. Even when the Increment is fully ready to release (that is, it meets the Definition of Done), the Product Owner may decide to postpone it when a release:

- Would bring the product into a state where it is more likely that users will run into issues, problems, or bad performance. For instance, a critical business rule may not be working well or feedback from stakeholders during the Sprint Review wasn't positive.
- May require work from stakeholders that is unacceptable at this time. This is particularly evident in products that also (or entirely) involve hardware. Stakeholders would probably run away in droves if they had to replace the hardware every Sprint.
- Would bring the product into a state where it doesn't comply with legal or fiscal requirements.
- Would bring an avoidable risk for the brand, organization, or product based on current market conditions. For example, releasing new cash register software during the peak of the Christmas shopping season could be postponed by one Sprint if nothing is broken.

In organizations that suffer from Zombie Scrum, each reason could easily turn into an excuse to release once a year or only when the product is "entirely done." But in environments of healthy Scrum, Product Owners understand that frequent releases are the best way to mitigate the risk of complex work. They also understand that the reasons not to release indicate deeper, hidden impediments that need to be resolved. For example, if releases frequently don't take place because it is difficult to continuously retrain users, it begs the question why small incremental changes necessitate continuous retraining in the first place; perhaps the Scrum Team needs to work on improving the usability of the product so that users don't need to be retrained.

Releasing Is No Longer a Binary Action

Product Owners are continuously making trade-offs; they understand that there is a whole field of options between "release nothing at all" and "release everything." Organizations that suffer from Zombie Scrum often see a "release" as something that either happens or it doesn't. But when organizations practice healthy Scrum, they understand that there are many different release strategies. For example, a Scrum Team can do the following:

- Deploy Increments to production while keeping new features disabled with so-called "feature toggles" that are "turned on" once a coordinated marketing campaign gets underway.
- Deploy new increments in a staged manner, starting with users who are eager to experiment and accept the risks of new features, then moving on to more risk-averse users. The practice of deploying new releases in a series of alpha, beta, and final releases is a good example of this option. Another example: the "Labs" feature that many products offer to allow users to turn on experimental new features.
- Deploy new Increments as alternatives. For example, LinkedIn frequently deploys new features where users can choose between a new and an old version of a screen.

- Deploy new Increments to a small group of users first and monitor closely what happens. When this "canary in the coal mine" doesn't show problems, expand the release to ever-larger groups.
- Deploy a new Increment as a version that users can opt in to. This is particularly common among hardware-based products, where users can decide to stay with their current (and supported) version or switch to a newer one.
- Deploy new Increments through a "soft launch" where new features are made available to users, but the marketing campaign to draw more attention to it starts later.

What these strategies have in common is that they enable teams to release their Increments in many small releases over time, instead of a few large ones. By doing so, they reduce the risk of each release by limiting the blast radius in complementary ways. Scrum Teams can also test new ideas faster, as each strategy gives them rapid feedback on what is happening and how people are using the product. For example, tracking the number of users that revert back to an older version of a feature is a great indicator that the new version needs work.

Obviously, these strategies require a well-tuned process and technical infrastructure to make this approach possible. Not all products are initially capable of being released in this manner.

Experience: Frequently Releasing a Mission-Critical and Rigid Product

Here's another tale of firsthand experience from one of this book's authors:

One of our Scrum Teams was responsible for a comprehensive and mission-critical product for managing workers on flexible schedules. It included features to match workers to jobs, to submit and approve hour sheets, to track vacation days, and generate detailed management reporting. The product also communicated with a variety of external systems. Any disruptions would immediately cause ringing phones in our office, as thousands of people depended on it to do their day-to-day jobs.

> The first version of the product evolved over a two-year period, where the bulk of the work was done by a single developer. When that developer left, a Scrum Team took ownership of it. This confronted them with a challenge. The poorly structured, monolithic code base meant that it was impossible to release parts of the product; it was really all or nothing. And the risk of failure was high. Wanting to stick to frequent releases, the team initially did its releases during off-hours—usually at night or during weekends. To make this approach easier, the Scrum Team strategically started rebuilding parts of the product in parallel with technologies that allowed isolated deployments and automated testing. The team made clever use of technology to keep the experience for users integrated. In many cases, they would lift out entire parts of a commonly used dashboard and move it into a separate web application, while keeping it visually part of the same dashboard. In other cases, new versions of a screen were transitioned by initially offering them as a suggestion, then making them the default (with the option to go back) and finally as the only option. At the same time, the team worked hard to automate their deployment pipeline.
>
> This concerted effort to keep releasing frequently, and to build the muscles and skills needed to do so, allowed this team to move to a state where they can now release during work hours, with almost no risk, and as often as they want.

Shipping during a Sprint

The biggest benefit of improving shipping speed, even when it involves big changes to process and infrastructure, is that it helps organizations build the muscle to respond ever more quickly to what matters to stakeholders. This is not just reactive, in which Scrum Teams respond to stakeholders' requests, but also proactive, in which Scrum Teams monitor how users interact with the product to gain insights into ways to improve user experiences before the users ask for them.

To respond to these new opportunities, Scrum Teams need not wait for the end of the Sprint to release some new improvement. The Scrum Framework encourages teams to be able to release at least at the end of a Sprint. If they can release more often, even better! So it's only natural that Scrum Teams eventually move into a process where tiny releases happen continuously throughout the Sprint. This has the added benefit of making the various

Scrum Events even more focused on inspection and adaptation based on realistic, live data.

NO MORE "BIG-BANG" RELEASES

Scrum Teams that have developed the capability to ship fast sometimes confide in us that there's one thing they miss: the big yearly release party. In the old days, a release was a nerve-racking activity where teams would clear their schedule (and their evenings) to deploy huge Increments to production. With such a huge number of changes, the potential for disaster was equally huge, meaning that teams often scrambled to find fixes for a host of unexpected issues. For such a high-stress, high-pressure activity, it makes sense that the release party was that one moment to collectively sigh with relief for having survived another one. Yes, it's true that teams that ship fast don't "live on the edge" anymore.

Thankfully, release parties can still be had. Even in environments where the product is in a constant state of flux, Scrum Teams still have important milestones to meet, targets to achieve, and stakeholders to satisfy. Instead of celebrating the admittedly awkward achievement of having "survived a release," they have more valuable things to celebrate.

NOW WHAT?

In this chapter, we explored common symptoms and causes for why Zombie Scrum Teams are not shipping fast enough. Instead of a luxury or a nice-to-have, shipping fast is one of the most effective ways to mitigate the uncertainty and risk of complex work. It is at the heart of Empirical Process Control. By shipping fast, there are many opportunities to validate assumptions about your product and make adjustments as needed. In the world of complex work, shipping fast really is both a survival strategy and an asset.

Is your Scrum Team or organization struggling to ship fast? Don't worry. The next chapter contains a slew of experiments, strategies, and interventions you can use to start your recovery.

8 Experiments

A zombie film is not fun without a bunch of stupid people running around and observing how they fail to handle the situation.

—George A. Romero,
creator of *Night of the Living Dead*

In This Chapter

- Explore ten experiments to start shipping faster.
- Learn what impact the experiments have on surviving Zombie Scrum.
- Discover how to perform each experiment and what to look for.

In this chapter, we share practical experiments to start shipping faster. Some are designed to create transparency around what happens because you can't ship fast, while others are designed to start taking the first small steps. While the experiments vary in their difficulty, each one will make taking further action easier.

EXPERIMENTS TO CREATE TRANSPARENCY AND URGENCY

The whole point of shipping fast is often difficult to understand for organizations where Zombie Scrum is prevalent. They believe either that shipping fast is impossible for them or that it is less efficient than releasing everything in one go. To bridge this gap, the following experiments are about creating urgency by showing what happens when teams can't ship fast(er).

MAKE A BUSINESS CASE FOR CONTINUOUS DELIVERY

Continuous Delivery is the practice of automating your release pipeline—from code commit to release. Without it, shipping fast is difficult and time-consuming, if not impossible. Unfortunately, Continuous Delivery is one of those dreams that teams often keep postponing by doing everything "manually one more time." Or management doesn't want to invest in Continuous Delivery because it would take time away from delivering more features; they forget that each manual release already costs the team valuable time.

When the promise of Continuous Delivery doesn't convince others to invest in it, one thing that can help is to turn that promise into something quantifiable. How much money and time can actually be saved by automating your deployment pipeline? This experiment is a great example of how Scrum Masters can use transparency to drive inspection *and* adaptation.

Effort/Impact Ratio

Effort	★★★☆☆	This experiment requires some preparation, calculation, and research on the current and desired state of Continuous Delivery.
Impact on survival	★★★★☆	Nothing shocks zombies out of their slumber like confronting them with the financial consequences of their decisions.

Steps

To try this experiment, do the following:

1. For a typical release, map out your current deployment process on a timeline—both inside and outside your team. Make sure to consider the entire process up to the point when users can interact with it. Which manual tasks does it involve? For example: "Writing release notes," "Going through the prerelease test procedure," "Creating a deployment package," "Performing a backup before deployment," or "Installing packages on the server." You can prepare this timeline either on your own or with the Development Team.
2. If you have the opportunity, time the actual hours that each manual task requires for a few releases. This gives you the most reliable data. Otherwise, ask people to estimate how much time they typically spend on each task.
3. Based on the data you collected, calculate the hours that each step takes on average. If more than one person is involved, sum their hours. Also, sum the total amount of time spent on all the manual tasks of a single release. You now have a metric that tells you how much time is potentially wasted on manual work per release.
4. When you have data from an actual release, you can also include the time it took to fix bugs, perform rollbacks, and address rework that resulted from the release.
5. Determine the hourly rate of developers in your organization. If you don't have access to this information, use an online calculator to translate an average salary to an hourly rate. For most Western countries, an example would be $30 per hour. Multiply the hourly rate with the total time of each task in the entire release to calculate how much that release costs.
6. You now have the cost of all the manual work involved in a single release, as well as the time it takes everyone involved. For example, it might take 200 hours to release a new version to production; that's $6,000 if you use a $30 hourly rate. If your organization releases twelve times a year, this cost becomes a whopping $72,000.

7. With the Product Owner, consider the total time spent on manual tasks. Very roughly, how much value could have been delivered if people were able to spend that amount of time on implementing more work from the Product Backlog?
8. Convene the people involved and ask them where automation can both reduce manual effort and create time to get more valuable work done. The purpose here is not to automate everything, but to start where the team thinks it is possible and where the gain is the most substantial. Obviously, automating tasks requires investment. And you can now offset that cost with how much the organization stands to benefit from making that investment.

Our Findings

- One knee-jerk response to the high costs of releasing may be to do it less frequently. You can counter reaction this by emphasizing that bundling releases only makes them more risky and expensive as the number of changes—the complexity—increases. By automating parts of your process, you're effectively enabling your organization to decrease the risk and cost of each subsequent release. That makes automation an investment in your future.
- A side effect of tedious manual work is that people tend to forego it even though it's necessary, or they use shortcuts that lead to additional unintended work. Automated processes don't get bored and don't suffer from this limitation. To add this dimension to your calculation, you can estimate how much time is spent after each release on fixing issues that would've been prevented if the manual steps were performed as they should.

Measure Lead and Cycle Times

Zombie Scrum flourishes in environments where people are unaware of how much time items from the Product Backlog are "in progress" somewhere in the organizational pipeline. Product Backlog Items are valuable only when they are released to stakeholders. Not releasing them early is essentially a form of waste, as those items have to be tracked, managed, and coordinated throughout their lifetime in the pipeline.

This experiment is all about creating transparency around this type of waste with two related metrics: **lead time**, or the time that transpires between when a stakeholder request enters the Product Backlog and when it is fulfilled to that stakeholder through a release, and **cycle time**, or the time that transpires between when work begins on an item and when the item ships. The cycle time is always a part of the lead time. Lead and cycle times are great measures for agility; the shorter they are, the faster you ship and the more responsive you are. In environments with Zombie Scrum, these timings are much longer than in environments where Scrum works well. Figure 8.1 illustrates this point.

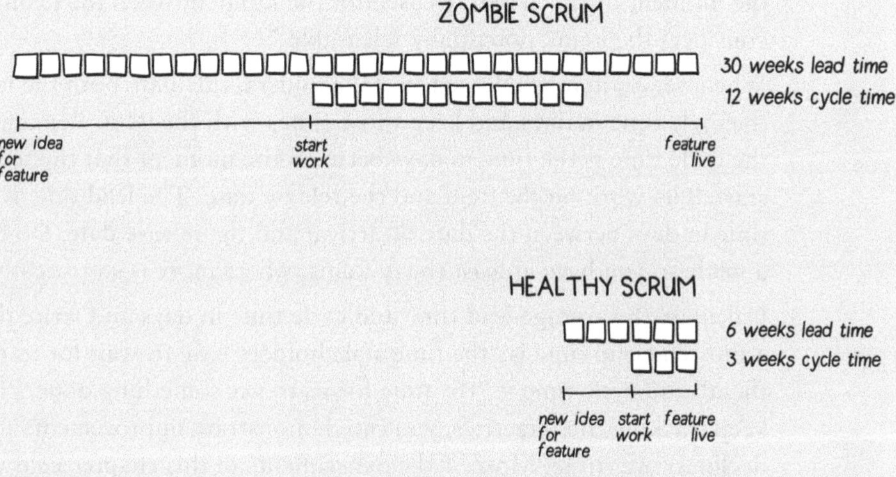

Figure 8.1 An example of lead time and cycle times compared between Zombie Scrum and Scrum as it is intended. The numbers are from two actual teams.

Effort/Impact Ratio

Effort	★☆☆☆☆	This experiment requires some data gathering, calculations, and patience. Nothing too fancy.
Impact on survival	★★★★★	Ultimately, cycle and lead times are incredibly helpful metrics to drive change where it matters. Expect a boost in survival!

Steps

To try this experiment, do the following:

1. For this experiment to work, you need to track three dates for every item on your Product Backlog that you want to analyze. You can track the dates for all the items or for a sample. For each item, add the date of arrival. This is the moment when an item is added to the Product Backlog.[1] Whenever an item is put on the Sprint Backlog, put the current date on the item, to track when the team started work on it. Finally, record the date when the item is made available to stakeholders. This is the moment of the actual release, not the moment when the team considers the item "potentially releasable."
2. Whenever an item is released to stakeholders, calculate both the lead and the cycle time in days and keep those times with the item. Remember that the cycle time is the time in days between the moment that the team started its work on the item and the release date. The lead time is the time in days between the date of arrival and the release date. Do this for a while so you have at least thirty items, where more is statistically better.
3. Calculate the average lead time and cycle time in days and write them on a flip. The lead time is "the time stakeholders have to wait for us to help them" and cycle time is "the time for us to get something done." If you keep tracking these metrics, you can demonstrate improvements (or declines) over time. Most of the experiments in this chapter help you drive both metrics down.
4. Use the cycle and lead times as inputs to Sprint Retrospectives and organization-wide workshops focused on reducing these times. What actions can be taken to shorten both? Who needs to be involved to do so? Where are impediments making it hard to shorten the lead time?
5. Recalculate the cycle and lead times every Sprint (or even more often) to monitor progress and identify further improvements.

---

1. If a lot of time usually transpires between the identification of the item and when it ends up on the Product Backlog, track the moment the item was identified instead for a more accurate picture.

Our Findings

- Incoming requests from stakeholders may be big enough to warrant refinement. In that case, maintain the same arrival date to the smaller items coming out of this refinement.
- Some Scrum Teams require other departments, teams, or people to do additional work before something can be released to stakeholders. For example, another team may need to perform Quality Assurance, run a security scan, or perform the actual installation. In all cases, the release date of an item remains the date when that item is actually made available to stakeholders. Using the date when your team hands off work to others is a great way to fool yourself (and the organization) that things are going well.
- Calculating an average cycle time is a rough indicator that we included for the sake of simplicity. A more precise approach is to use scatter plots and confidence intervals.[2]
- Don't worry if the items you picked are not the same size. Since we're working with averages, differences even out. Just make sure that the work is small enough for (roughly) a Sprint.

Measure Stakeholder Satisfaction

Asking how satisfied a stakeholder is essentially amounts to asking them how valuable your work is to them. Do they think you are responsive enough to their needs? Do they believe that their investment of time or money results in sufficient value? This experiment is a simple way to use Empirical Process Control in your work with stakeholders. Rather than make assumptions about how satisfied stakeholders are, you can now make decisions based on objective data.

Effort/Impact Ratio

Effort	★☆☆☆☆	Asking one stakeholder is easy. Asking a thousand is harder. Make this as difficult as you want.
Impact on survival	★★★★★	Starting to track stakeholder satisfaction—and how much value is being delivered to them—is like shock therapy for Zombie Scrum.

2. Vacanti, D. S. 2015. *Actionable Agile Metrics for Predictability: An Introduction*. Actionable Agile Metrics Press. ISBN: 098643633X.

Steps

To try this experiment, do the following:

1. Determine your most important stakeholders. Don't fool yourself by including people who don't actually have a stake in your product. Refer back to Chapter 5 to tell the difference.
2. Start by frequently measuring stakeholder satisfaction. Use the questions below these steps as inspiration. You don't have to ask everyone; a sample is fine. The larger the sample, the more reliable your results will be as the distribution of scores becomes more normal and less prone to extremes. We like to keep the score—as well as the historical trend—visible in the team room. It's also something to inspect during the Sprint Review or Sprint Retrospective.
3. A natural opportunity to measure stakeholder satisfaction is at the end of a Sprint Review, when your stakeholders are physically present.
4. Set up a short survey to measure stakeholder satisfaction. A survey can be as simple as a paper form or a digital one. Keeping surveys anonymous and short removes barriers for people to participate. Make sure to explain how getting this data will help you be more effective as a team.

You can use the following questions as a starting place or substitute your own. The satisfaction for each stakeholder is represented by their average score on the four questions (on a scale from 1 to 7). You can calculate the satisfaction of groups by averaging the individual scores.

1. On a scale from 1 to 7, how satisfied are you with how responsive we are to your questions, needs, or issues?
2. On a scale from 1 to 7, how satisfied are you with the results we deliver for the money or time, or both, that you invest?
3. On a scale from 1 to 7, how satisfied are you with how fast we deliver features, updates, or fixes?
4. On a scale from 1 to 7, how satisfied do you expect to be six months from now if we continue to work as we do now?

Our Findings

- When you calculate averages for groups of stakeholders, keep in mind that averages are sensitive to extreme scores. One extremely satisfied or dissatisfied stakeholder will distort the results. As a very rough guide, for groups with fewer than 30 participants, the median is more reliable than the average. For groups with fewer than 10 participants, the mode is more reliable than the median.[3]
- Don't use the numbers as a way to compare teams. Every team is different. Instead, involve everyone—including stakeholders—in making sense of the numbers and how you can work together to improve them if they are low.

Experiments for Starting Shipping More Often

Once Scrum Teams learn how shipping fast enables them to reduce the risks of complex work, their next challenge is to remove what is getting in the way of that. The experiments that follow help you make improvements in these areas to enable you to ship faster.

Take the First Steps to Automating Integration and Deployment

Automation is the primary enabler of shipping fast. Without it, the repetitive manual work that a team must perform for every release becomes a huge barrier. This drudgery may lead them to cut corners, especially on the time they spend on manual testing, and compromise the integrity of the product.

But automation can overwhelm teams too, especially when they are working on a legacy application that was never designed with automation in mind. Where should they begin? What if they don't have control over important parts of the process? How can they start untangling the huge web of dependencies and technologies?

3. The median is the middle value when you order all values from low to high. Or the average of the two middle values if you have an even number. The mode is the value that appears most often.

Rather than avoiding the journey altogether, they are better off starting with something simple that is within their control. This experiment is based on "15% Solutions,"[4] a Liberating Structure intended to trigger big change by starting small. A 15% Solution is any first step that you can do without approval or resources from others and that is entirely within your discretion to act. It is a good way to build confidence, celebrate small successes, and build the muscle to get through the hard stuff.

Effort/Impact Ratio

Effort	★★☆☆☆	Automation is hard, but identifying and executing the first steps isn't.
Impact on survival	★★★★☆	Since you can't really ship faster when you don't automate, your chances of survival will get a good boost.

Steps

To try this experiment, do the following:

1. Schedule a room where you have space to work for two hours and invite your team(s). Allow people to opt in to the meeting, rather than being required to join. Prepare a "value/effort" canvas on the wall or on the floor, based on the example with this experiment (see Figure 8.2).
2. Start by traveling to a hopeful future instead of remaining stuck in the dreary present. Ask people to stand up, form pairs, and talk about what their work would look like if more of it were automated. What would be easier? What would become possible that isn't now? Repeat this process two more times in different pairings. After three minutes, ask people to form new pairs. Repeat until people have been in three pairings. With the whole group, take a few minutes to share the most surprising, impactful, or important changes.
3. Now that you've helped the group create a vision of a hopeful future, return to the present. Ask people again to take a few minutes of silence to write down their 15% Solutions for moving towards that future. A 15%

4. Lipmanowicz, H., and K. McCandless. 2014. *The Surprising Power of Liberating Structures: Simple Rules to Unleash a Culture of Innovation*. Liberating Structures Press. ASN: 978-0615975306.

Solution is something that teams can do right now, without requiring approval or resources they don't currently have access to. For example, "Replace external libraries with packages," "Create one passing unit test for X," or "Ask Dave to give us access to the cloud-based deployment server." After a few minutes, invite people to share their ideas in pairs and to come up with more. After four minutes, ask pairs to form quartets and continue sharing and building on their ideas for a few more minutes. Ask the quartets to capture their five to eight most promising ideas on stickies for the next round.

4. Introduce the value/effort canvas. To give the group a reference, ask for one example of a solution that is very easy to implement (e.g., "Automatically check if site is up every hour.") and one that is very hard (e.g., "Automatically roll back when a new version fails during deployment."). Put the examples on the canvas. Do the same for a solution that has a small impact and one that has a huge impact. Then ask the small groups to take 10 to 15 minutes to decide for each of their solutions where they think the solution falls on the canvas compared to the rest.
5. When all the solutions are mapped, take 15 to 20 minutes with your team to select the solutions you want to work on in the next Sprint. Start with "quick wins" (low effort, high impact) and stay away from "time and money drains" (high effort, low impact). If there are many options, let people vote by placing a limited number of dots on the items they feel provide the highest benefit. Put the options on the Sprint Backlog if you are doing this experiment as part of a Sprint Retrospective. Or on the Product Backlog if you're using this experiment outside of a Sprint Retrospective.
6. Repeat this experiment as needed to continue making progress on automation. Use the "quick wins" to build confidence that making change is possible, and build out from there by venturing into the "low-hanging fruit" and the "big wins."

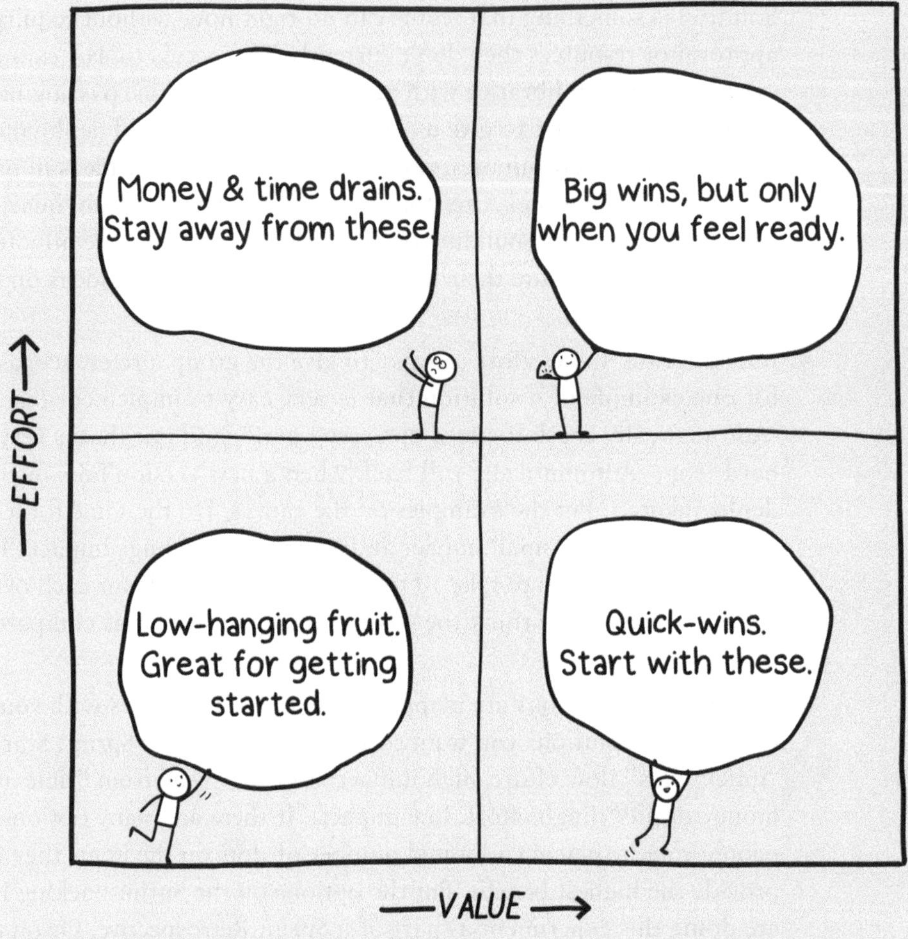

Figure 8.2 The value/effort canvas is a great way quickly to pick the most viable options.

Our Findings

- Items that end up in the "high effort" half of the canvas are probably not 15% Solutions. You can refine them by doing another round to identify what first steps make sense to start work on these solutions.
- Work hard to include the Product Owners, as you probably need their help and mandate to make the solutions possible. It's also a good way for

Product Owners to understand the complexities involved in shipping fast while offering their own perspective on what is the most valuable.

Evolve Your Definition of Done

Your Definition of Done is the set of rules that governs the implementation of every Product Backlog item. To be considered "Done," every item must conform to the Definition of Done. This definition reduces rework and problems with quality by setting clear goalposts around what quality and professionalism mean to your work. There are three steps to using a Definition of Done successfully:

1. Having a Definition of Done
2. Actually using a Definition of Done
3. Gradually evolving your Definition of Done to make it more professional

If you don't have a Definition of Done or don't use it, you will have to take care of that first. Then you can gradually expand the definition to ship faster.

Effort/Impact Ratio

Effort	★★★☆☆	The experiment is simple. However, creating transparency around your deployment process might not be.
Impact on survival	★★★★☆	A working, ambitious Definition of Done can be a powerful tool that guides you on your way towards shipping fast.

Steps

To try this experiment, do the following:

1. Gather your Scrum Team and familiarize yourselves with your current Definition of Done. Make sure it accurately represents what you are currently doing. A good opportunity is to do this periodically during a Sprint Retrospective.

2. Ask the question "If we wanted to release immediately after a Sprint, what rules should be added to our Definition of Done to ensure a high-quality result?" What checks would be necessary in addition to the current Definition of Done so that each Product Backlog item, and the Increment as a whole, is "Done" to the extent that the Increment can be released immediately after the Sprint? Include even the rules that seem completely infeasible at this time but are vital to guarantee high-quality releases. Collect the additional rules on a second list.
3. You now have two lists: your current Definition of Done, and a list of rules you are not yet following or cannot yet follow. The second list represents the gap between what you are doing now and what is necessary to reduce the risk of complex work (see Chapter 4). Each item on that gap list would take away or reduce a risk that is present today. The bigger the gap, the more risks you accept and the more work will be needed. Most Zombie Scrum Teams start with a big gap. When you find yourself in a heavily zombified environment, the best strategy is to start broadening your Definition of Done by making small improvements instead of going for huge shifts.
4. Ask your team "What would be our first step towards being able to release immediately after the Sprint?" What is something that your team can do right now, without needing approval or resources they don't have access to? Who needs to be included? Where can you find help and support? The experiments "Take the First Steps to Automating Integration and Deployment" and "Ship Every Sprint" in this chapter help when your team is struggling. Make sure to come up with specific, actionable steps such as automating certain tasks or involving people to broaden your Definition of Done.
5. Add one or two action steps to the Sprint Backlog of upcoming Sprints. Keep both your Definition of Done and the gap list clearly visible in your team room. Collaborate with stakeholders about your Definition of Done and your gap list. They are your natural allies. An expanding Definition of Done increases quality and allows stakeholders to receive value sooner. Continuously ask: "What creative solutions can we find to include items from our gap list into our Definition of Done and prevent the associated risks?"

Our Findings

- Break up bigger improvements into items that you can actually accomplish within a Sprint. It is more helpful to take several smaller steps than one big leap.
- If you are already able to release immediately after a Sprint, you can make your experiment more ambitious by asking your team to consider adding rules or steps that improve your ability to release individual Product Backlog items during the Sprint.
- Make sure your improvement activities are aligned with your business needs. Dedicate large portions of a Sprint to improvement only when everyone on your Scrum Team and your stakeholders are on board.

Ship Every Sprint

When you're developing a new product, you may be tempted to postpone shipping until everything in the planned release is done. Development Teams may fear that the quality of their work isn't good enough, and so they delay releasing the product. Product Owners may want to delay shipping to add more features to deliver more value. These decisions may sometimes be the right call, but Scrum Teams that perpetually postpone releases are setting themselves up for failure. Releasing infrequently removes the pressure that helps the Scrum Team improve their product and their own way of working, and lets bad habits take hold. It allows Product Owners to pile more and more features of unknown value into a larger and larger release, delaying feedback, increasing waste, and delaying the realization of value that users will receive from the features that turn out to be actually useful.

This experiment is about bringing the pressure of releasing front and center. Instead of considering shipping fast a luxury, this experiment makes it a principle to enable learning based on feedback that Scrum Teams can only acquire by shipping fast (see Figure 8.3).

Figure 8.3 Development Teams continue adding more details to the product while the customer urgently needs a much simpler version.

Effort/Impact Ratio

Effort	★★★☆☆	This experiment is an important leap. It requires trust, focus, and courage.
Impact on survival	★★★★★	When you're currently releasing very infrequently, this experiment acts like a vitamin booster shot. It will make clear where the impediments are.

Steps

To try this experiment, do the following:

1. With your Scrum Team, explore what happens when they release infrequently. What mistakes do they make? Where do risks increase? As an experiment, set a goal to release, at a minimum, at the end of every Sprint for five or more Sprints.
2. Together, explore the different release strategies discussed at the end of Chapter 7. From the principle that you are going to release every Sprint, which strategies are the most feasible?

3. Together, agree how you will celebrate a release to production. Will the Product Owner bring snacks? Will you go for drinks afterwards? Will you watch a zombie movie together? Involve your stakeholders in the celebration.
4. Keep track of the number of Sprints since your last release, and draw attention to that number during your Sprint Review and your Daily Scrum. Use your Sprint Retrospectives to investigate what you achieved by releasing more frequently.
5. If you are unable to release, capture your reasons for not doing so; these are impediments you want to focus on. For example, the team may lack the skill to perform releases or may depend on others to do it. The technology and infrastructure may not support it. Or the Product Owner doesn't have a mandate to release.
6. Make the number of Sprints since the previous release, as well as impediments that got in the way, transparent in the team room.

Our Findings

- This experiment is a leap that requires the respect and trust of the Scrum Team. When you—the one initiating this experiment—don't have it, focus on other experiments first.
- Your team may have no control over releases. If you can't change the frequency of releases or exercise more control over them, you may have to settle for an imperfect alternative: releasing to a staging or acceptance testing environment. Although you will not realize the same benefits as releasing to actual stakeholders, you can still learn more than not releasing at all. Use this environment during your Sprint Review to inspect your Increment with stakeholders.
- Your stakeholders are your natural allies. Involve them to help you remove the impediments that are getting in the way of delivering value to them faster.

Ask Powerful Questions to Get Things Done

Shipping fast is difficult when Scrum Teams struggle to create a "Done" Increment every Sprint. This often occurs because team members are working on too many items at the same time and have difficulty completing any of them. As the end of the Sprint approaches, stress rises as team members rush to complete all their work in progress. This experiment helps you ask powerful questions to help Development Teams remain focused on the Sprint Goal.

You can gently challenge the way that members of the Development Team collaborate during a Sprint. Like a psychologist, you can ask the powerful questions that everybody knows should be answered but are avoided because the answers may be inconvenient. The Daily Scrum is a natural opportunity to ask these questions, as this is where collaboration is (at the very least) coordinated.

Effort/Impact Ratio

Effort	★☆☆☆☆	No special skills are needed for this, other than asking questions during the Daily Scrum.
Impact on survival	★★★★☆	When Scrum Masters shift their role to asking the kinds of questions described in this experiment, everything starts to change.

Steps

Before engaging in this experiment, have an open conversation with the Development Team about whether it's okay for you to help them think by occasionally asking powerful questions. Here are some examples of questions you (or others) can ask while people talk about the items they're working on, or planning to work on:

- How does working on this Product Backlog item help us achieve the Sprint Goal?
- If you were a stakeholder, what would be the most valuable thing for us to work on today in order to achieve the Sprint Goal?
- Instead of picking up something new, where can you help others get work done that is already in progress?
- Where can others help you get this item done?
- What is keeping us from completing this item? Where do we need help?

- If we stopped our work on this item, how would it impact our Sprint Goal?
- What is the biggest bottleneck in our current work together? What can we do today towards removing it?
- If we pick up new work instead of working on things that are already in progress, how does this increase our likelihood of achieving the Sprint Goal?

Try it for several Sprints and see what happens. You'll probably notice that others start asking similar questions of each other. Learning to ask the right questions, and how to ask them, is a skill the Development Team also has to learn.

Our Findings

- Asking powerful questions isn't hard. The challenging part of asking powerful questions is doing so in a friendly and inviting way that doesn't sound condescending and pedantic. Practice and ask for feedback.
- If you feel uncomfortable interrupting with questions, or if you notice resistance to your presence, you can make an agreement with the Development Team on a signal they can use to let you know that they're open to a powerful question.

Experiments for Optimizing Flow

It's hard to ship fast when teams struggle to get items from their Sprint Backlog completely done within a single Sprint. There are many reasons for this friction. A team may be missing skills, or they may be working on items that are too large, or they may be working on too many things at the same time. The experiments that follow help you optimize flow by removing bottlenecks and working on fewer things at the same time.

Increase Cross-Functionality with a Skill Matrix

Is your team experiencing bottlenecks because only one person is capable of testing work? Is a developer on your team struggling to implement something that is blocking everyone else until she is done? Do team members start work on unrelated and low-value tasks simply because they have nothing else to do? These symptoms arise when teams are not cross-functional enough, causing work to pile up for some people and creating delays for others.

The Scrum Framework is built on cross-functional teams because they are better able to overcome the unpredictable challenges that arise when working on complex problems. Your team is cross-functional enough when items flow smoothly through your workflow. Cross-functionality does not mean that everyone can perform any kind of task or that you must have at least two experts for every kind of skill on your team. Often, just having another person who has a particular skill, even when they are slower and less experienced at it, already improves flow enough to prevent most problems.

This experiment offers your team practical strategies to help them improve their cross-functionality (see Figure 8.4).

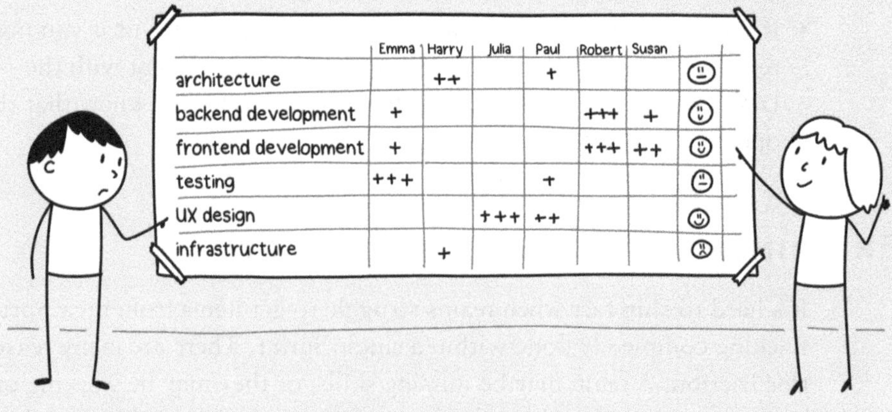

Figure 8.4 Increase cross-functionality with a skill matrix.

Effort/Impact Ratio

Effort	★★★☆☆	This experiment aims at one of the toughest causes of Zombie Scrum. You may have to deal with resignation and cynicism.
Impact on survival	★★★★★	Finding ways to distribute skills in your team not only improves flow, it is also good for morale.

Steps

To try this experiment, do the following:

1. With your team, map the skills you need during a typical Sprint. Together, create a matrix on a flip chart where you plot the members of your team against the skills you identified. Invite people to decide for themselves what skills they possess and to self-rate their proficiency with it using plus signs (+, ++, and +++).
2. When you're done with the matrix, ask "What do you notice about how the skills on our team are distributed? What is immediately obvious?" Invite people to reflect on this question individually for two minutes, then for a few minutes in pairs. With the whole group, capture important patterns on a flip chart.
3. Ask "What does this mean for our work as a team? Where should we focus our improvements?" Let people reflect on this question individually, then in pairs for a few minutes, and then capture the biggest insights on the flip.
4. Ask "Where should we start improving? What first step is possible for us without needing approval from others or resources we don't have?" Let people reflect on this individually, then in pairs for a few minutes, and then capture the biggest insights on the flip chart. Use the strategies as described in the next section as inspiration when people struggle to see possibilities.
5. Keep the skill matrix in your team room and update it frequently. You can tie it to flow-based metrics such as throughput and cycle time, which should improve over time as cross-functionality increases. See the experiment "Limit Your Work in Progress" to learn how to do this.

There are many strategies for improving cross-functionality on your team.

- You can add people to your team who already have skills that you need. Although a seemingly obvious solution, adding skilled people isn't always possible. It's also doubtful how structural this solution really is, as it can cause "Skill Whac-A-Mole," where other skills then become bottlenecks and you have to add even more specialized people. Instead of maintaining high degrees of skill specialization, it's often more effective to distribute skills.

- You can automate tasks that require scarce skills. For example, creating a backup of a database or deploying a release are critical tasks that are often performed by database specialists and release engineers. When you automate these tasks, you improve not only the speed of the activity, but also how frequently these tasks can be performed, while also removing the constraint.
- You can purposefully limit your team's work in progress, putting constraints on how much new work can be started, to encourage cross-functionality. Instead of starting a new Product Backlog item, because there isn't anything else to do, ask "How can I help others complete their current work?" or "How can others help me complete this work?" The Daily Scrum is a natural opportunity to offer and request help.
- You can encourage people to pair on tasks that only a few people can perform. When you pair experienced and inexperienced people, the less experienced people develop new skills, and both people find better ways to support each other. For example, pairing developers who typically work on the front end with developers who work on the back end makes it easier for them to support each other when bottlenecks occur.
- You can use approaches such as "Specification by Example"[5] to allow customers, developers, and testers to work together to develop automated test cases. In a similar vein, front-end frameworks (e.g., Bootstrap, Material, or Meteor) can make it easier for designers and developers to work together with a common design language for elements.
- You can organize skill workshops where people who are skilled at a particular task demonstrate how they perform it and help others perform it.

Our Findings

- When Scrum Teams have been affected by Zombie Scrum for a long time, they may have come to believe that nothing ever changes. You may even face understandable cynicism. If this is the case, start with the smallest

5. Adzic, G. 2011. *Specification by Example: How Successful Teams Deliver the Right Software*. Manning Publications. ISBN: 1617290084.

possible improvements to show people that change is possible and worth the time spent making it happen.

- When the skills of team members are narrowly specialized, they may struggle to see how broadening their skills will benefit the team. They may also fear losing their uniquely visible contribution to the team. Make an effort to celebrate the successes of the team to emphasize the collective outcomes over individual contributions.

Limit Your Work in Progress

Intuitively, multitasking feels like a way to get more work done. But when people, especially when they work on teams, try to work on many things at the same time, they usually struggle to get any of it actually finished. They are certainly busy, but they lose a lot of time reestablishing context when they pick up a task again. When you consider how teams work, and analyze how much work they really complete, you find that teams get more done when they work on less at the same time. Optimizing flow by limiting work in progress (WIP) is built on this counterintuitive truth. It fits well with the Scrum Framework because it gives teams direction on how to optimize their work during a Sprint.

This experiment is a good starting point for limiting your work in progress and seeing what happens because of that. For more information and potential pitfalls, we highly recommend *The Kanban Guide for Scrum Teams* by Scrum.org.[6]

Effort/Impact Ratio

Effort	★★★☆☆	This experiment puts pressure on the right spots and may surface some painful impediments that require creativity and cleverness to resolve.
Impact on survival	★★★★★	Limiting your work in progress is the best way to get more work done in a Sprint.

6. Vacanti, D. S., and Y. Yeret. 2019. *The Kanban Guide for Scrum Teams*. Scrum.org. Retrieved on May 26, 2020, from **https://www.scrum.org/resources/kanban-guide-scrum-teams**.

Steps

To try this experiment, do the following:

1. With your Scrum Team, set up a Scrum Board that represents how Product Backlog items move through the team's current workflow (see Figure 8.5). For example, when an item is pulled from the Sprint Backlog, it begins in "Coding," then moves to "Code Review," "Testing," and "Releasing," and ends in "Done." Don't start with a dozen columns; start with the minimum.
2. With your Scrum Team, decide on a limit to the number of items that are allowed to be in any one column at a given time. For example, you may decide to limit to three items in Coding and Testing and two items in each of the other columns. Although you want to limit your work in progress as much as possible, a limit of one may be unfeasible. Finding the optimal limits is an empirical process, so experiment with different limits and measure how they affect the amount of work done during a Sprint. A good starting point is to look at how much work is usually "in progress" for a particular column in a regular Sprint and lower the work in progress to see what happens.
3. Agree with your Scrum Team to respect the WIP limits for the upcoming Sprints. In practice, this means that work can only be pulled into a column when the number of items in that column is lower than its limit. When every column is at maximum capacity, members who are available pair up or support work that is already in progress rather than picking up more. You will notice that the limits induce pressure on the system by constraining what is possible. Instead of simply adding more work, the team learns that collaboration is now essential. The limits also surface impediments as certain bottlenecks become apparent. For example, work may quickly pile up in a Testing column when there is only a part-time member who can take care of testing.
4. Tracking two related flow-based metrics will help you determine where and how to optimize your limits. The first is the *throughput*, or the number of items completed each Sprint. The second is the *cycle time*, or the number of days that items spend on the board between the column

for the Sprint Backlog and the one for Done. A simple approach to track cycle time is to dot the items for every day they are in progress and calculate the number of dots at the end. As cycle time decreases, your team becomes more responsive and more predictable at the same time.[7] Throughput should also increase as more items get completed and more value is delivered.

5. Use these metrics as input for your Sprint Review and Sprint Retrospectives and to drive decisions you make about changing your limits to work in progress.

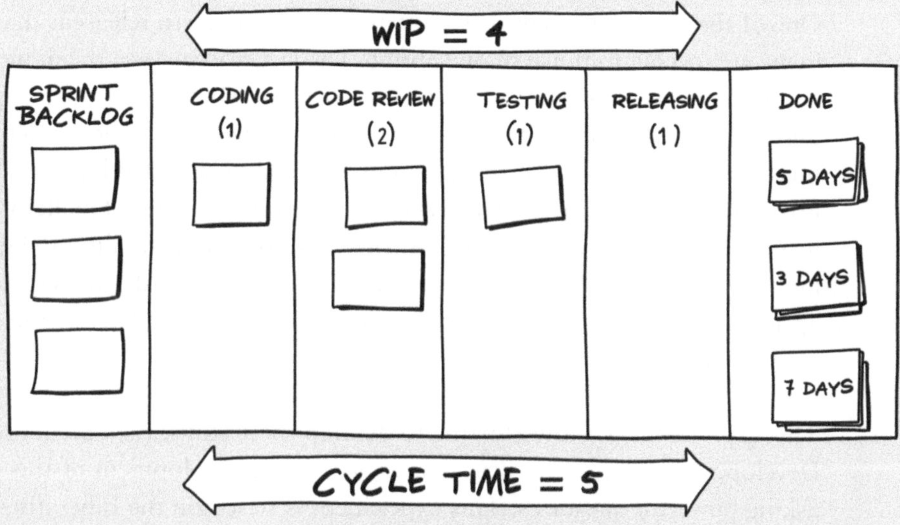

Figure 8.5 An example of a Scrum Board with work-in-progress limits and flow-based metrics

Things to Watch Out For

- Resist the temptation to change limits during the Sprint, but use your Sprint Retrospectives to make such changes. Track the impact of those changes on your flow measures. More often than not, increasing your work-in-progress limit essentially obscures underlying impediments. For example, increasing the work-in-progress limit for your Testing column to reduce the pressure on the one tester on your team would hide the fact that you don't

7. Vacanti, *Actionable Agile Metrics for Predictability.*

have enough people who can test. Instead, find ways to add more of that skill to your team (e.g., with training, new members, or other ways of testing).

- Recruit your Product Owner and your stakeholders to help you remove the impediments that emerge by enforcing work-in-progress limits. Help them see how removing impediments will improve throughput and lower cycle time, and why this is beneficial to them.

Slice Your Product Backlog Items

One of the most persistent reasons why teams struggle to release is that their items are too big to finish in one Sprint. The larger items are, the more risk and uncertainty they hide. When teams work on two, three, or four huge items during a Sprint, every setback or delay can result in the inability to deliver an Increment at all. So one of the most important skills for Development Teams is to learn how to break down larger items into smaller ones. Smaller items increase the flow of work through a team, improve predictability, and give more flexibility to decide where to add or drop items in order to achieve the Sprint Goal. This is exactly what the ongoing activity of *refinement* in the Scrum Framework is all about.

This experiment is about starting to develop these skills. As a Scrum Master, Developer, or Product Owner, you encourage the development of this skill by asking powerful questions. This experiment is based on the Liberating Structure "Wise Crowds."[8]

Effort/Impact Ratio

Effort	★★☆☆☆	Asking the questions is easy. Coming up with creative solutions to slice items that seem "unsliceable" isn't.
Impact on survival	★★★★☆	Learning to work on many small items instead of a few large ones is one of the most enabling skills you can acquire.

8. Lipmanowicz and McCandless, *The Surprising Power of Liberating Structures.*

Steps

To try this experiment, do the following:

1. Work with the Development Team to organize a refinement workshop. Allow people to opt in, instead of requiring everyone to show up. Select the largest items. If possible, identify one member of the team, potentially the Product Owner, who is most likely to have a good understanding of what the item entails. Print the questions outlined in this experiment on cards, adding more if you want.
2. For the first item, invite the member (the client) who knows most about the item to present it briefly for a few minutes. The team (the consultants) can ask clarifying questions for another few minutes. Then invite the client to turn their back to the team so they don't influence what's coming next. Invite the team to take 15 minutes to talk about how the item can be sliced, using the questions that follow as inspiration. The client is free to take notes, but they don't engage in the discussion.
3. The client turns back to the team and takes a few minutes to share what they discovered while listening. Which strategies seemed the most feasible? Give the whole group 10 minutes to capture their ideas.
4. Repeat as often as people feel they are still getting value from the exercise. You can also do multiple rounds on a single item, building on ideas from earlier rounds.

Here are some powerful questions you can ask:

- If we had to implement this item in only one day, what would we focus on? What could be done later?
- What is the smallest and simplest possible way to implement this item?
- Which steps do users go through when using functionality described in this item? Which steps can we implement now? Which can be implemented later?
- Of the business rules that are important for this item, which are the least vital or impactful? Which can we let go of for now or work around creatively?

- What do the "unhappy paths" for this item look like: What are some unintended ways that users could interact with this functionality? Which are the least common ways?
- Which of the acceptance criteria for this item can we get away with by implementing later?
- Which groups of users will be using this item? Which group is the most important? What can we let go of if we focus on that group?
- Which devices or modes of presentation do we need to support for this item? Which ones are least common or important?
- Which CRUD (create, read, update, delete) interactions do users have with this item? Which could be implemented later without much impact now?

Our Findings

- Most developers love their craft and care deeply about the work they do. They don't want to deliver something that feels incomplete—and that's a good thing. If developers start to express concerns that slicing a Product Backlog item will result in something that is incomplete, or of low quality, emphasize that the goal of slicing isn't to deliver incomplete work, but to find the smallest possible implementation of a larger item that is, in itself, complete and of high quality.
- Perform the actual administrative work of updating the Product Backlog, especially when you work with tools such as Jira or TFS, outside of this workshop. Waiting for people to write something down is a huge energy drain for groups.
- The goal is not to end up with a Product Backlog where all the items have the same size. Instead, focus on breaking down each item as much as possible.

Now What?

In this chapter, we explored experiments that help your team and organization to ship fast(er). Although the experiments differ in difficulty, each should create a noticeable improvement. Signs that you are recovering include increased stakeholder satisfaction, higher quality, and lower stress levels. And if you're still stuck, there are more experiments in the following chapters that help you sort out other issues first. Don't give up hope. The road to recovery can be long, but it is a road worth walking.

"Looking for more experiments, recruit? There is an extensive arsenal available at ***zombiescrum.org****. You can also help expand our collection by suggesting what worked well for you."*

IV

Improve Continuously

9 Symptoms and Causes

Everything's better with zombies—NOT.

—Lily Herne, *Deadlands*

In This Chapter

- Learn what continuous improvement means.
- Explore the most common symptoms and causes that make it hard to improve.
- Discover how healthy Scrum Teams have embraced continuous improvement.

An Experience from the Field

The Development Team has gathered, unenthusiastically, for their Sprint Retrospective. They grumble about the time it takes. One developer sums up how the rest feel when he says, "What's the point, really?" But since they agreed to give this Scrum thing a try, they resolve to make the best of it.

The door flies open and in rushes their Scrum Master, Jessica. "Sorry!" she begins. "The Sprint Retrospective for one of my other teams took longer than expected." It doesn't take her long to set up though; they've done this many times before. Jessica draws two columns on the whiteboard, marking the left one with "Going Well" and the right one with "To Improve." This is a format she found online, and she's been relying on it with all of her six teams ever since their agile transformation started three months ago. When she's done, she asks people to write down whatever comes to mind on stickies and put them in the associated column.

After a few minutes, the column with possible improvements is overflowing. The Going Well column, on the other hand, is empty except for a sticky mentioning that the cafeteria now has better burgers. Honestly, the same pattern has emerged over the past seven Sprints. Most of the suggestions are attempts to deal with their inability to get anything done. The team's tester, Pete, has been burned out and at home for the past three Sprints. Despite requests from the team, HR declined to find them a new tester. Instead, they feel that the team should just continue doing Scrum until Pete is back and can work his way through the backlog of items to test. Another improvement has to do with the Product Owner, who keeps pushing items into the Sprint or removing items that the team is already working on. Although the Product Owner never attends the Sprint Retrospectives, the team knows that he doesn't really have a choice. When the agile transformation started, management decided to assign the requirements analysts to become Product Owners, as they saw them as the most capable of turning needs from stakeholders into clear requirements for the Development Team. In doing so, management did not empower these analysts-turned-Product-Owners to make decisions. So when stakeholders need something immediately, the "Product Owners" feel that they have no option but to add it to the Sprint Backlog straightaway.

The Development Team considers the Sprint Retrospective a mostly pointless affair. All of the improvements they identify have been raised many times before. "Give the Product Owner mandate" and "Get a new tester" are their favorites. When Jessica asks them how to do this, the team points at management and HR as the ones who should be fixing these impediments. But nothing ever changes. As a result, members of the team are losing their interest in working with Scrum.

Sadly, many Scrum Teams struggle to identify tangible improvements, and instead find only superficial or vague opportunities to improve, or find only improvement opportunities that are entirely outside of their control. During their retrospectives, they express beliefs and attitudes that show they are far from being self-managing and cross-functional teams (for more on this topic, see Chapter 11). For example, team members stick to the skills they've honed over the years. They are unwilling or unable to try something new, and they may feel uncomfortable sharing their knowledge with other team members.

In this chapter, we explore how Zombie Scrum prevents Scrum Teams from continuously improving, including recognizing the symptoms and potential causes.

How Bad Is It, Really?

We are continuously monitoring the spread of Zombie Scrum around the world with our online Symptoms Checker at **survey.zombiescrum.org**. Of the Scrum Teams that have participated at the time of writing:*

- 70% of the teams never or infrequently use metrics to identify improvements.
- 64% of the teams don't actively engage with people outside their team to learn something new or have discussions about their professions.
- 60% of the teams never or very rarely celebrate small or large successes they've achieved.
- 46% of the teams never or rarely encourage people to learn new things, read professional books, or join meetups and conferences.
- 44% of the team's Sprint Retrospectives don't result in improvements for the next Sprint.
- 37% of the teams find it difficult to take risks by trying something new.

* The percentages represent teams that scored a 6 or lower on a 10-point scale. Each topic was measured with 10 to 30 questions. The results represent 1,764 teams that participated in the self-reported survey at **survey.zombiescrum.org** between June 2019 and May 2020.

Why Bother Improving Continuously?

Few teams start from a position where the Scrum Framework works perfectly from the beginning. Like learning to play an instrument, Scrum takes practice and improvement over time. As we've seen in earlier chapters, Scrum is radically different from the way that teams have built products and worked with stakeholders in the past. Scrum Teams usually need to improve in many different areas, and overcome many barriers, in order to reach their goals of higher customer satisfaction. Overcoming these barriers challenges teams to find their own solutions. Because every team, every challenge, and every context is unique, it doesn't suffice to simply copy "best practices" from elsewhere and expect them to work. Instead, teams need to experiment with different approaches to find what works best for them.

When teams work with the Scrum Framework, we've noticed that they often start from a position of relatively poor performance. But if they use feedback to continuously learn and improve, they will achieve higher levels of performance over time. The Scrum Guide clarifies that the Sprint Backlog should at least include one high-priority improvement that was identified from the previous Sprint Retrospective. When teams focus on removing at least one barrier every Sprint, either fully or partially, those small incremental improvements accumulate to large change over time.

WHAT IS CONTINUOUS IMPROVEMENT?

Continuous improvement is a form of learning that applies not only to individual teams, but also to entire organizations as a whole. In his book *On Organizational Learning*, organizational theorist Chris Argyris defines organizational learning as a type of error detection.[1] Learning happens when a group of people achieves an outcome they were seeking without introducing (new) errors. It also happens when a mismatch is detected and a solution is produced to correct it. For example, a Scrum Team discovers that they frequently exceed the time box for the Daily Scrum because side discussions continue creeping into the conversation. They decide to limit their conversation to only what matters to the Sprint Goal. In other words, learning requires both discovering an error as well as implementing a solution for it.

1. Argyris, C. 1993. *On Organizational Learning*. Blackwell. ISBN: 1557862621.

The Scrum Framework is essentially a mechanism for detecting two types of errors. The first type are errors that the Scrum Team detects in the product they are developing, ranging from bugs to incorrect assumptions about what is needed. The second type are gaps between what would be necessary to detect those errors earlier and what is actually done to detect them. These are the impediments that teams identify towards working (more) empirically. Focusing on these two types of errors allows teams and organizations to learn in two complementary ways, according to Argyris: single-loop learning for errors of the first type, and double-loop learning for errors of the second type.

As shown in Figure 9.1, single-loop learning focuses on solving a problem within an existing system that is defined by sets of beliefs, structures, roles, procedures, and norms. Double-loop learning challenges the system itself. As an example of single-loop learning, a Scrum Team might explore different techniques for estimating their Product Backlog for the purpose of forecasting. The Scrum Team might also use double-loop learning to challenge the purpose of forecasting itself and look for other ways to satisfy the need to forecast. Another example of single-loop learning is when developers try to fix broken unit tests faster, whereas double-loop learning would see them question why their unit tests are so prone to breaking in the first place. A final example of single-loop learning is when a Product Owner tries to better capture requirements on the Product Backlog, whereas double-loop learning might make her question the need for detailed requirements in an empirical process in the first place. Where single-loop learning improves what is possible within the current system, double-loop learning is about challenging and changing the system. Double-loop learning helps people change (sometimes deeply held) assumptions and beliefs.

Although both types of learning are important for continuous improvement to happen, Argyris emphasizes double-loop learning as particularly important for non-routine, complex work where teams have to constantly challenge not only how they do the work, but also why. The many changes that organizations have to go through to transition from plan-based approaches to empirical ways of working mean that organizations need to employ a high degree of double-loop learning to change underlying beliefs about risk, control, management, and professionalism. Organizations that find themselves unable to change the rules, norms, and beliefs that stand in their way will struggle to stay competitive. Unfortunately, Argyris also notes that highly trained professionals in particular often struggle to practice double-loop learning, as it involves challenging the practices and skills that have made them successful in the past.

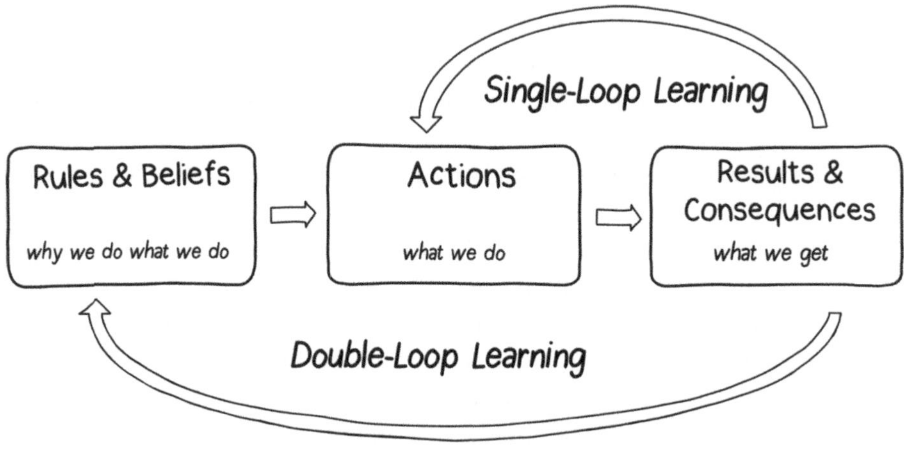

Figure 9.1 The distinction between single- and double-loop learning[2]

Fortunately, using the Scrum Framework purposefully helps teams leverage both types of learning by creating transparency around how work is done, and by creating opportunities for inspection and adaptation. Although all Scrum Events help teams to learn by inspecting and adapting, the Sprint Retrospective is the one that most directly reflects on how work is done. The benefits of this reflection are limited when it focuses only on finding new practices and techniques (single-loop) and doesn't involve challenging underlying beliefs and rules (double-loop). Teams affected by Zombie Scrum tend to limit themselves to single-loop learning and can't benefit from double-loop learning because their existing beliefs about management, products, how to manage people, and how to control risk remain unchallenged.

2. Source: Argyris, *On Organization Learning.*

Continuous Improvement or Agile Transformation?

Many organizations begin their journeys into Scrum with an "agile transformation" focused on reducing costs, improving responsiveness, or appeasing stakeholders. Management brings in external consultants and coaches, sends teams to training, and changes roles and structures accordingly. Like a butterfly that emerges from a caterpillar, "transformation" suggests that it is possible to transition from one state (e.g., waterfall-based development) to another (e.g., agile and other value-driven approaches) in a relatively short amount of time through a concerted organizational change program.

These transformations are rarely successful in making teams more responsive. Although high-quality research is hard to find, our Zombie Scrum Survey suggests that over 70 percent of Scrum Teams don't frequently collaborate with stakeholders, and that 60 percent don't frequently deliver working software. We don't know from our data if these teams are (or have been) involved in agile transformations, but the results don't point to huge shifts in responsiveness. It fits with our own observations from the organizations we've visited where agile transformations have taken place. More often than not, little has actually changed in terms of responsiveness and collaboration with stakeholders. And without meaningful results, organizations quickly move to transform to the next promising trend that comes along, only to repeat the process again.

A model that helps us understand why change is so difficult is Kurt Lewin's Force Field Model[3] (see Figure 9.2). Lewin, one of the pioneers of group dynamics and action research, argues that social systems—of which organizations are one example—exist in a state of equilibrium where some forces drive for change on an issue while others prevent it. Forces consist of beliefs that people have, social norms about how work is done, things that are happening in the environment, or the actions that people or groups take. In any case, change happens when the forces driving for change exceed those

3. Lewin, K. 1943. "Defining the 'Field at a Given Time.'" *Psychological Review* 50(3): 292–310. Republished in *Resolving Social Conflicts & Field Theory in Social Science*. Washington, D.C.: American Psychological Association, 1997.

restraining it. This balance fluctuates as forces grow stronger or weaker over time, or change direction altogether.

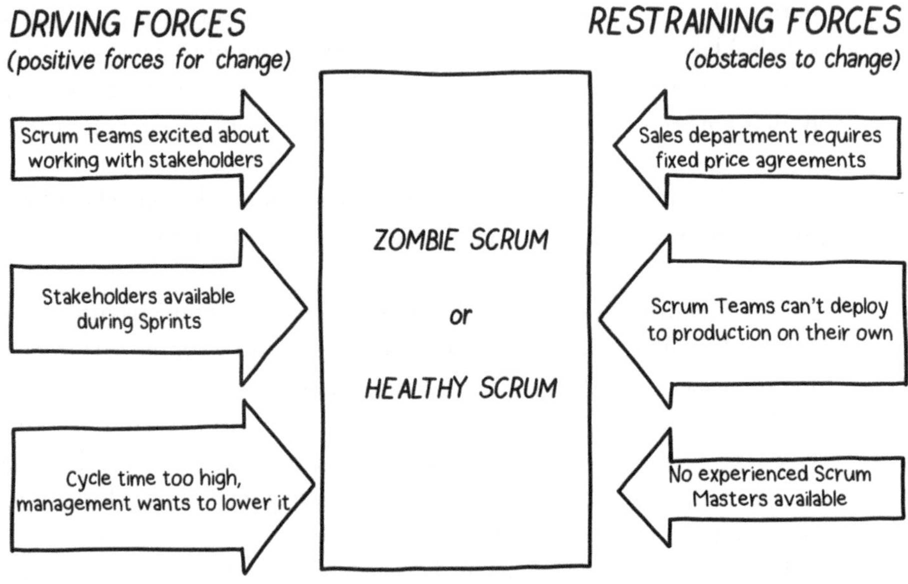

Figure 9.2 The status quo is often hard to change, as forces driving for change are not strong enough to counter forces restraining it.[4]

This model helps us understand three important realities about organizational change. The first is that a change is never done (or "implemented"), as any change simply regresses back to an earlier state when the forces pushing against it become stronger. The second is that changing the status quo can be very difficult, as there are countless visible and invisible forces pushing for and against it. The third is that underlying beliefs and assumptions about how work is done are some of the most constraining forces we find in organizations.

The Force Field Model shows how important double-loop learning is for challenging those beliefs. If Scrum Masters believe that they are essentially project managers, with a clear responsibility for the outcome, they will continue to

4. Source: Lewin, "Defining the 'Field at a Given Time.'"

act in ways that disempower the ability of the Development Team to self-manage and continuously improve. And when people see mistakes as something to avoid at all cost, it becomes impossible to create an environment where Scrum Teams can learn from their mistakes without fear of punishment.

The Scrum Framework not only helps teams to become more responsive, it also gives them a process by which they can learn and improve over time. Some changes involve single-loop learning, where teams and organizations discover new techniques and practices to do their work. Other changes involve double-loop learning, where the purpose of the work and its governing rules are themselves questioned. Deep learning enables the forces that push towards increased agility to overcome those forces that restrain it, creating the conditions to sustain the change.

Why Are We Not Improving Continuously?

If continuous improvement is so important, why doesn't it happen in Zombie Scrum? Next, we explore common observations and their underlying causes. When you are aware of the causes, it is easier to select the right interventions and experiments. This awareness also builds empathy with teams and organizations suffering from Zombie Scrum, and helps to better understand how it often emerges, despite everyone's best intentions.

In Zombie Scrum, We Don't Value Mistakes

Making mistakes is inevitable when you are dealing with complex work. As we explored in Chapter 4, complex work is inherently uncertain and unpredictable, and the people doing that work have fallible memories, make imperfect decisions, don't have access to all the facts, and often draw incorrect conclusions when they do. Bugs will be introduced, incorrect assumptions that seem obvious after the fact will be discovered, and people will forget important information. Thankfully, Scrum offers a framework to discover these mistakes early and learn how to prevent them. Trying new things, having them not turn out as planned, learning what went wrong, applying that learning, and trying again: this is continuous improvement in a nutshell.

Organizations that suffer from Zombie Scrum avoid making mistakes at all costs or don't recognize what they can learn from them. For example, when Scrum Teams can't deploy their Increment on their own because there is too much risk. Or releases don't happen every Sprint because it seems too difficult, and new technologies are avoided because they are too daring. When you say that the Scrum Framework is a way to fail fast, people respond with wide-eyed wonder: "Why would you ever want to fail in the first place? Instead, let's call it 'succeed fast.'" And "Let's not talk about 'experiments' or 'minimum viable products'—it makes people uncertain." Instead of seeing mistakes as opportunities to learn, they see mistakes as things to avoid.

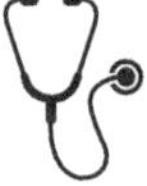

Signs to look for:

- Management wants experiments to be called "initiatives," because the term "experiments" gives the impression the outcome is uncertain and mistakes might be made.
- The Product Owner tells the Development Team not to release the product until they can guarantee it is 100 percent bug-free.
- During Sprint Planning, only the easy but not-so-valuable Product Backlog items are selected. The more valuable, riskier items are ignored.
- The outcomes of Sprints are batched into large, infrequent releases. Or teams deliver Increments that they consider "Done," but in reality need a lot more work by others before they can be deployed to production.

When a big-bang rollout results in significant issues, it can permanently damage reputation. Like the disastrous initial launch of HealthCare.gov[5] or the storm of negative reviews that followed the long-awaited release of the game *No Man's Sky*."[6] A recurring pattern behind these massive,

5. Cha, A. and L. Sun. 2013. "What Went Wrong with HealthCare.gov." *Washington Post*. October 23. Retrieved on May 27, 2020, from **https://www.washingtonpost.com/national/health-science/%20what-went-wrong-with-healthcaregov/2013/10/24/400e68de-3d07-11e3-b7ba-503fb5822c3e_graphic.html.**
6. Schreier, J. 2016. "The *No Man's Sky* Hype Dilemma." Kotaku.com. Retrieved on May 27, 2020, from **https://kotaku.com/the-no-mans-sky-hype-dilemma-1785416931.**

reputation-threatening mistakes is that all the risk is at the end of development—when the product is finally released. Despite everyone's best efforts, any mistake—like a breaking bug or poor performance—has a huge blast radius. Mistakes can bankrupt or permanently damage a brand. One knee-jerk reaction is to engage in even more up-front planning and analysis in an attempt to identify potential risks. Unfortunately, this approach provides a false sense of security: due to the nature of complex work, most risks are completely unknown until you actually do the work.

As we explored in Chapter 4, the Scrum Framework offers a better strategy for reducing risks by containing the blast radius to a single Sprint (or less). Instead of trying to avoid the mistakes that inevitably happen, Scrum helps teams reduce the damage by giving them a process to discover mistakes earlier, fix them faster, and reduce their impact. More important, it allows teams to improve their process, collaboration, and technology by delivering a working product Increment and measuring the result. By taking this approach, they will sometimes find that what they built wasn't the right solution, or it doesn't work quite as expected. But these mistakes will be small and easier to correct than if the team had gone on for a very long time before delivering something and measuring the result. By making many small corrections, they reduce the impact and likelihood of having to make much bigger ones. Just as our immune systems usually become stronger when we're exposed to pathogens, teams become more resilient when they make mistakes and recover from them. But organizations that suffer from Zombie Scrum ironically are so involved in removing all pathogens from their surroundings that they end up getting life-threatening illnesses from a common cold.

Try these experiments to improve with your team (see Chapter 10):

- Ask Powerful Questions during Sprint Retrospectives
- Dig Deeper into Problems and Potential Solutions, Together
- Create a Low-Tech Metrics Dashboard to Track Outcomes

"Everyone makes mistakes. You delete the wrong document. Or you buy stickies that don't stick. Or you use permanent markers on a whiteboard. It happens. We can't have each other's backs when we also blame each other for our mistakes."

In Zombie Scrum, We Don't Have Tangible Improvements

The Scrum Framework provides a clear criterion for success: deliver a potentially releasable Increment every Sprint. And because that requires addressing many of the hard challenges we talk about in this book, you won't be able to do it overnight. Improving incrementally, in small steps, is your best strategy to keep change manageable and motivating.

We run into serious problems, however, when the small steps that people come up with are vague and nonspecific, like "improve communication" and "increase collaboration with stakeholders." Although these are good goals, they don't tell you where to begin and what success looks like. Teams with improvements like this should ask themselves: "When we communicate better, what will be different?" and "What would it look like if we increased our collaboration with stakeholders?" Specific improvements, with metrics, help people know what they are committing to; vague improvements are easily agreed on, and harder to judge whether they have missed their goal. They make it very difficult to actually succeed in improving and building confidence.

Another example of this dynamic is what we call "Happy-Clappy Scrum" (see Figure 9.3). Here, Scrum Teams focus their energy on making the Scrum Events as fun, lighthearted, and energizing as possible, leveraging the many games and facilitation techniques that can be found online. This phenomenon often happens when teams cannot influence impediments, and their well-intentioned improvements remain superficial. Although there is great value in creating inclusive and engaging environments, this approach doesn't help when the team is not actually inspecting their results and adapting their product and their approach based on feedback. Rather than use the Scrum Events as opportunities to remove larger impediments to inspecting and adapting, the Scrum Team focuses on reenergizing people to survive another Sprint amidst a wasteland of Zombie Scrum. But no matter how fun the Sprint Retrospective is, teams won't feel better when they have no feedback about the impact they're having on real users. No matter how energizing and fast your Sprint Planning is, it won't make your stakeholders happier when they still have to wait a year for the work to reach them.

Figure 9.3 Although fun and happiness are certainly part of Scrum Teams, they shouldn't be more important than delivering value to stakeholders.

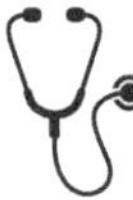

Signs to look for:

- The Sprint Retrospective doesn't result in any improvements at all.
- For the actions that come out of a Sprint Retrospective, it is unclear where to start or what success looks like.
- Scrum Teams or Scrum Masters focus their improvements mostly on making the Scrum Events more fun, with more games and more facilitation techniques.
- Scrum Teams don't inspect metrics during Sprint Retrospectives to identify improvements.
- Team members put the responsibility of performing an action on others, often people outside of the team.

One important skill for Scrum Teams to learn is how to be specific about what to improve, and how to break down improvement into small steps. Just as refining large items on the Product Backlog into smaller items makes it easier to complete them, breaking down large improvements into small steps makes it more likely your improvements will succeed. Teams that suffer from Zombie Scrum tend to either get stuck in huge, demotivating improvements like "Product Owner should have a greater mandate" or they get lost in vague improvements that don't tell them where to start.

Try these experiments to improve with your team (see Chapter 10):

- Create 15% Solutions
- Focus on What to Stop Doing
- Create Improvement Recipes

In Zombie Scrum, We Don't Create Safety to Fail

Teams can't improve when they experience no room for uncertainty, doubt, or criticism. Teams that suffer from Zombie Scrum operate in environments that signal that doubt and uncertainty are unacceptable. They often develop all kinds of defensive strategies to prevent uncertainty. From subtle strategies, such as changing the topic or casually dismissing opposing views, to very blatant ones, such as ostracizing or criticizing dissenters.

Teams are social systems. Past behavior of people inside and outside the team shapes the social norms that govern how people interact (and vice versa). When doubts and uncertainty are met with dismissal, it creates and reinforces a social norm that being critical is "not something we do here." The same goes for when people notice how others never ask for help when they're stuck, so that everyone muddles through instead of asking for guidance. These signals shape the organizational culture.

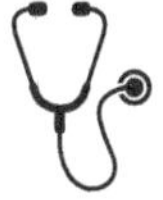

Signs to look for:

- The concerns, doubts, and uncertainties that people have about a proposed action are dismissed or ridiculed by others.
- Members complain about each other privately but never voice those complaints to the group, out of fear of being "negative."
- When members of the team are stuck at a task, they don't ask for help from others. Or it takes them several days of muddling through before they do so.
- The conversations during Sprint Retrospectives focus on tiny improvements, instead of the important things that are obviously not going as well as they could.
- Concerns and doubts are never expressed when the team is together but are mostly gossiped about.
- During team meetings, body language is protective. Arms are crossed, people lean back (instead of in), and are turned away from each other.

The social scientist Edgar Schein described organizational culture[7] as an onion of three layers (see Figure 9.4). The outer layer consists of the artifacts and symbols that you observe in an organization, from the titles that people have or the size of their offices to how people are seated or who speaks first at

7. Schein, E. H. 2004. *Organizational Culture and Leadership*. 3rd ed. San Francisco: Jossey-Bass.

meetings. The core of the onion consists of deeply held, often unconscious, assumptions that people make about each other and their work. For example, "More-experienced people are more worthy of attention than you." Or that "Colleagues will support you when you get in trouble." In between the outer layer (the observable elements) and the core (the assumptions) are the beliefs and values that are actively espoused by people when you ask them. These are the things that often end up in culture manifestos or work agreements.

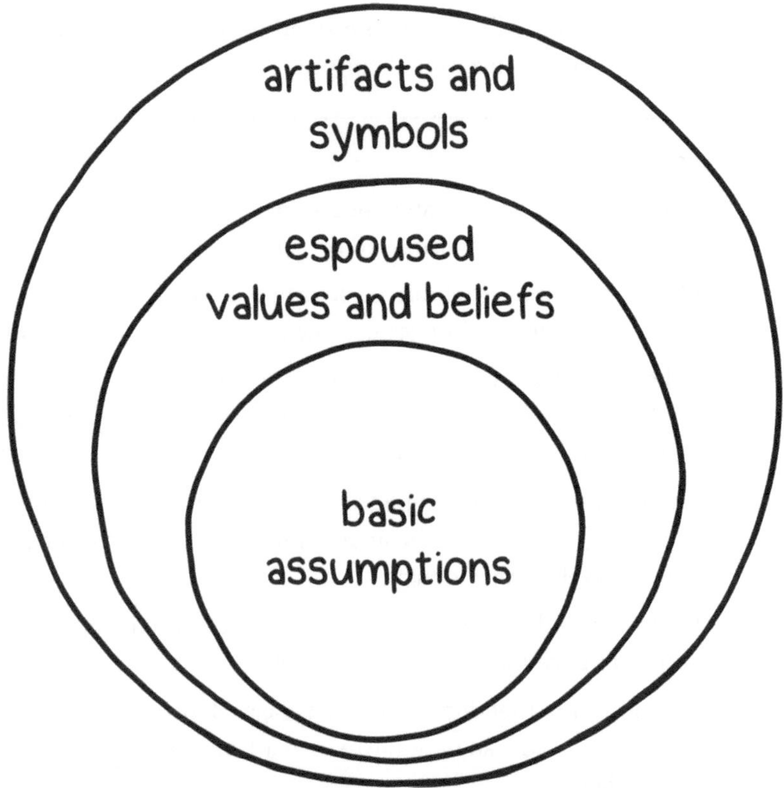

Figure 9.4 Organizational culture can be understood as an onion, from the very visible artifacts and symbols to deeply held beliefs and basic assumptions.[8]

Organizations experience problems when the layers don't align. This is particularly pronounced in how they deal with mistakes and uncertainty. Few organizations and teams actively espouse values that discourage doubts or

8. Source: Schein, *Organizational Culture and Leadership.*

uncertainty, even when they put rules in their working agreements such as "Raise concerns when you have them." When the espoused values (the middle layer) don't match what actually happens (the outer layer), people's beliefs change accordingly over time (the core).

If the team manifesto says that you should "Ask for help when you need it" but nobody ever offers to help when you ask for it, people will stop asking for help eventually. If an espoused value is "Admit it when you don't know something" but leaders never admit to not knowing something themselves, people will eventually start presenting false certainty as well. In their desire to belong to the social group—which every team is—people start to self-censor in order to fit in. The resulting artificial harmony gets in the way of continuous improvement, as people stop looking for, or challenging, things that are not going well.

Organizational culture is like the ruts in a well-trodden path. The deeply held beliefs of people about making mistakes, showing uncertainty, and being vulnerable are reinforced over time by behavior and artifacts in their environment, both by themselves and by others. The deeper the rut, the harder it is to change course. And for teams that suffer from Zombie Scrum, the ruts have become particularly deep. That makes it very hard to create environments where people can safely learn.

Try these experiments to improve with your team (see Chapter 10):

- Share an Impediment Newsletter throughout the Organization
- Focus on What to Stop Doing

In Zombie Scrum, We Don't Celebrate Success

Sometimes, teams can focus so much on potential improvement that they ignore all the positive things that they are already doing. As we saw from the data presented at the beginning of this chapter, few teams find the opportunity to celebrate small and large successes as they happen. How demotivating is it for people when their contributions to success are never recognized?

Signs to look for:

- People don't compliment each other when something went well, or was done well.
- Even when something has gone well, people immediately jump to new things to improve.
- When a Sprint goes well, stakeholders don't make positive comments.

Some people stumble over the word "celebration," fearing fake compliments or gratuitous high spirits. Or they may feel that they need to solve the whole problem before they can celebrate small steps towards a solution. This puts the bar too high if every problem first needs to be completely solved before you can be happy about the progress you made as a team. A celebration simply recognizes progress towards a goal; it doesn't have to mean that the work is over, nor that the pressure is off.

Celebrating success can be as simple as saying, "Thank you for doing a good job" or even "Thanks for trying to make an improvement." Or bringing snacks to the Sprint Review and going for drinks at the end of a Sprint. Many teams that suffer from Zombie Scrum are stuck in the mud to such an extent that all they can see is the mud.

Try these experiments to improve with your team (see Chapter 10):

- Bake a Release Cake
- Share Success Stories and Build on What Made Them Possible

In Zombie Scrum, We Don't Recognize the Human Factors of Work

As we explored earlier, Scrum Teams that lack psychological safety find it hard to learn and improve. Both require trying new things and talking openly about mistakes. The organizational psychologist Amy Edmondson describes psychological safety as "a shared belief about the consequences of interpersonal risk-taking."[9] Her research shows that psychological safety is an important enabler for learning to take place in groups and individuals.

Organizations that suffer from Zombie Scrum spend little time on human factors. Either they don't see the need or they simply assume that employees will behave professionally, and so they implicitly and explicitly signal that spending time on work agreements, talking about tension, getting to know each other, and building a team are not considered "real work." They fail to appreciate that teams are social systems with important social needs.

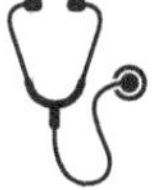

Signs to look for:

- The composition of Scrum Teams is frequently changed by people outside the team, without taking time to reestablish interpersonal safety and trust.
- Team composition is entirely based on skills and experience, and not also on personal preferences, diversity of backgrounds, or behavioral styles.
- Teams are not given time or support to learn how to make decisions, to navigate interpersonal conflict, and make work arrangements.

It's impossible to summarize the decades of work done by social, cognitive, and organizational psychologists into the vast influence of human factors on work, but we have learned that:

- People are likely to self-censor criticisms and doubts in favor of being part of a cohesive group, to the point of unethical or irresponsible decisions (groupthink).[10]

9. Edmondson, A. 2009. "Psychological Safety and Learning Behavior in Work Teams." *Administrative Science Quarterly* 44(2): 350–383.
10. Janis, I. L. 1982. *Groupthink: Psychological Studies of Policy Decisions and Fiascoes*. Boston: Houghton Mifflin. ISBN: 0-395-31704-5.

- People attribute successes to their own actions, and failures to their environment—even when this is demonstrably not the case (fundamental attribution error).[11]
- Making people work on different complex tasks at the same time negatively impacts their performance for each individual task.[12]
- People quickly conform to decisions by their group, even when they know the decisions are blatantly wrong (peer pressure).[13]
- People reject obvious facts that don't align with their beliefs (cognitive dissonance).[14]
- Groups compete with each other, and start forming negative judgments about each other, when their only distinguishing characteristic is as trivial as a name (minimal group membership).[15]
- Our ability to arrive at rational decisions is severely limited by countless biases,[16] such as our limited grasp of probabilities, how we generalize from recent examples, and how our estimations tend to be way too optimistic.
- Conflicts—both latent and overt—have a profound negative influence on group functioning.[17]

This is just a selection of well-researched and replicated effects that shape our own thinking and work in groups. They help us understand why adding more people or teams often doesn't help at all. Or that changing team composition has far-stretching social consequences. The point here is that a team can't continuously improve without recognizing that they are social systems. It is

11. Ross, L. 1977. "The Intuitive Psychologist and His Shortcomings: Distortions in the Attribution Process." In L. Berkowitz, ed., *Advances in Experimental Social Psychology*, pp. 173–220. New York: Academic Press. ISBN: 978-012015210-0.
12. Rogers, R., and S. Monsell. 1995. "The Costs of a Predictable Switch between Simple Cognitive Tasks." *Journal of Experimental Psychology* 124: 207–231.
13. Asch, S. E. 1951. "Effects of Group Pressure on the Modification and Distortion of Judgments." In H. Guetzkow, ed., *Groups, Leadership and Men*, pp. 177–190. Pittsburgh: Carnegie Press.
14. Festinger, L. 1957. *A Theory of Cognitive Dissonance*. California: Stanford University Press.
15. Tajfel, H. 1970. "Experiments in Intergroup Discrimination." *Scientific American* 223(5): 96–102.
16. Kahneman, D., P. Slovic, and A. Tversky. 1982. *Judgment Under Uncertainty: Heuristics and Biases*. New York: Cambridge University Press.
17. De Dreu, K. W., and L. R. Weingart. 2003. "Task Versus Relationship Conflict, Team Performance and Team Member Satisfaction: A Meta-analysis." *Journal of Applied Psychology* 88: 741–749.

simply not enough to put "the best people" in teams and expect them to work miracles by virtue of their individual professional skills.

Try these experiments to improve with your team (see Chapter 10):

- Share Success Stories and Build on What Made Them Possible
- Share an Impediment Newsletter throughout the Organization
- Use Formal and Informal Networks to Drive Change

In Zombie Scrum, We Don't Critique How We Do Our Work

Organizations that suffer from Zombie Scrum don't leverage the Scrum Framework to critique and change how work is done in the organization. This often begins with what the organization expects of a Scrum Master, and the Scrum Master's own understanding of what is important about their role.

For many Scrum Masters, this understanding translates exclusively into the facilitation of Scrum Events for one or more Scrum Teams. And although there is value in that, it is also a very narrow definition. The broader purpose of Scrum Masters is to create transparency around the ability of teams to deliver valuable outcomes to their stakeholders, and the impediments that get in the way. One way to do this is by helping teams gather data to assess how they are doing. By shining a light on where it hurts the most, Scrum Masters encourage double-loop learning, when it comes to building what stakeholders need and shipping fast.

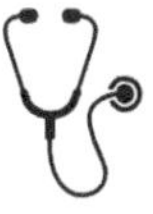

Signs to look for:

- Scrum Masters spend most of their time facilitating Scrum Events.
- Scrum Teams are measured and compared based on how much work they complete (e.g., velocity and the number of items completed) instead of how much value that work actually generates for stakeholders and organizations.

- Scrum Teams don't spend time together, and with their stakeholders, to make sense of the outcome-oriented metrics they track and what improvements seem sensible.
- Scrum Teams don't dissect product or process data, such as stakeholder happiness or cycle time, to identify improvements.

One way to start critiquing is by tracking relevant metrics. Unfortunately, Zombie Scrum Teams usually don't measure improvements at all. When they do, they focus on areas that don't support, or even hinder, empiricism, such as when Scrum Teams measure the amount of work they deliver every Sprint, as expressed by the velocity or the number of items completed, rather than the value that they delivered. Organizations may also track the number of people and teams working on a product, and the number of hours they put in, looking at reductions in the number of people or hours as an indicator of improvement. We've explored the reasons behind this approach in more detail in Chapter 5.

The problem with metrics like these is that they are concerned only with how much work is done in a given amount of time—the output—but not with how valuable that work actually is for stakeholders and the organization—the outcome. And while the former may be easier to track, it's largely irrelevant in terms of the value that the organization delivers. After all, it is entirely possible to see huge improvements in velocity over time and still go bankrupt when the product doesn't deliver enough value to stakeholders. It's also entirely possible to work on a product with a dozen teams yet deliver a product of such low quality that teams are essentially only fixing bugs and drowning in technical debt. While you can achieve stellar scores on output and horrendous scores on outcomes, the reverse is unlikely.

Fortunately, the Scrum Framework provides both a process for discovering and implementing improvements as well as areas to focus on:

- **Responsiveness.** The time it takes between the discovery and the fulfillment of an important stakeholder need, as expressed by cycle time and (low) work in progress, decreases over time (or remains low).

- **Quality.** The quality of the work delivered, as expressed by the number of defects, code quality, customer satisfaction, and other quality metrics, increases over time (or remains high).
- **Improving.** The way work is done and experienced, as expressed by team morale, innovation rate, lower dependencies, and other metrics, improves over time.
- **Value.** The amount of value, as expressed in revenue, return on investment, and other business metrics, increases (or remains high over time).

In order to leverage the Scrum Framework to drive change throughout organizations, Scrum Teams and Scrum Masters do well to create transparency around outcome-oriented metrics. By periodically inspecting them with stakeholders, they can identify where it hurts, what to improve, and what happens because of these improvements. This is what empiricism is all about.

Try these experiments to improve with your team (see Chapter 10):

- Focus on What to Stop Doing
- Share an Impediment Newsletter throughout the Organization
- Create a Low-Tech Metrics Dashboard to Track Outcomes

In Zombie Scrum, We Consider Learning and Work As Different Things

In organizations suffering from Zombie Scrum, people are implicitly taught that learning and work are separate things. Work generates value, while learning only costs time and money that could've been spent doing more "real" work. For example, management expects people to participate in training on evenings or on weekends. The implicit message is that people get paid for work, and since learning isn't real work, they have to do it on their own time.

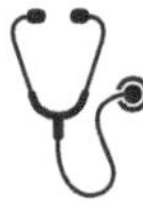

Signs to look for:

- People don't visit external meetups or trainings, or read professional books or blogs, and they certainly are not encouraged to do so.
- Scrum Teams don't stay up to date with developments in their professions. For example, developers don't know about continuous delivery, virtualization, and microservices, or Scrum Masters are unaware of Kanban and Liberating Structures.
- Product Owners keep pushing items focused on innovation further down the Product Backlog in favor of adding more features, without actually measuring how effective that is.
- Scrum Teams make their Sprint Retrospectives as short as possible.
- Management discourages people from going outside and learning from others by requiring detailed business cases about what value this would generate.

The point here is not to spend more time on learning, but to remove the artificial separation between learning and work. Long gone are the days when you could learn a skill at school and then put learning behind you. This has never been more true than in software development, where new technologies, languages, and practices emerge ever faster. Though not all are equally helpful, some offer new paradigms, such as continuous delivery and containers, that make it easier to ship faster and improve quality. The uncertainty of complex work, and the challenges it throws at teams, requires them to constantly learn how to navigate that complexity better. Organizations that suffer from Zombie Scrum push learning to the fringes of work. Therefore, they never benefit from what happens when teams have time and space to try new things and see what becomes possible because of that.

It's hard to improve when you're rarely exposed to new ideas and different perspectives, yet for many teams that suffer from Zombie Scrum, this is exactly what happens. With so much work to do, they have little time for learning. Although organizations frequently describe themselves as "learning organizations," few actually exhibit the characteristics of a true learning organization. When "getting work done" is always valued more than participating in training and meetups, or when organizations don't invest in knowledge-sharing workshops because they see more value in keeping teams busy, or when reading professional blog posts during work is frowned upon, the organization clearly sends a message that it doesn't value learning.

Try these experiments to improve with your team (see Chapter 10):

- Use Formal and Informal Networks to Drive Change
- Share Success Stories and Build on What Made Them Possible (especially with multiple teams present)

"You think that learning and working are different things, recruit? As Henry Ford said: 'Anyone who stops learning is old, whether at twenty or eighty.' You're never done learning when it comes to Scrum. And tie your shoelaces: we're going for a run!"

HEALTHY SCRUM

Experience: Not Scrum by the Book

Here's a tale of firsthand experience from one of this book's authors:

When one of the authors started with Scrum, all he did was host a Daily Scrum every other day. For him and his team, that seemed like the most useful part of the Scrum Framework. Coming from a situation where detailed specification documents—written by the author—guided the work, the Development Team initially didn't see much value in Sprint Planning and Sprint Review. The team believed that all the work was already known, and they wouldn't be releasing the product for months anyways.

> As the team started working with Sprints, they learned how useful it was to show intermediate results to their customers. They also learned that while many ideas from the specification document seemed good at the time of writing, they were often interpreted differently by customers and developers. Or better ideas emerged when the customers got to interact with the results. The benefit was mutual. In fact, one of their corporate customers—normally dressed in a crisply tailored suit—would visit every other week wearing shorts and flip-flops to see what the Development Team had come up with.
>
> Where the relationship was initially very much framed as customer and vendor, it became more informal and collaborative over time. Increasingly, key users would tag along to benefit from the opportunity to offer ideas that would make their work in the resulting product easier (and join in after-work drinks). Developers started making parts of the product available before its scheduled "launch date" to address users' natural need to benefit immediately from the work done. This situation paved the way for continuous delivery and ever closer collaboration. Only in hindsight we realized that this team was increasingly learning to work empirically. They learned from experience and changed existing beliefs about specifications, about collaboration, and about the need to ship fast.

In the story, we see double-loop learning when stakeholders change their belief that the Development Team is merely a supplier of their product. We also see double-loop learning when the team learns that releasing Increments actually allows them to build a better product.

Although this story is only one example, there is a clear commonality with other successful Scrum Teams we've worked with. Few of them start with Scrum by the book. Instead, their desire to deliver valuable outcomes to their customers, users, and stakeholders drives their learning. In turn, stakeholders respond by being more available as they learn how this approach benefits them too. And management actively encourages both movements by removing impediments that get in the way and giving teams autonomy to improve where they deem necessary. The process of continuously inspecting and adapting the work, along with how and why that work is done, contributes to their success.

Self-Critical Teams

From the story, it might seem that the growth over time was smooth and free of conflict. It wasn't. And that is another commonality we've found with other successful Scrum Teams. They have spirited disagreements on how to move forward. Where some passionately argue to deploy faster, others argue to take it slower to guarantee quality and stability. Where some want to spend more time writing code, others want to spend more time thinking about what to write. But although preferences and strategies diverge, the focus remains on delivering high-quality outcomes to stakeholders.

Healthy Scrum Teams are critical of themselves. They use their Sprint Retrospectives to reflect on their ability to create a high-quality, releasable version of their product to stakeholders. They use objective data to support this reflection, ranging from cycle time to bug count. Although their Sprint Retrospectives can use creative formats to achieve this goal, a good conversation with powerful questions is often better. Scrum Masters support this reflection by keeping the focus on delivering valuable outcomes and helping teams to navigate the inevitable conflicts that surface while doing so.

See the Forest and the Trees, Together

In their drive to deliver value to stakeholders, healthy Scrum Teams are acutely aware that impediments often transcend individual teams. Shared tooling may not support continuous delivery, for example. The sales department continues to sell work against fixed prices and deadlines. Or teams find that the way their office spaces are organized is making collaboration difficult.

Healthy Scrum emerges where people take time to see both the forest *and* the trees. While making improvements in their own teams (the trees), they also take time to reflect and improve how the system as a whole (the forest) is making it possible for them to deliver value. Instead of leaving this task up to Scrum Masters or dedicated agile transformation teams, this is done with whoever wants to be involved. After all, impediments in one area are often linked to others elsewhere in the organization. That makes it beneficial to bring in as many minds as possible, so as to maximize the resolution of the reflection and the creativity of possible solutions. This can take the shape of multiteam Retrospectives to workshops attended by everyone who wants to help. For example, the authors of this book are frequently involved in workshops where fifty or more participants—ranging from management to developers—use a day to reflect on, and resolve, impediments to empiricism that are surfacing across their organization.

Now What?

In this chapter we explored the most common observations that help you conclude that continuous improvement isn't taking place. We also covered the important underlying causes that we often find in our work with teams that suffer from Zombie Scrum. Although everyone agrees that continuous improvement is a good idea, the problems start when you are dealing with impediments that seem to be outside the control of your team. Instead of focusing on where you don't have control, we find it more useful to focus on where you do and start from there. No matter how small, where do you have responsibility and control? And who can you draw in to help you remove what you can't control yourself? In the next chapter, we explore experiments that help you do just that.

10 Experiments

It is a truth universally acknowledged that a zombie in possession of brains must be in want of more brains.

—Seth Grahame-Smith,
Pride and Prejudice and Zombies

In This Chapter

- Explore ten experiments to improve continuously.
- Learn what impact the experiments have on surviving Zombie Scrum.
- Discover how to perform each experiment and what to look for.

This chapter presents experiments to help teams advance their ability to improve. Some experiments offer inspiration on how to run a Sprint Retrospective differently. Others take continuous improvement to the organizational level.

Experiments for Encouraging Deep Learning

Double-loop learning is a form of deep learning where existing rules, procedures, roles, and structures are challenged (see Chapter 9). Because this doesn't come naturally to most people, we're sharing our favorite experiments to get started.

SHARE AN IMPEDIMENT NEWSLETTER THROUGHOUT THE ORGANIZATION

The impediments that make it hard for Scrum Teams to work empirically often involve people across the organization. Helping these people understand the impediments and the problems they cause creates awareness that enables double-loop learning, which can lead to systemic improvements.

Effort/Impact Ratio

Effort	★★★☆☆	This experiment calls for nothing but courage and a dash of tact.
Impact on survival	★★★★☆	Although painful, this experiment is a great way to create urgency around the biggest problems.

Steps

To try this experiment, do the following:

1. With your Scrum Team, ask everyone to silently write down impediments they see that are making it hard for them to build what stakeholders need or ship fast(er), or both. What skills are missing? Where is protocol getting in the way? Which people do they need, but don't have access to? After a few minutes, invite people to pair up to share and build on their individual ideas. Together, share all impediments and pick the three to five impediments that are most impactful (e.g., with dot-voting).
2. For the biggest impediments, ask "What is lost because of this? What would we and our stakeholders gain when this impediment is removed?" Capture the consequences for the various impediments.
3. For the biggest impediments, ask "Where do we need help? What would help look like?" Collect the requests for help for the various impediments.
4. Compile the biggest impediments, including their consequences and requests for help, in a format that you can easily distribute to everyone who has a stake in your work. It could be a mailing, a paper newsletter, a

blog post on your intranet, or a poster that you put in a heavy-traffic corridor. Include the purpose of your team and how to contact you. You can also include the accomplishments of your team, of course.

Our Findings

- Make sure to include (higher) management and consider informing them up front. Also, they will probably appreciate a shorter, more concise version of the newsletter.
- Transparency can be painful. Be honest but tactful in your messaging, and don't blame others or be negative. State what is happening and make clear requests for help.
- If you are planning to do this experiment frequently, make sure to include the accomplishments of your team as well. What is going well? What has changed since the previous newsletter? And most important: from whom did you receive (unexpected) help?

Ask Powerful Questions during Sprint Retrospectives

As we explored in the previous chapter, people's deeply held beliefs, assumptions, and values influence how successful they will be in changing. For example, when Development Teams feel that talking to customers is the responsibility of Product Owners, they limit their opportunities for collaboration. When people assume that their feedback is only useful when the entire Product Backlog has been implemented, they will struggle to embrace empiricism. Many of these assumptions are subconscious and need to be surfaced in order to be challenged. This experiment is designed to help teams by asking powerful questions that reveal hidden assumptions.

Effort/Impact Ratio

Effort	★★☆☆☆	Asking questions isn't difficult, but asking the "right" questions and creating an environment in which the team is willing to answer them openly is.
Impact on survival	★★★★☆	This experiment sets an example of how people can challenge their own beliefs and those deeply held by the organization.

Steps

To try this experiment, listen for statements about whether or not something is possible. The Sprint Retrospective is a good opportunity, but so are other moments when teams are together. Ask "What do you believe to be true that makes you say that?" Work together to reframe the answer into a statement that starts with "I believe that . . . ." See Table 10.1 for examples.

Table 10.1 Examples of What People Say and What Underlying Beliefs Can Make Them Do So

What you hear someone say	A possible underlying belief
"When we ask people for input on this change, they're only going to complain."	"I believe that people resist change."
"Only management can remove this impediment."	"I believe that I can't change this without authority."
"We can't deliver a new Increment every Sprint."	"I believe that our product is too complex."
"This task is important, so I will take care of it myself."	"I believe others lack the knowledge and quality I have."
"We don't have to ask the customer for feedback."	"I believe that I know exactly what customers need."
"We need to add more teams."	"I believe that more people will get more work done."

When you have identified a belief, use the following powerful questions to gently challenge it. We took inspiration from work done by people in the Liberating Structures community (primarily Fisher Qua and Anja Ebers) on "Myth Turning":[1]

- What would need to happen for you to let go of this belief?
- Who else believes this to be true?
- Where does this belief benefit you?

1. Lipmanowicz, H., and K. McCandless. 2014. *The Surprising Power of Liberating Structures: Simple Rules to Unleash a Culture of Innovation*. Liberating Structures Press. ASN: 978-0615975306.

- Where do you see this belief confirmed?
- What are the signs that others are starting to question this belief?
- What is irrevocably lost when we don't do this?
- What happens when this belief turns out to be wrong?

Asking these questions won't convince people to change their beliefs, but it may help them learn and reflect on why they hold those beliefs. In doing so, they may discover that changing a belief benefits them, but that decision is up to them.

Our Findings

- People may be overwhelmed and frustrated if they are not used to deep questions such as these. Ask permission from your team to help them reflect and learn by asking a deep question every now and then.
- Don't tell people what their belief should be. Don't share your own, unless people specifically ask you to. Invite people to challenge yours too. Make the identification of underlying beliefs a team effort or something for people to reflect on themselves.

Dig Deeper into Problems and Potential Solutions, Together

Effectively analyzing and removing impediments is important for deep learning and continuous improvement. Teams have to learn how to ask or write questions that include different perspectives, and to identify specific and actionable solutions. The Liberating Structure "Discovery and Action Dialogue"[2] is ideal for this exploration. It contains a sequence of questions that teams can ask to understand the problem, come up with solutions, and specify steps that need to be taken.

2. Lipmanowicz and McCandless, *The Surprising Power of Liberating Structures.*

Effort/Impact Ratio

Effort	★★☆☆☆	We give you the specific sequence of questions the team can use, which makes this a low-effort experiment. This specific sequence will help you guide the process.
Impact on survival	★★★★☆	This experiment helps people solve the right problems *and* builds the skill set to more effectively analyze those problems.

Steps

In Discovery and Action Dialogue, groups answer the following sequence of questions together:

1. How do you know when the problem is present?
2. How do you contribute effectively to solving the problem?
3. What prevents you from doing this or taking these actions all the time?
4. Do you know anybody who is able to frequently solve this problem and overcome barriers? What behaviors or practices made their success possible?
5. Do you have any ideas?
6. What needs to be done to make it happen? Any volunteers?
7. Who else needs to be involved?

Follow these steps for Discovery and Action Dialogue:

1. As input for Discovery and Action Dialogue, help your team or teams identify their biggest impediments. Many of the other experiments in this book are helpful here. Either choose the most important topic with one team or have participants from multiple teams form groups around different topics.
2. Give the group(s) enough time (at least 30 minutes) to answer the sequence of questions. If it makes sense, groups can deviate from the order or revisit earlier questions when new insights emerge.
3. When you run a Discovery and Action Dialogue with multiple teams, add opportunities for teams to share their findings with the whole group

and gather feedback. A Liberating Structure such as Shift & Share[3] is ideal for this.

Our Findings

- Encourage the team(s) to spend enough time on the first question. Asking additional questions such as "What's so challenging about this problem?", "Is there a deeper problem we're not seeing?" or "What happens when we don't solve this problem?" will help you dig deeper (see Figure 10.1).
- Keep in mind the concept of 15% Solutions—described next in this chapter—when asking what needs to be done to make the solution happen.
- Use a host when the team is struggling to maintain a good pace and flow for answering the questions. The host asks the questions in order and gives everyone the opportunity to speak to each question, while the host keeps track of time.

Figure 10.1 Dig deeper into problems and potential solutions with Discovery and Action Dialogue.

3. Lipmanowicz and McCandless, *The Surprising Power of Liberating Structures*.

Experiments for Making Improvements Tangible

It's easy for teams to remain stuck in vague and promising improvements such as "Communicate more" and "Involve stakeholders." But when improvements are this imprecise, it is hard to know where to start and hard to validate when you're done. The experiments in this category all revolve around making your improvements as tangible and small as possible.

Create 15% Solutions

Continuous improvement works best when changes are small and start from what people can change on their own. To help with this focus, the organizational theorist Gareth Morgan proposed the concept of "15% Solutions."[4] Working from the assumption that people don't have control over 85% of their work situation, the focus shifts to the 15% they do have control over. Not only is this more motivating, it also keeps improvements small and free of the barriers that make the 85% so difficult to control, such as organizational culture, existing hierarchies, and rigid procedures. If everyone starts with where they have autonomy and opportunity to change, all those 15% changes together easily snowball into significant change across the organization.

This experiment helps your Scrum Team define 15% Solutions and create change even in environments where little seems possible. It is based on the Liberating Structure "15% Solutions."[5]

Effort/Impact Ratio

Effort	★☆☆☆☆	If you can rein in your temptation to go for bigger change, sticking to what you can control isn't difficult.
Impact on survival	★★★★☆	Although individual 15% Solutions won't change the world, many small changes together can.

4. Morgan, M. 2006. *Images of Organization*. Sage Publications. ISBN: 1412939798.
5. Lipmanowicz and McCandless, *The Surprising Power of Liberating Structures*.

Steps

To try this experiment, do the following:

1. Use 15% Solutions at the end of every meeting. This helps people turn what they've learned into actionable steps. Preferably, use a shared impediment or challenge to give focus to the 15% Solutions.
2. Ask everyone to generate a list of 15% Solutions for themselves. Ask "What is your 15 percent? Where do you have discretion and freedom to act? What can you do without more resources or authority?"
3. Invite people to share their ideas in pairs for five minutes. Encourage them to help each other make their 15% Solutions as tangible as possible. Questions that help are: "What is the first step to do this?" or "Where would you start?"
4. For maximum transparency, collect the 15% Solutions in the team room, for example, around a Scrum Board if your team uses one.

Our Findings

- Don't restrict the use of 15% Solutions to Sprint Retrospectives. Use them to identify where to start refactoring large and complex code bases, to identify next steps after a Sprint Review, or to conduct multiteam retrospectives.
- Help people resist the temptation to define actions for others or for the group as a whole, effectively moving away from what they control themselves. 15% Solutions work when people focus on their own contribution. It's okay if solutions overlap or when they are not clearly related.

Focus on What to Stop Doing

Continuous improvement can easily devolve into adding more things to an already overcrowded to-do list: one more check to the Definition of Done, one more workshop to an overcrowded agenda, or one other technology to research. But as you add more, you are less likely actually to get any of it done.

Instead of adding more things to do, find things that you are doing that are unproductive and eliminate them. The Liberating Structure "TRIZ"[6] is a huge help, as it invites creative destruction of activities that limit innovation and productivity by engaging everyone in a playful way. The name TRIZ is an abbreviation of the Russian version for "theory of the resolution of invention-related tasks."

Effort/Impact Ratio

Effort	★★★★☆	Letting go of behaviors and activities is often harder than adding more to an ever-expanding list.
Impact on survival	★★★★☆	Letting go of unwanted activities and behaviors creates space.

Steps

To try this experiment, do the following:

1. Create three rows on a flip chart, leaving space open in each of them. Don't add labels to the rows as this might spoil the twist of the second round.
2. Give everyone ten minutes to make a first list of everything they can do to guarantee the worst possible outcome. Ask: "How can you personally contribute to making our team so zombified in its ability to ship fast and collaborate with stakeholders that it becomes the prime example of 'Zombie Scrum' on Wikipedia?" Do this step first individually and in silence for a few minutes, then in pairs for a few minutes more. Encourage people to be creative and practical while keeping things within the boundaries of the law. Then invite people to share and build on their ideas for a few more minutes in pairs. Take five minutes to collect the most salient examples on stickies and place them into the top row.
3. Give the participants ten minutes to make a second list of activities the team is already doing that resemble or are closely related to items on the first list. Ask: "If you're brutally honest, which items represent things we're already doing or are moving in that direction?" First, give people a few minutes of individual reflection before they pair up to share their

6. Lipmanowicz and McCandless, *The Surprising Power of Liberating Structures.*

thoughts and notice patterns. Capture the most salient patterns of Zombie Scrum by moving the items from the top row to the middle one.

4. Give the team ten minutes to make a third list of all the activities or behaviors from the second list that they want to stop from now on. Start this step individually, then do it in pairs, and then repeat with the whole group. In the third row, capture the items that the team is going to stop doing from now on. Resist the temptation to *add* actions to stop something.

Our Findings

- Invite participants to have serious fun, go a bit over the top, and have a laugh while they're doing it. This helps create a safe environment where people feel comfortable being honest.
- For deeper reflection, replace the activities and behaviors in TRIZ with beliefs and norms. Which beliefs should we have about each other, our work, and our stakeholders to guarantee the worst possible outcome? Which beliefs are already present or similar? Which should we let go of?

Create Improvement Recipes

Vague improvement ideas such as "More collaboration" or "Use Sprint Goals," or ideas that have no clear start and end, won't propel teams forward. This experiment is about translating vague improvements into something specific by building on each other's intelligence and creativity. Just as a cookbook gives you detailed instructions on how to cook a dish with local ingredients, *improvement recipes* clarify the ingredients, the steps, and the expected outcomes. This experiment is based on the Liberating Structure "Shift & Share."[7]

Effort/Impact Ratio

Effort	★★☆☆☆	Creating the recipes isn't hard. Having the team use the recipes can be more difficult.
Impact on survival	★★★★☆	Being clear about where you are going to improve as a team, and what this entails, is a vital skill for continuous improvement.

7. Lipmanowicz and McCandless, *The Surprising Power of Liberating Structures*.

Steps

To try this experiment, do the following:

1. During a Sprint Retrospective or a multiteam Retrospective, identify a handful of areas for improvement. Ask everyone to self-organize into small groups (three to five people) by picking the improvement they care about the most. Provide each group with an empty whiteboard or flip that designates their "station."
2. First individually and in silence, invite everyone to think about what the recipe might look like by asking: "If we want to achieve this, what would help us do that? What practices come to mind? What have you tried elsewhere that might work here?" (two minutes). Then invite people to share their ideas in small groups and pick one (five minutes).
3. Explain the Definition of Done for a recipe. Each recipe needs to clarify: What is it trying to achieve ("purpose")? Who needs to be involved ("people")? What steps need to happen and in what order ("steps")? And how do you know that the recipe is working ("success")? If you want, you can prepare a canvas for each of the recipes.
4. Give the groups ten minutes to create a first increment of their recipe. Encourage groups to use their full creativity by writing, drawing, and using symbols.
5. Invite each group to pick one station owner. That person remains with their station for the remaining rounds. The others move clockwise to the next station. The station owner updates the new group on the progress and works together with them to build on the increment, adding improvements and clarifications as needed (five minutes).
6. Repeat as many times as necessary for each group to visit each station.
7. Ask the groups to return to their original station and take a look at the final version of their recipe that was created incrementally by the various groups.

8. Ask people to write their name on a sticky note and put it on one recipe they're willing to commit to making possible. Give people a few minutes to synchronize how and where to start for the recipe they've picked.

Our Findings

- Improvement recipes often capture recurring patterns or local strategies to resolve impediments. Sharing useful recipes with other teams—both inside and outside the organization—is a great way to learn.
- If you notice that the recipes are superficial and vague, encourage groups to keep asking "How will we do this?" when they visit a new station.
- For initiatives that span more Sprints, encourage groups to frequently synchronize their work and progress until the purpose has been fulfilled.

Experiments for Gathering New Information

Sometimes we tell teams that "it's hard to squeeze juice from dry oranges." It is our—admittedly blunt—way of telling them that their toolbox or the flow of new ideas has dried up to the point that their continuous improvement has stalled. In this category, we share experiments that help bring in new ideas or people to see possibilities where you couldn't see them before.

Use Formal and Informal Networks to Drive Change

Changing the environment of Scrum Teams can be difficult when you're trying to do it alone, especially in large organizations where the people with influence are difficult to get in touch with. When working to remove an impediment, you should first find people in your organization who are facing similar impediments and work together to remove them. This experiment is about leveraging the informal and formal networks in organizations to create change. It is based on the Liberating Structures "Social Network Webbing" (for an example, see Figure 10.2) and "1-2-4-All."[8]

8. Lipmanowicz and McCandless, *The Surprising Power of Liberating Structures.*

Effort/Impact Ratio

Effort	★★★★☆	Finding creative ways to expand the network is challenging, especially in large, complex organizations.
Impact on survival	★★★★★	We've seen significant shifts when people start tapping into formal and informal networks to create change.

Steps

To try this experiment, do the following:

1. Start by inviting Scrum Masters, Product Owners, and members from Development Teams who are eager to start removing organizational impediments to Scrum.
2. First individually (one minute), then in pairs (two minutes) and in groups of four (four minutes), ask people to answer "What are the biggest impediments we face? What in this organization is making it difficult for us to work empirically?" Collect the biggest impediments.
3. Create a wall or use the floor for the social map. Bring stickies with different colors.
4. Start creating the social network map by asking the participants to write down their name on stickies. Put them in the center of the social network. These people are the "core group."
5. First individually (one minute), then in pairs (two minutes) and then with another pair (four minutes), ask people to identify the key groups or departments you need support from to remove impediments. Limit to a maximum of ten groups and create a legend where each has a different color or symbol (ten minutes).
6. Invite everyone to write down the names of people they know in the organization on separate stickies, making use of the legend. Ask people to place the stickies on the map based on how close or distant they are to the people currently present (ten minutes).
7. First individually (one minute), then in pairs (two minutes), and then with another pair (four minutes), ask people to answer "Whom would you like to include to remove the impediments we're facing? Who has influence, a fresh perspective, or the skills we need?" Write down the names on separate stickies, making use of the legend. Map the stickies on the

network based on their current and desired involvement. Update the legend as new groups are identified (fifteen minutes).

8. Ask everyone to take a look at the map that is emerging and ask: "Who knows whom? Who has influence and expertise? Who can block or boost progress?" Draw lines between people and groups to connect them based on the answers (fifteen minutes).
9. Use the experiment "Create 15% Solutions" elsewhere in this chapter to generate strategies for involving influential people who are distant or to work around blockages. How can you leverage your network to involve the right people? This can be as simple as making a phone call, sending an email, or asking someone closer to you to make the connection. You can use the experiment "Share an Impediment Newsletter throughout the Organization" to inform people in the network.

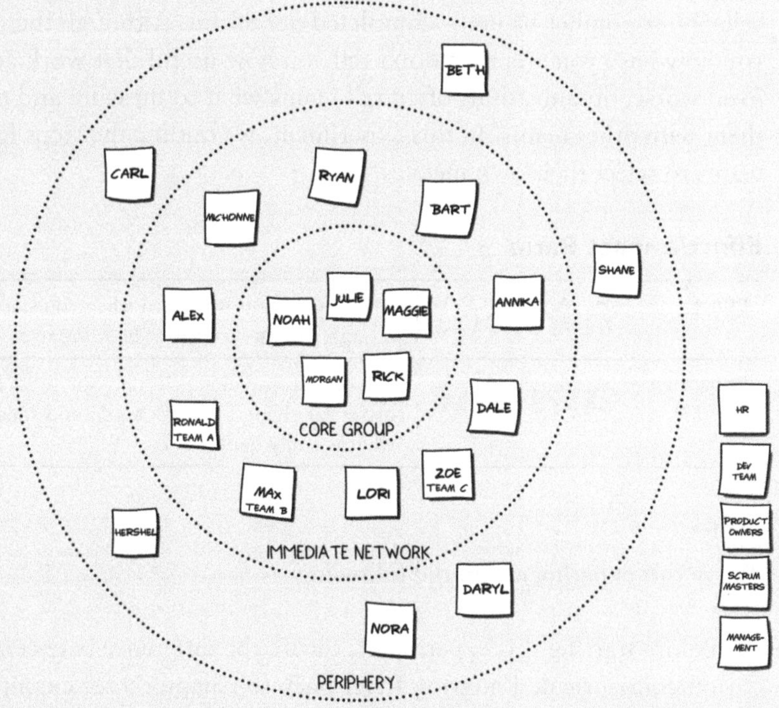

Figure 10.2 An example of a social network web[9]

9. Source: Lipmanowicz and McCandless, *The Surprising Power of Liberating Structures*.

Our Findings

- Pay close attention to black holes in the map. These are the departments or groups you need support from, but where you don't know anyone (directly or indirectly).
- This experiment works best when you repeat it every so often. Try to expand your "core group" with people who are willing to help. As your network grows, it becomes progressively easier to remove blockages or boost progress.

Create a Low-Tech Metrics Dashboard to Track Outcomes

How well is your team performing? Do you know what outcomes you're delivering? More often than not, teams try to answer these questions by tracking velocity or number of items completed per Sprint. Although these metrics tell you how busy you are, they don't tell you how useful that work actually is. Even worse, organizations often tell teams what to measure and then compare them with other teams. In this experiment, we outline the steps for helping teams to select their own metrics.

Effort/Impact Ratio

Effort	★★☆☆☆	This experiment isn't hard when you start small—even a single metric—and start building from there.
Impact on survival	★★★★★	Creating transparency around outcomes is a significant driver for change, as both teams and stakeholders see what is really happening.

Steps

To try this experiment, do the following:

1. Before starting this experiment, clarify the difference between output- and outcome-oriented metrics. Refer back to Chapter 9 for examples.
2. First individually (one minute), then in pairs (two minutes), then in groups of four (four minutes), ask people to consider how they would

know that their team is doing better. Ask: "How do we know that we're responsive to our stakeholders? What metrics would go up when we do a good job and down if we don't?" Together, collect relevant metrics with the team (five minutes).

3. Repeat for quality. Ask: "How do we know that our work is of high quality? What metrics would go up when we do a good job and down if we don't?"
4. Repeat for value. Ask: "How do we know that we're delivering value through our work? What metrics would go up when we do a good job and down if we don't?"
5. Repeat for improvement. Ask: "How do we know that we're finding time to improve and learn? What metrics would go up when we do a good job and down if we don't?"
6. Together, look at the selected metrics and remove obvious duplicates. First individually (one minute), then in small groups (four minutes), ask people to remove metrics that the team can do without, while still being able to measure their progress on responsiveness, quality, value, and improvement. Together, keep the most minimal set that covers these areas (five minutes).
7. For each of the metrics left, explore how to quantify them well and where to get the data from. If additional research or setup is needed, you can add this work to the Product or Sprint Backlog.
8. Set up a dashboard—preferably just a whiteboard or flip—that the team updates (at least) once every Sprint. Create graphs for the various metrics to track trends. Resist the temptation to set up overwhelming dashboards in digital tools. First build the discipline to track a handful of metrics and inspect them every so often. Low-tech dashboards, such as whiteboards, promote experimentation because they're easier to change in terms of presentation, content, and format.
9. Inspect the dashboard together during Sprint Reviews or Sprint Retrospectives. What trends are obvious? When you run an experiment, what would you expect to see change? A Liberating Structure such as "What, So What, Now What?"[10] is well-suited for this.

10. Lipmanowicz and McCandless, *The Surprising Power of Liberating Structures.*

Our Findings

- When it comes to metrics, it is easy to try to measure too much. Be purposefully minimalistic by starting with the essentials: for example, stakeholder happiness and cycle time. Add more metrics when it helps your learning and when teams develop a rhythm in maintaining and inspecting them.
- Don't turn metrics into key performance indicators (or KPIs) and work hard to prevent others from doing so. When metrics are used to appraise the performance of teams, it incentivizes them to "game" the numbers. Instead, use metrics purely for learning what works and what doesn't.
- Don't hide your dashboard from stakeholders. Instead, engage them in making sense of the data and finding opportunities for improvement. They benefit from the data just as much as your team does.

Experiments to Create a Learning Environment

Continuous improvement requires trying new things, some of which will lead to improvements and some will not. People who have to worry about the repercussions of making mistakes or being criticized will avoid trying new things, which means they can't learn and improve. In this part of the chapter, we share experiments that make it easier to promote a culture of learning.

Share Success Stories and Build on What Made Them Possible

Instead of focusing on the things that don't go well—as is all too easy in Zombie Scrum—you can help teams focus on what is already working and improve from there. Sharing successful experiences, stories, and strategies from the past is a good way to both build safety and uncover unseen paths forward. This experiment is based on the Liberating Structure "Appreciative Interviews."[11]

11. Lipmanowicz and McCandless, *The Surprising Power of Liberating Structures.*

Effort/Impact Ratio

Effort	★☆☆☆☆	It doesn't take much effort to share a success story. Most people like sharing their personal successes.
Impact on survival	★★★★☆	Sharing successful experiences gives hope that fighting Zombie Scrum is worth the effort.

Steps

To try this experiment, do the following:

1. This experiment can be done anytime. The Sprint Retrospective is a natural opportunity, but so is the start of a Sprint Planning or Sprint Review. You can do it with a single team or with multiple teams to spread stories and learnings.
2. Ask everyone to form pairs and sit face to face. Make sure that everyone has something to write on and something to write with.
3. In turn, invite people to interview each other for five minutes per person. Ask: "Share a story of a time when we worked together to overcome a small or large challenge and you are proud of what we accomplished. What made the success possible?" Interviewers primarily listen, asking a clarifying question now and then. Make sure they also take notes, as they'll need those in the next step.
4. Invite the pairs to find another pair. In ten minutes, everyone retells the story of their partner (about two minutes each). When one person is retelling the story, the others listen closely for patterns in what made the stories possible. Afterwards, gather key insights from the whole group and collect them on a flip (ten minutes).
5. First individually and in silence, ask people to think about what they can do to have more of these stories in the future (two minutes). Ask: "How can we build on the root causes of success? How can we be successful more often?" Then invite people to share their ideas in small groups (four minutes). Collect the most salient ideas with the whole group (ten minutes).

6. Use the experiment “Create 15% Solutions” or “Create Improvement Recipes” elsewhere in this chapter to translate potential improvements into specific actions.

Our Findings

When you do this experiment, watch out for the following:

- When you have an uneven number of participants, you’ll end up with one group of three. Let this group creatively work within the same time box as the other groups.
- Pay close attention to group dynamics and posture when people share their stories or retell those of others. Not only is it nice for groups to reminisce about their successes, it is also a positive experience to hear someone else retell your story in their own words.

BAKE A RELEASE PIE

A great way to build team spirit is to acknowledge small successes as they happen. For example, teams can celebrate every time they release to production, or when they automate another part that would require manual work otherwise. We’ve found it helpful to celebrate these successes in a simple and playful way while also giving everyone on the team the opportunity to contribute.

Effort/Impact Ratio

Effort	★☆☆☆☆	Aside from picking a worthy action to celebrate, this experiment is a piece of cake.
Impact on survival	★★★☆☆	This experiment won’t change the world. But it is one way to build team spirit and safety on a team.

Steps

To try this experiment, do the following:

1. With your team, identify a specific achievement that is worthy of celebration when it happens during a Sprint. Pick an action that helps you

work more empirically and that is challenging or frequently postponed. For example, a release to production. Or verifying an assumption with a real user. Or pairing up with others instead of adding more work to "In Progress."

2. Find a big sheet of paper or a whiteboard and draw a big circle on it. Divide the circle into six or eight slices so that it represents a "release pie" (see Figure 10.3). Put the diagram in a visible spot in the team room.
3. Every time your team completes the action it identified, mark one of the slices. You can add the initials of the person who completed it, but only when everyone on your team has the opportunity to actually complete or contribute to the action.
4. When all the slices of the pie are marked, go out and get a real pie. Or something else that the team enjoys and gets them together.

Figure 10.3 Celebrate releases by creating a release pie!

Our Findings

- You want to set goals that are challenging but possible to achieve multiple times a Sprint. Adjust the number of slices and the difficulty to the capabilities of a team.
- Pick actions where achieving them is visible to others in the team. Otherwise, the decision to mark a slice becomes too subjective and based on individual motivations.

NOW WHAT?

In this chapter, we explored a set of experiments that are designed to help your team, and the entire organization, improve continuously. In part this involves double-loop learning. But it also requires a safe environment, new inspiration from external sources, and tangible improvements. Use these experiments, or draw inspiration from them, to start improving continuously now.

"Looking for more experiments, recruit? There is an extensive arsenal available at ***zombiescrum.org****. You can also help expand our arsenal by suggesting what worked well for you."*

V
Self-Organize

11 Symptoms and Causes

We're trying to rebuild society, not plunge it back into chaos.

—Andrew Cormier,
Shamblers: The Zombie Apocalypse

In This Chapter

- Learn what self-organization looks like and how self-managed teams make it possible.
- Explore the most common symptoms and causes of poor self-organization.
- Discover what self-organization and self-management look like in healthy Scrum Teams.

Experience from the Field

"Let's start our Scrum Journey!" exclaimed Jeff, CEO of Widget Inc., at the start of the annual corporate retreat. It was an important strategic move for the company. In recent years, Widget Inc. experienced an increase in the number of competitors in their field. Jeff had been reading a lot about how Scrum could help the company compete, and it had been recommended to him by several of his peers.

> A few weeks later, the agile transition started in earnest. Together with a team of external Scrum consultants, Jeff worked behind the scenes to get everything in order. One of the first challenges was forming Scrum Teams. As it turned out, dismantling the current departments for testing, coding, and design to form cross-functional teams would be too much of a hassle. To complete the transition sooner, Jeff tasked his department heads to create Scrum Teams within their departments: three for development, one for design, and two for testing. The department heads would also act as the Product Owners for their teams. The new role of Scrum Master was assigned to people who weren't fully planned in yet. Another big challenge was to get everyone trained and certified quickly. Thankfully the external consultants provided certified training. They also offered to train each Scrum Team in common best practices, such as writing User Stories, Planning Poker, using a Definition of Ready, and something with LEGO. With that arranged, Jeff relaxed in the realization that it was now up to the Scrum Teams to take responsibility and control.
>
> A cry for help reached us six months later. We entered an organization in disarray. In contrast to what Jeff had hoped for, there was an atmosphere of cynicism and low morale. The teams complained about management, other teams, and the consultants. It was impossible for them to get anything done within a single Sprint, as they depended on other teams to do work for them. They had proposed reforming the Scrum Teams with cross-functional skills, but the department heads resisted. In turn, the department heads and Jeff each complained about the lack of commitment from teams. They'd made a huge effort to get the teams started, only to see that effort go to waste. Instead of the self-organization they were promised, all they got were complaints, problems, and cynicism. From now on, they'd take control again. The Scrum Framework had failed.

This case vividly illustrates self-organization, or the complete lack thereof. Self-organization is an important characteristic of the Scrum Framework, but it is remarkably difficult to define, and that causes confusion. People who don't fully understand how challenging it is to create and sustain self-organization can see it as a remedy for all kinds of organizational ailments. Some people see self-organization as a means for people to choose their own role and define how they do their work. Others see it as a means for people to set their salary and conduct performance appraisals with their peers. Some people even use self-organization as a means to elect a new management team every year, or to make teams responsible for their own profit-and-loss performance, or to give teams full authority over their own composition.

In this chapter, we approach self-organization from the perspective of the Scrum Framework. We also share common symptoms of low levels of self-organization as well as what might be causing them. At the end of this chapter, we give examples of what self-organization looks like in healthy Scrum Teams.

How Bad Is It, Really?

We are continuously monitoring the spread of Zombie Scrum around the world with our online Symptoms Checker at **survey.zombiescrum.org**. Of the Scrum Teams that have participated at the time of writing:*

- 67% of the teams have members who only or mostly do work in their specialization.
- 65% of the teams have no or limited say in the composition of the team.
- 49% of the teams never or rarely have a clear goal for their current Sprint.
- 48% of the teams work on multiple projects or products at the same time.
- 42% of the teams have no or limited say in their tooling and infrastructure.
- 37% of the teams have no or limited redundancy in skills on their team to buffer against team members who are suddenly unavailable.
- 19% of the teams have very little say in how to do their work during a Sprint.

* The percentages represent teams that scored a 6 or lower on a 10-point scale. Each topic was measured with 10 to 30 questions. The results represent 1,764 teams that participated in the self-reported survey at **survey.zombiescrum.org** between June 2019 and May 2020.

Why Bother Self-Organizing?

Self-organization is a concept that is central to the Scrum Framework. For all its significance, it is remarkably hard to define. It is often confused with "self-management," or the idea that teams should make their own decisions. This distinction may seem trivial, but it helps to understand two essential truths about Scrum that we explore in more detail in this chapter. The first is how Scrum uses self-organization to act as a lever to make organizations more agile. The second is how Scrum Teams require a high degree of self-management to make this happen.

WHAT IS SELF-ORGANIZATION?

In different scientific domains, from biology to sociology and from computational sciences to physics, self-organization is the process by which order arises spontaneously from something that is initially disorganized.[1] This order is the result of self-organization only when it emerges from the interactions of the smallest units of the system and isn't imposed by outside influences. Self-organization happens all around us and on many different levels. It happens when the wind creates beautiful shapes in the sand. It happens when ants work together to build massive colonies, without a clear intelligence guiding them. And it happens when people effortlessly avoid walking into each other when large crowds intersect.

A good example of this phenomenon is when you bring a large group of employees together. Initially there will be chaos, because they don't know how to work together. Managers can create order by giving instructions. But because this order is imposed, it isn't self-organization. Alternatively, employees can come to a shared understanding of how to perform and coordinate their work without direction from outside. Although this example uses "employees" as its smallest unit, you can replace them with Scrum Teams for the same effect. There too, rules, structures, and collaborations will form spontaneously when you put fifty teams together. Whether they are also effective is another question though.

The success of self-organization, and whether or not it turns into chaos or useful solutions, depends on two major ingredients. The first is the simple rules the teams follow. And the second is the autonomy they actually have.

1. Camazine, S., et al. 2001. *Self-Organization in Biological Systems*. Princeton University Press.

Self-Organization through Simple Rules

The first ingredient for successful self-organization is the simplicity and quality of the rules that are followed by the smallest units of a system. A common example is the flock of birds that creates elaborate and complex patterns in the sky called murmuration. For all their beauty, these patterns are the result of a few simple rules that all birds adhere to: they maintain the same speed and stay at a similar distance from a handful of birds close to them.[2] As each individual bird follows these simple rules, tiny variations in speed, distance, and direction cause big changes as the flock rapidly elongates, turns, and flips. Without these simple rules, chaos would ensue. Self-organization does not reflect the autonomy of individual birds, but rather how group-level patterns spontaneously emerge when individual members of a group follow a few simple rules.

The Scrum Framework purposefully defines one essential rule for Scrum Teams to follow: Deliver a "Done" Increment every Sprint that achieves the Sprint Goal. This Increment is the primary driver of transparency, inspection, and adaptation. It gives purpose to all the structural elements that make up the Scrum Framework: its roles, artifacts, and events. Although following this rule is certainly not as simple as maintaining the same speed and distance from the birds around you, maintaining it will cause systemwide changes.

The people who build the product—the Scrum Teams—will discover things that get in their way of releasing a Done Increment every Sprint. They may discover that they lack skills or depend on people outside the team to do work for them. Or a lack of mandate makes it hard for Product Owners to define a clear Sprint Goal. As Scrum Teams identify and remove impediments, it becomes progressively easier to conform to the single rule. This enables them to improve their way of working more quickly in response to the increasing amount of feedback they are getting on their work, and the speed at which they are obtaining this feedback. In other words, they are becoming

2. Hemelrijk, C. K., and H. Hildenbrandt. 2015. "Diffusion and Topological Neighbours in Flocks of Starlings: Relating a Model to Empirical Data." *PLoS ONE* 10(5): e0126913. Retrieved on May 27, 2020, from **https://doi.org/10.1371/journal.pone.0126913.**

increasingly flexible and agile to their environment. The Scrum Framework acts as a lever for system-level change by having Scrum Teams focus on releasing a Done Increment every Sprint.

Unfortunately, teams that suffer from Zombie Scrum are either unwilling or unable to follow this single rule. Here, the lever doesn't work, and self-organization doesn't happen, or not in a direction that matters to agility.

Self-Organization through Self-Management

The second ingredient for successful self-organization lies in the autonomy that people and teams have to determine their own rules. One way to think about this is to consider the work that a team does as a river. An impediment or challenge may appear in the form of a rock that is put in its path. The more constrained the river is, the fewer options there are to flow around the rock. Increased autonomy gives teams the ability to allow their work to flow around rocks that get in their way. Organizational scientists often describe this as "self-management." In this philosophy on management, teams are responsible for a complete product, an isolated part of a product, or a particular service.[3] Instead of having a manager who decides for them, or having to adhere to strict policies and protocols, teams have a degree of autonomy in areas such as the following:[4]

- How new members of a team are selected and recruited
- How teams and its members are rewarded and evaluated
- How teams create a safe and collaborative environment
- How teams are trained in important skills, and by whom
- How teams spend their time
- How teams synchronize their work with other teams, departments, and units
- How teams set goals

3. Hackman, J. R. 1995. "Self-Management/Self-Managed Teams." In N. Nicholson, *Encyclopedic Dictionary of Organizational Behavior*. Oxford, UK: Blackwell.
4. Cummings, T. G., and C. Worley. 2009. *Organization Development and Change*, 9th ed. Cengage Learning.

- What facilities and tools teams need to do their work
- How decisions are made on the team
- How teams distribute their work
- Which methods, practices, and techniques teams use

For each of these areas, the autonomy of a team ends up somewhere between "no autonomy at all" and "full autonomy."

The concept of self-managed teams might seem novel, but it has been around for a long time. Self-management is an important part of the sociotechnical systems (or STS) approach that was developed by the Tavistock Institute of Human Relations during the Second World War.[5] As a result of this work, self-managed teams started appearing everywhere, including in many car manufacturing plants.[6] Instead of the traditional assembly-line manufacturing that had previously prevailed, teams took responsibility for the completion of entire subsystems of a car (the brakes, electronics, and so on). Teams were also responsible for their own planning, scheduling, task allocation, recruitment, and training—without involvement from management. The extensive research that has been done on sociotechnical systems over the years shows a huge boost in job satisfaction, motivation, productivity, and quality.[7] The Toyota Production System (or TPS) that would later inspire the Scrum Framework and Lean methodology is an example of such a sociotechnical system.

Although the Scrum Guide defines Scrum Teams as being "self-organizing," it means them to be "self-managing" in order for the process of "self-organization" to happen. Scrum Teams have all the roles and responsibilities needed to make decisions about their product and how to do their work. In reality most Scrum Teams are severely limited in their ability to self-manage, however. In an attempt to reduce the potential chaos and disorder that they expect will happen when teams self-manage, many organizations tightly control how

5. Hackman, J. R., and G. R. Oldham. 1980. *Work Redesign*. Reading, Mass. Addison-Wesley.
6. Rollinson, D., and A. Broadfield. 2002. *Organisational Behaviour and Analysis*. Harlow, UK: Prentice Hall.
7. Bailey, J. 1983. *Job Design and Work Organization*. London: Prentice Hall.

teams do their work instead. They either don't understand the mechanisms of self-organization or don't trust the outcomes—with Zombie Scrum as a result.

SELF-ORGANIZATION IS A SURVIVAL SKILL IN A COMPLEX WORLD

Complex environments are characterized by high degrees of unpredictability and uncertainty. This makes them volatile and rife with risk. Markets shift in the blink of an eye, new technologies achieve widespread popularity seemingly overnight, and as they do they may be found to harbor security vulnerabilities that need to be fixed immediately. New competitors enter the market with a superior product, undermining seemingly unassailable market positions. And then there are global catastrophes, such as the financial crisis of 2008 and COVID-19 in 2020, that upend economies overnight and take companies entirely by surprise. As our world becomes increasingly globalized and interconnected, so does the chance of unpredictable and highly impactful events that demand immediate adaptation. The statistician Nassim Taleb calls these events "Black Swans."[8]

Taleb goes on to describe how organizations often optimize for what he calls "robustness."[9] In an effort to reduce volatility, they rely on standardization and centralized coordination to reduce harmful variation both within and outside the organization. For example, all teams have to use the same technologies or follow the same procedures when solving specific problems. Or they create centralized steering committees to guide multiteam product development. By adopting rigid standards and coordination structures, organizations are able to limit the impact of variation when the changes are small. But in a world that is increasingly volatile, this rigidity prevents them from adapting to change and can even break them entirely.

8. Taleb, N. N. 2010. *The Black Swan: The Impact of the Highly Improbable*, 2nd ed. London: Penguin. ISBN: 978-0141034591.
9. Taleb, N. N. 2012. *Antifragile: Things That Gain from Disorder*. Random House. ISBN: 978-1400067824.

Another way is to optimize for "antifragility." Instead of trying to resist variation and shocks, antifragile systems grow stronger when they are pressured. For example, engineering teams at Netflix created a tool called "Chaos Monkey"[10] to randomly terminate services in their infrastructure. Every time a terminated service ends up causing disruptions to end users, engineering teams redesign the architecture to reduce the impact. Over time, responding to these kinds of random shocks helped Netflix make its infrastructure more resilient.

Space Exploration Technologies (or SpaceX) has a launch cadence that is purposefully higher than that of other launch providers.[11] Every time a launch fails, their self-managed teams update technology, protocols, and processes to avoid similar failures in the future. Other organizations, including Procter & Gamble, Facebook, and Toyota, run many small experiments at the same time to explore different alternatives. Although most experiments fail, some strike gold. More important, their self-managed teams learn from failures and grow stronger because of them.

Three threads are apparent in antifragile organizations:

1. They rely on self-managed teams to self-organize around problems as they appear (see Figure 11.1).
2. They encourage experimentation to grow stronger through failures.
3. They spend effort to learn from failure through single- and double-loop learning (see Chapter 9).

Taken together, organizations develop the skills, technologies, and practices to not only survive the uncertainty of complexity but actually thrive on it, because they can adapt faster than others. Unfortunately, and as we explore later in this chapter, the variation and redundancy that is necessary for antifragility is often seen as inefficient and wasteful by organizations where Zombie Scrum is flourishing.

10. Izrailevsky, Y., and A. Tseitlin. 2011. "The Netflix Simian Army." *The Netflix Tech Blog*. Retrieved on May 27, 2020, from **https://netflixtechblog.com/the-netflix-simian-army-16e57fbab116.**

11. Morrisong, A., and B. Parker. 2013. PWC, *Technology Forecast: A Quarterly Journal* 2.

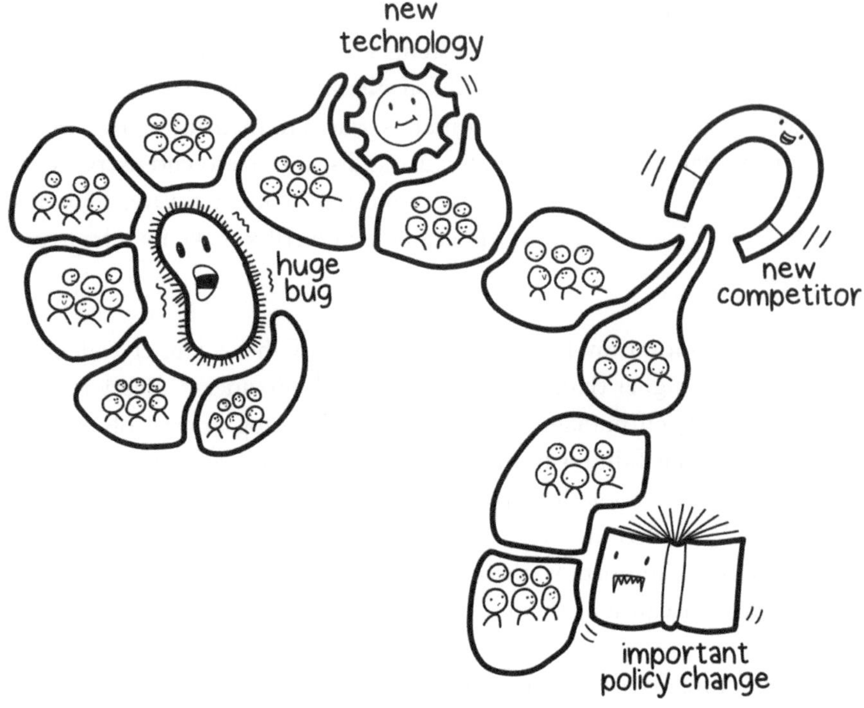

Figure 11.1 Like an organizational immune system, self-managing teams can quickly self-organize around challenges and opportunities as they emerge.

The concept of antifragility ties together much of what we're writing about in this book. The Scrum Framework actively promotes it. It relies on self-managed teams to self-organize around challenges that get in their way. By following the single rule of releasing a Done Increment every Sprint, everything that makes it hard for teams to do so becomes apparent, including many of the factors that optimize for robustness, but not antifragility, such as rigid control structures, lack of mandates, long feedback loops, and highly specialized (but not distributed) skills. By releasing a Done Increment every Sprint, teams effectively introduce more opportunities for success and failure, giving them opportunities to reflect on their results and learn. When enough teams in an organization do this, the whole system becomes increasingly antifragile.

The Bottom Line

In his novel *Seveneves*, author Neil Stephenson[12] describes a catastrophic event where a dense field of debris suddenly appears around the Earth and is about to rain down and eradicate all life. In an effort to save humanity, engineers start building a space station for a few thousand souls that can continue to orbit the Earth until it becomes habitable again. Instead of building one giant station, the engineers design a massive swarm of smaller and autonomous stations that can connect and disconnect as needed. With all the debris still orbiting the Earth—even a tiny grain of debris would have a catastrophic result—a single station would be too dangerous. Although each unit in the swarm is still susceptible to disaster, their smaller size makes it easier to avoid incoming debris. Furthermore, the loss of individual units doesn't immediately threaten the survival of the swarm as a whole. The swarm can now self-organize around impending disaster more effectively than a single space station can.

This is a great metaphor for what the Scrum Framework tries to achieve. It aims to break down traditional structures where work is standardized and tightly controlled through centralized management in order to avoid risk and variation. Like the large space station in the metaphor, these structures work well in stable environments. But our world is increasingly complex, and increasingly filled with unexpected debris that may cause havoc. Instead, the Scrum Framework enables antifragility by making self-managing Scrum Teams the metaphorical swarm from this story. As a self-managed team, every Scrum Team adds variability and thereby survivability.

Why Are We Not Self-Organizing?

If self-organization is so important, why doesn't it happen in Zombie Scrum? Next, we explore common observations and their underlying causes. When you are aware of the causes, it is easier to select the right interventions and experiments. It also builds empathy with Zombie Scrum, and how it often emerges despite everyone's best intentions.

12. Stephenson, N. 2015. *Seveneves*. The Borough Press. ISBN: 0062190377.

"Well recruit, now you see how important self-organization is. It may sound fluffy, but it's your best survival strategy."

In Zombie Scrum, We Are Not Self-Managing Enough

As we explored earlier in this chapter, it is difficult for Scrum Teams to self-organize around shared challenges if their ability to self-manage their work is limited. In organizations that suffer from Zombie Scrum, most or all of the areas tilt towards "no autonomy at all." Instead of being able to make decisions about their own work, when, and by whom it should be done, Zombie Scrum Teams have others who make those decisions for them, they need to get approval first, or they are required to adhere to existing standards or "the way we do things here."

Signs to look for:

- Scrum Teams have no role in deciding who is part of their team. Such decisions are made either by external managers or by a human resources department.
- Scrum Teams cannot change their tools or work environment to suit their needs.
- Product Owners have limited mandate over "their" product. Either they are not allowed to make decisions or they frequently have to ask for permission.
- There is a lot of negative gossip about, and blaming of, other teams, departments, or people that a Scrum Team depends on. And vice versa.

- People respond with cynicism to the purpose of their work and the product they are developing together. Team morale is low.*

* A free tool to measure team morale is available at teammetrics.theliberators.com.

Self-management works in environments where the professionals doing the work are trusted for their ability to make the right decisions. Unfortunately, organizations infected by Zombie Scrum often don't demonstrate that trust. When it comes to self-management, this lack of trust shows in the use of external experts to design how work is to be done, instead of letting the professionals figure that out themselves. And it shows when Product Owners have to go through long approval chains before they can release to production. In subtle and not-so-subtle ways, professionals are not trusted to use their autonomy in a way that is careful, considerate, and in the interest of the organization.

This lack of trust fuels a vicious cycle of finger-pointing, where Scrum Teams complain that management is not giving them enough space to move, while management in turn complains about Scrum Teams not taking responsibility. The low morale and cynicism that management senses in teams are usually a response to a perceived lack of control. When people feel that their ability to do their work well is limited by others, they have different strategies for dealing with the resulting tension. Complaining about or blaming others is a good example of such a strategy. It allows people to relieve tension by offloading their frustrations on others and feeling less responsible themselves. Another strategy is to withdraw from collective commitments, as captured by low team morale, or "the enthusiasm and persistence with which people do work as part of a team."[13]

Self-management and trust require and reinforce each other. It's not an easy transition, and teams will make mistakes, some worse than others. But if people don't have the freedom to make those mistakes, they will never learn, and

13. Manning, F. J. 1991. "Morale, Unit Cohesion, and Esprit de Corps." In R. Gal and A. D. Mangelsdorff, eds., *Handbook of Military Psychology*, pp. 453–470. New York: Wiley.

they will never commit themselves to achieving their goals. There will always be "bad actors" who actively sabotage the company or pursue self-interests to the detriment of others. But instead of enacting rigid hierarchies and policies to prevent mistakes and sabotage, it is more helpful to limit the blast radius of mistakes. It is better to support a process by which teams feel the consequences of their mistakes and then learn to avoid them in the future.

The point of self-management is not to remove all the rules or to allow teams to do whatever they want. The point is to empower teams in designing and shaping how their work is done, while also becoming accountable for those decisions. A part of this process happens inside teams; another part happens as teams work together to clarify their dynamics. This is when self-organization emerges.

Try these experiments to improve with your team (see Chapter 12):

- Find a Minimum Set of Rules for Self-Organization
- Make the Cost of Low Autonomy Transparent with Permission Tokens
- Break the Rules!
- Observe What Is Happening
- Find Actions That Boost Both Integration and Autonomy

IN ZOMBIE SCRUM, WE USE OFF-THE-SHELF SOLUTIONS

Organizations that suffer from Zombie Scrum like to follow standardized methods, well-defined frameworks, and "industry best practices." To them, this preference feels more efficient than developing their own approaches. They believe that they are learning from the experiences of others, as in the case when organizations implement the "Spotify Model" in the hope of replicating Spotify's top-notch engineering culture. But there are three big problems with "copying" from others:

- Copying what works for one organization to another completely ignores the unique circumstances that enabled the solution to work for the original organization. For example, Spotify has a completely different culture and environment from the banks and insurance companies that try to copy its "model." What works for Spotify may be completely unsuited to other organizations.

- The very nature of complex systems means that there are no "models" or "best practices." Organizations such as Spotify are in a constant state of flux as double-loop learning and self-organization continuously reshape how people work together. Although you can take a snapshot of what Spotify looks like at a given moment and copy its roles, structure, and rules to your own organization, the actual model at work here is not its structure but its focus on learning and self-organization. In fact, Spotify went out of its way to show that their structure always changes and shouldn't be copied.[14]
- Copying "best practices" from other organizations effectively sidesteps the double-loop learning and self-organization that gave rise to those recipes in the first place. By simply copying the (supposed) result, organizations never develop the ability to learn that is essential to solving complex challenges. Copying actually impedes self-organization and double-loop learning as predefined solutions from elsewhere are rolled out across the organization (see Figure 11.2).

Figure 11.2 But it feels so convenient to have a one-stop shop with precooked solutions.

14. Floryan, M. 2016. "There Is No Spotify Model." Presented at Spark the Change conference. Retrieved on May 27, 2020, from **https://www.infoq.com/presentations/spotify-culture-stc/**.

The example of Spotify is an obvious one, but the same argument applies to other attempts to copy best practices from elsewhere. It also applies to scaling frameworks that emphasize a particular structural solution for scaling over double-loop learning and self-organization.

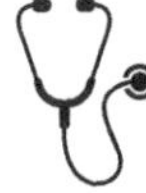

Signs to look for:

- People say things such as "Let's not reinvent the wheel."
- External experts are hired to implement their best practices or "roll out" change initiatives that were planned without concerted involvement of employees.
- Approaches that worked for other organizations are copied onto the entire organization without trying them in one small area first.
- You don't get a clear answer when you ask people what problem they are trying to solve with an external framework or solution (e.g., SAFe, LeSS, or the Spotify model).

You can certainly find inspiration in solutions from other organizations. But instead of jumping straight to replicating their recipes, it's more helpful to create environments where people can learn and fail. Don't copy the plant, copy the soil it grew from. Create environments where people are encouraged to explore why a problem exists, where they have autonomy over their work, and where they can experiment with different approaches. This is where double-loop learning starts and when all sorts of wildly creative solutions start emerging from self-organization.

Try these experiments to improve with your team (see Chapter 12):

- Find a Minimum Set of Rules for Self-Organization
- Develop Local Solutions with Open Spaces
- Find Actions That Boost Both Integration and Autonomy

In Zombie Scrum, Scrum Masters Keep Resolving All Impediments

The Scrum Master is responsible for helping Development Teams resolve impediments. When they are sufficiently self-managing, Development Teams should increasingly be able to resolve impediments on their own as they become more experienced. In Zombie Scrum, this doesn't happen, and Scrum Masters remain busy with the same kinds of impediments. These teams have become dependent on their Scrum Masters to fix all the problems that get in their way. And their Scrum Masters have contributed to the problem, either by actively offering to solve impediments or by accepting all requests from the Development Team to do so. Although they have done this with the best intentions, Scrum Masters are not helping their teams to build the skills to do so on their own.

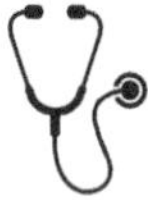

Signs to look for:

- During Sprint Retrospectives, the Scrum Team looks to the Scrum Master to resolve most of the challenges identified.
- Scrum Masters routinely perform tasks such as renewing certain software licenses, updating Jira, getting office supplies for the team, or booking meeting rooms.
- Scrum Masters are always facilitating the Scrum Events.
- When the Development Team runs into dependencies on others—including the Product Owner—the Scrum Master usually resolves them.

Scrum Masters who believe that resolving problems is their responsibility are causing more problems than they are solving. Not all problems are automatically impediments. We like to define impediments as those challenges that (1) block Development Teams from (2) achieving the Sprint Goal and (3) exceed their capability to resolve on their own. Typically, the kind of impediments where help from Scrum Masters is needed should evolve over time (see Figure 11.3). Initially, their efforts focus on helping Scrum Teams and the organization understand the purpose of the Scrum Framework: Why is it important to release a Done Increment every Sprint? How do Sprint Goals help teams become more effective in complex environments? And how do the various events, roles, and artifacts of Scrum allow teams to work empirically?

As their understanding of Scrum grows, teams may need help changing their composition—they may need different skills or people—to be able to work more empirically. They may also discover that bringing these skills together in one team requires a different way of working and different engineering practices to benefit from them (e.g., automated testing, Lean UX, emergent architecture, continuous deployment).

As Scrum Teams become more capable of working empirically within their team, they may run into broader impediments that involve other departments and teams. For example, HR practices may reward individual contributions over working together as a team. Or Scrum Teams may struggle to synchronize their work with other Scrum Teams. Or the sales department continues to sell fixed-price/fixed-scope projects. Finally, impediments may involve the way work is organized in the organization as a whole, such as when yearly product strategy definitions no longer remain relevant as market conditions change, or when management struggles with how best to support self-managing Scrum Teams.

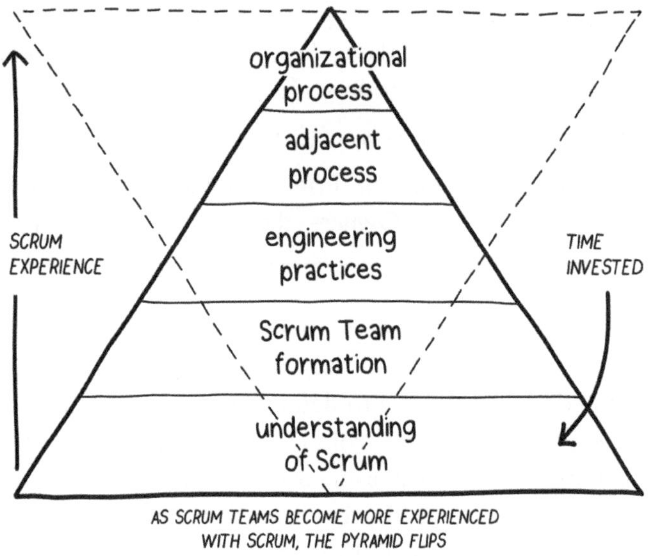

Figure 11.3 The Impediment Pyramid by Dominik Maximini[15]

15. Source: Maximini, D. 2018. "The Pyramid of Impediments." Scrum.org.

Although Scrum Masters likely face impediments of all kinds from the start, a first priority is to get the Scrum Teams—and the empirical process—started. Once these "engines of empiricism" are running, they create transparency around other kinds of impediments that need to be resolved. Over time, the pyramid should flip as Scrum Masters shift most of their efforts to broader, organization-level impediments. But in Zombie Scrum, Scrum Teams remain stuck in the lower parts of the pyramid.

Try these experiments to improve with your team (see Chapter 12):

- Observe What Is Happening
- Express Clear Requests for Help
- Find a Minimum Set of Rules for Self-Organization

In Zombie Scrum, Scrum Masters Focus Only on Scrum Team(s)

When Scrum Teams follow the single rule of releasing a Done Increment every Sprint, they are bound to run into many impediments that get in the way of working empirically. Although some of these obstacles are constrained to individual Scrum Teams, most of them involve other teams, departments, and suppliers.

Because of this reality, Scrum Masters are in a perfect position to help their organization work more empirically. They see on a daily basis what impedes Scrum Teams and where they need to improve. Working together with other Scrum Masters, Product Owners, Development Teams, and stakeholders, they guide the organization towards increased empiricism and agility by influencing it from the inside out.

Unfortunately, organizations with Zombie Scrum don't leverage this potential of Scrum Masters to change their organization. Sometimes Scrum Masters misunderstand their role and focus only on their teams. Other times, Scrum Masters are expected to be team-focused and leave larger impediments to other people or external experts.

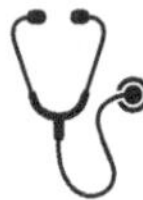

Signs to look for:

- Scrum Masters don't spend time with other Scrum Masters to overcome impediments shared by their teams.
- The job description of Scrum Masters specifically emphasizes their responsibility for their teams, and nothing beyond that.
- Agile Coaches and Enterprise Coaches are responsible for supporting the environment around the Scrum Teams.
- Scrum Masters don't coordinate their work on impediments with management.

But how can Scrum Masters change entire organizations? They probably can't on their own, and that is why they work with other Scrum Masters, as well as with natural allies such as Product Owners, Development Teams, and stakeholders. They distribute time between working with their team and working with others to encourage self-organization across teams. And since no two Scrum Masters are the same, some will spend more time working across teams or with management, while others are more content working with their own team. Like a cross-functional team, the community of Scrum Masters within an organization needs to have the skills to drive change both on the level of individual teams as well as on an organizational level. And more-experienced Scrum Masters can train and help less-experienced ones.

How Scrum Masters drive change across the organization depends on the situation. It can take the shape of sense-making workshops where (representatives of) teams make sense of important metrics and devise strategies to improve. It can take the shape of visits to other companies to see how they use Scrum there. Scrum Masters can also purposefully create transparency around a critical issue (such as low cycle time or low code quality) and invite teams to inspect and adapt.

Whatever the case, when organizations invest more in hiring experienced Scrum Masters and growing the skills of their internal Scrum Master community, their need for external experts and other coaches will diminish.

Try these experiments to improve with your team (see Chapter 12):

- Observe What Is Happening
- Organize Scrum Master Impediment Gatherings
- Find Actions That Boost Both Integration and Autonomy
- Develop Local Solutions with Open Spaces

In Zombie Scrum, We Have No Goals or They Are Imposed

Provided they have sufficient autonomy, teams and people go in many different directions when there are no clear goals to direct self-organization. This is what often happens in Zombie Scrum, and it can be a huge source of frustration to everyone involved.

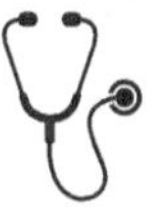

Signs to look for:

- There is no clear goal during a Sprint that helps teams align their work, both within the teams and between teams.
- If there is a Sprint Goal, the team is unable to explain in certain terms how stakeholders benefit from achieving this goal.
- People mostly work on their own items from the Sprint Backlog. When problems arise in that work, they resolve them mostly without help from others.
- Scrum Teams are not aware of what other Scrum Teams are doing, even when their work is for the same product.

One of the primary challenges that all organizations face is that of alignment. In traditional management, a core task of managers is to ensure that work done by their teams, departments, and employees aligns with plans, objectives, and strategies set out for the organization. For example, when multiple teams work on one product, managers can use weekly status-update reports or meetings to know what is happening and to decide what to start and stop. Or a manager asks a team to work on something else that has become more important. This appears to be efficient, but it also turns managers into bottlenecks. A manager may not have up-to-date information about what is happening in the field, or problems that are experienced by users, or potential business opportunities that teams are seeing. This makes it harder for them, and the organization as a whole, to respond to sudden changes in their environment. Also, making managers responsible for alignment means that their creativity, intelligence, and experience determine how successful that alignment is.

Self-managed teams use a different mechanism to align work and drive self-organization within and across teams. Instead of dedicated roles (managers) or standardized structures (hierarchies and policies), they self-align through compelling goals and an inspiring purpose.

Shared goals act as guide rails to self-organization. To facilitate rapid decision-making and making use of the knowledge of the people doing the work, product-related goals should be set by the Scrum Teams themselves. Sprint Goals are a good example of this. When Scrum Teams set a clear and valuable goal for their current Sprint, it helps them make decisions about what on their Sprint Backlog matters the most to achieving that goal. When a member discovers that something is impeding the goal, this gives the team a good opportunity to step back and reflect on how best to move forward and how to adapt their Sprint Backlog. Aside from Sprint Goals, Scrum Teams should be able to set technical goals together. Or improvement goals. Product strategy, and intermediate product goals, should be set by the Product Owner in coordination with stakeholders. Together, this maximizes the ability of Scrum Teams to respond quickly to changes that impact their product and to maximize the value of their work.

High-level goals, such as business objectives and strategic goals, are probably set by others (e.g., management). But even there, involving everyone in creating those goals builds support for them and allows the inclusion of more perspectives. It also makes it easier for people to self-organize in the desired direction when they understand why the goals are there.

Try these experiments to improve with your team (see Chapter 12):

- Create Better Sprint Goals with Powerful Questions
- Find a Minimum Set of Rules for Self-Organization
- Find Actions That Boost Both Integration and Autonomy

In Zombie Scrum, We Don't Use the Environment As External Memory

Self-organization becomes progressively easier when teams use their environment as external memory. Scrum Teams that work in environments with Zombie Scrum often can't do this well. This prevents an important type of self-organization, "stigmergy."

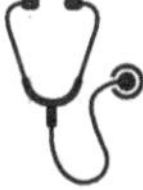

Signs to look for:

- Scrum Teams don't have a physical Scrum Board. Instead, organizational guidelines require all teams to use the same digital tool.
- Teams are not allowed to put informative posters on the walls. The "clean-desk policy" also applies to the walls.
- Communication between team members occurs primarily digitally via Slack, email, and so on. There are no physical information radiators to gather around and start a conversation about.

Stigmergy was first discovered by the biologist Pierre-Paul Grassé in termite colonies.[16] Although termites don't possess individual intelligence, they construct huge and complex nests together. This happens as termites create balls of mud infused with pheromones and initially leave them in random locations. Other termites deposit similar mud balls where they smell the pheromones, causing mud balls to cluster in the same location over time. As the piles grow, they become increasingly attractive to other termites in a form of positive feedback.

16. Bonabeau, E. 1999. "Editor's Introduction: Stigmergy." *Artificial Life* 5(2): 95–96. doi:10.1162/106454699568692. ISSN: 1064-5462.

Stigmergy happens when one agent (e.g., a person, an ant, a robot) leaves a trace in the environment that is so clear about what needs to happen next that another agent that comes along can do so without direct communication or control.

Examples of stigmergy in human organizations include Wikipedia and open-source projects:[17] Individuals perform small tasks and leave traces (commits, ideas, bug reports) that are picked up by other volunteers. Together, they are capable of building a free encyclopedia, sophisticated software, and complex frameworks without anyone telling them what to do. Constant direct communication isn't necessary to coordinate complex work. The quality of traces left in the environment and how accessible they are determine the quality of the actions that follow, and the degree to which self-organization happens. A trace must be so specific that it basically necessitates the next action (or *stigmergic* action).[18]

Stigmergic action is an important mechanism by which Scrum Teams coordinate work (see Figure 11.4). The Product Backlog, the Sprint Backlog, and the Increment are traces of the work that has been done or will be done. During a Sprint, the clearer and better refined the next items on a Sprint Backlog are, the easier it is for teams to coordinate work without direct communication. It also happens when Scrum Teams synchronize their work through continuous integration, since a broken build or failed deployment indicates work that needs to be completed. Automated testing also encourages stigmergic action, as failing tests indicate specific problems that need to be fixed. Having a clear Sprint Goal on the wall helps Scrum Teams to distinguish between what is important and what isn't, and it gives directions to stigmergic actions.

Unfortunately, Zombie Scrum often blocks stigmergy; the physical environment does not reinforce external memory. Instead of putting a Sprint Backlog on a wall in their team room, teams have to use a company-mandated digital tool. Or the action items

17. Heylighen, F. 2007. "Why Is Open Access Development So Successful? Stigmergic Organization and the Economics of Information." In B. Lutterbeck, M. Bärwolff, and R. A. Gehring, eds., *Open Source Jahrbuch*. Lehmanns Media.

18. Heylighen, F., and C. Vidal. 2007. *Getting Things Done: The Science behind Stress-Free Productivity*. Retrieved on May 27, 2020, from **http://cogprints.org/6289**.

from a Sprint Retrospective end up in an email or in someone's drawer, and not clearly visible on the wall. Instead of drawing architectural diagrams on a movable whiteboard, the team stores them in a digital folder. Important metrics are in a digital dashboard that is only accessible to the Product Owner. This doesn't mean that digital tools are bad, but they can easily block stigmergy by hiding traces behind a login or in a virtual folder, making them less visible. You have to actively look for them in order to find them. That architectural diagram is stored in a specific folder on the network, the Sprint Backlog is under a certain tab in your browser, and the improvements from the previous Sprint are in an email sent two days ago. This makes these traces less active. Physically surrounding the team with the work that is happening or needs to happen helps to encourage self-organization within and across teams.

Figure 11.4 Literally surrounding ourselves with the traces of our work together makes it much easier to collaborate and build on each other's work.

Try these experiments to improve with your team (see Chapter 12):

- Use a Physical Scrum Board
- Observe What Is Happening
- Create Better Sprint Goals with Powerful Questions

In Zombie Scrum, We Are Impeded by Standardization

Because self-managed teams have a greater degree of autonomy to decide how to do their work, the efficiency mindset (see also Chapter 4) can lead to strong statements such as "It'll be a mess when every team works in a different way!", "It's really inefficient to reinvent the wheel multiple times!" or "It'll be chaos." An underlying belief here is that multiple solutions for the same problem are less efficient than a single, standardized one. But two questions are important here:

1. Why is it a problem when teams make different choices? Every team is different, and they face at least a slightly different environment; one team's solution to a problem may be different from the next, but if each team is effective, what difference does that make?
2. Why does the desire for standardized, centralized, and harmonized solutions override the desire to maximize the results that each team produces?

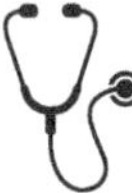

Signs to look for:

- Scrum Teams are unable to change their tooling or processes without approval from someone outside the team.
- Every Sprint, the Scrum Board shows a large number of items in a "Waiting" column, where someone other than a direct stakeholder of the product—such as another team, department, or supplier—needs to perform an action or give approval for this item to move to "Done" because standard procedure demands it.
- Scrum Teams are unable to change their physical or digital workspace because they need to adhere to default policies set by the organization.
- Scrum Teams are required to follow standardized practices, such as writing User Stories or estimating in Story Points, and standardized tools and technologies.
- Job descriptions for Scrum Masters, developers, and Product Owners are standardized and don't take their context into account.

In environments with high degrees of standardization, Scrum Teams are constrained in their ability to develop local solutions in response to what is happening in their immediate environment. When the standardized solution, tool, structure, or practice doesn't work well in response to changes in their environment, it impacts the team or even the entire organization. Such standardization makes the whole system decidedly more fragile against sudden change. Suppose that the one technology stack that is used by all teams is suddenly discovered to have a serious unpatchable security hole. What if requiring all teams to write User Stories makes it very frustrating for teams that work in areas where they don't make sense? What if that one person with highly specialized skills suddenly went to work for a competitor?

Not standardization, but variability in solutions, functions, practices, and structures makes organizations more antifragile against sudden change (see Chapter 10). Variability lessens the possibility that a problem will disrupt everything in the organization. It also allows for double-loop learning as each variation is essentially an experiment with different potential outcomes. This kind of redundancy can appear inefficient, like waste. But as Nassim Taleb puts it: "Redundancy is [. . .] like waste if nothing unusual happens. Except that something unusual happens—usually."[19] In complex environments, redundancy is a competitive advantage.

Variability in solutions emerges on its own when self-organization is given space. When self-managed teams have the autonomy to come up with local solutions, antifragility follows. At the same time, practices can be put into place that let teams share successful approaches that other teams can take inspiration from. Code libraries, an overview of ongoing change initiatives, internal blogs, and regular marketplaces for innovative solutions are only a few examples that help teams share knowledge actively.

19. Taleb, *Antifragile*.

Try these experiments to improve with your team (see Chapter 12):

- Find Actions That Boost Both Integration and Autonomy
- Break the Rules!
- Express Clear Requests for Help
- Organize Scrum Master Impediment Gatherings
- Make the Cost of Low Autonomy Transparent with Permission Tokens

HEALTHY SCRUM: WHAT SELF-ORGANIZATION LOOKS LIKE

Zombie Scrum often starts when the ability of Scrum Teams to self-manage their work, and the impediments that are getting in the way of that work, are limited. From there flow many of the other problems we've addressed in this book. Scrum Teams are often acutely aware of the impediments that are making it hard to ship fast, to build what stakeholders need, and to improve continuously. But without a sense of control over removing those impediments and no support in doing so, it is understandable that teams withdraw into Zombie Scrum.

In this part of the chapter, we explore what healthy Scrum Teams look like. What does self-organization look like? How do they self-manage their work? How do Scrum Teams work together to drive change across the organization? And what is the role of Scrum Masters and management?

SCRUM TEAMS HAVE PRODUCT AUTONOMY

Healthy Scrum Teams have full autonomy to make decisions over the product and how, when, and by whom work for that product is done. Within the Scrum Team, the Product Owner has autonomy over decisions regarding the "what" of the product and the Development Team regarding the "how." Product Owners have the final say in what goes on the Product Backlog and in what order, guided by a product vision or strategy of their devising. The Development Team has the final say in how the work is done and how much work is done in the scope of a single Sprint.

When Scrum Teams have full autonomy, it doesn't mean that they can ignore others and do whatever they want. The concept of "locus of control" is helpful here.[20] The locus of control is internal when teams make the decisions about the product, but it is external when decisions are made for them. Although the locus of control remains with the Scrum Team, they coordinate their work closely with stakeholders, other Scrum Teams, relevant departments, and management. With an internal locus of control also comes the responsibility for the outcomes of decisions—successful and unsuccessful.

A more complete overview is shown in Table 11.1. Other areas of self-management—such as setting your own salary, having a profit/loss balance as a team, and doing performance reviews within the team—may be a natural extension of this control, but they are certainly not required. In the same vein, some Product Owners may have the autonomy to set the product budget. Though very helpful, this budgetary power is not required. At a minimum, Product Owners should have autonomy over how to spend their allocated budget.

Table 11.1 Locus of Control and Accountability for Some Key Areas of the Scrum Framework

Locus of Control/Role	Scrum Team	Product Owner	Development Team	Scrum Master
Defining a strategy for the product		X		
Defining a Definition of Done	X			
Defining the Sprint Goal	X			
What goes on the Sprint Backlog and in what order			X	

20. Rotter, J. B. 1966. "Generalized Expectancies for Internal versus External Control of Reinforcement." *Psychological Monographs: General and Applied* 80: 1–28. doi:10.1037/h0092976.

Locus of Control/Role	Scrum Team	Product Owner	Development Team	Scrum Master
What goes on the Product Backlog and in what order		X		
How the work for a Product Backlog item is done			X	
Who is part of the Development Team			X	
Resolving impediments that the Development Team can't resolve on their own				X
Maintaining the integrity of the Scrum Framework in order to work empirically				X

In many organizations, more than one Scrum Team works on a single product. When this is the case, the decision on whether or not to scale work (and how) is up to the Scrum Teams. Adding more teams invariably increases complexity. The Product Owner has to find ways to scale his or her work across multiple Scrum Teams. Scrum Teams have more dependencies on other teams as they try to create a Done Increment every Sprint that integrates their collective work.

Healthy Scrum Teams work together to find the best way to scale their work. Instead of shortcutting their learning process by jumping straight to off-the-shelf scaling frameworks, they engage in double-loop learning by identifying where impediments are happening and why. In some cases, technology stacks may be getting in the way of releasing every Sprint. In other cases, teams may benefit from colocation to facilitate smoother coordination. Creative solutions emerge from double-loop learning. For example, Scrum Teams can discover that a product can be broken down into smaller products or services, thereby reducing the complexity of having many teams working on a single product. Or they decide to invest in a continuous deployment pipeline to make it easier to integrate and release their collective work.

This is where self-management and double-loop learning enable self-organization. Autonomous Scrum Teams create their own rules, structure, and solutions for the problems they run into, instead of being told what to do by management or external consultants.

MANAGEMENT SUPPORTS SCRUM TEAMS

In addition to Scrum Masters, managers play a pivotal role in supporting self-management and the resulting self-organization. Managers can be supportive or destructive. In healthy Scrum environments, managers don't force alignment through top-down control, off-the-shelf frameworks, or standardized solutions. Instead, they focus on setting larger strategic goals from which Scrum Teams can distill product-specific goals for their work. Instead of mandating that unit test coverage should be 100 percent, they set a goal to increase customer satisfaction with product quality by 25 percent. Instead of determining what should go on the Product Backlog for a new group of stakeholders, they set a goal to enter a new market within six months. Instead of requiring teams to adhere to an off-the-shelf framework or practice, they encourage teams to ask for what they need to become more effective, and then they support those needs.

Like Scrum Masters, managers are there to support self-management and self-organization. They don't lead by making decisions, but by creating an environment where Scrum Teams can decide things themselves.

"Recruit, self-organization is like a river. The more constrained it is by walls, floodgates, and detritus, the less capable it is of flowing around the obstacles that inevitably get in its way."

Now What?

In this chapter we explored what self-organization is and how it is made possible through self-managed teams. Instead of the abstract concept that it tends to be, we explained how self-organization is a critical survival strategy in complex, uncertain environments, where sudden change can disrupt everything. We also explored common symptoms that help you identify when self-organization is (too) low. Although there are many potential causes, we covered the most important ones.

But what can you do when you're faced with low levels of self-organization? Many of the causes in this chapter may lie outside of your control. In the next chapter, we offer practical experiments that help you create change nonetheless.

12 Experiments

Culture is just a shambling zombie that repeats what it did in life; bits of it drop off, and it doesn't appear to notice.

—Alan Moore,
comic book writer

In This Chapter

- Explore ten experiments to foster and promote self-organization.
- Learn what impact the experiments have on surviving Zombie Scrum.
- Discover how to perform each experiment and what to look for.

In this chapter, we share practical experiments to create more space for self-management by teams and to foster and encourage self-organization for teams and for the entire organization. Although the experiments vary in difficulty, each one makes subsequent steps easier.

Experiments to Increase Autonomy

The following experiments are designed to increase the autonomy of teams, or at least make the lack thereof transparent. Self-organization is more likely to take off when teams have autonomy to come up with their own solutions.

MAKE THE COST OF LOW AUTONOMY TRANSPARENT WITH PERMISSION TOKENS

The autonomy of teams decreases as their dependencies on external people increase. Some dependencies are explicit, such as when a Scrum Team needs someone outside the team to do something for them. Other dependencies are more implicit. Having to ask for permission or approval from someone outside the team in order to proceed is a good example. This experiment is about making transparent where and how often permission is required (see Figure 12.1).

Figure 12.1 Without considering all the things that constrain Scrum Teams, it's easy to expect miracles from them.

Effort/Impact Ratio

Effort	★★☆☆☆	This experiment requires only a jar, some tokens, and a few minutes during your Sprint Review.
Impact on survival	★★★★☆	Even in the most zombified environments, regaining some sense of control makes people sigh with relief.

Steps

To try this experiment, do the following:

1. Find an empty jar, or another container, and place it in the team room. Somewhere near the Sprint Backlog is the best spot.
2. Give everyone on your team a bunch of permission tokens. You can use marbles, LEGO bricks, magnets, or stickies. Use different colors for the various permission categories. For example, the permission to release something, to move an item to another column on your Scrum Board, or to change your tools or environment. We recommend a limit of five categories to keep things simple.
3. During the Sprint, put an approval token in the jar every time someone on the Scrum Team has to ask permission from someone outside the team. For example, put a token in the jar when an external architect needs to approve that an item is done. Or when the Product Owner has to vet an item with an external manager. Put a token in the jar when you need permission from office management to purchase stickies. And put a token in the jar when you need a configuration to be changed by an external administrator. Aside from requests for permission, also add a token every time you need someone outside the team to perform a specific action as well.
4. During the Sprint Review, and with stakeholders present, share the number of tokens in the jar. Ask: "How does this affect our ability to quickly adapt in the moment and do what is the most valuable? Where can we simplify things?" Invite people to first consider this question for themselves and in silence, then in pairs for two minutes, and then paired with another pair for four more minutes. Capture the most salient improvements with the whole group. The Sprint Retrospective is a great opportunity for digging into potential improvements.

Our Findings

- For another perspective, you can use different colors for everyone on your team. This allows you to identify who is most often in need of permission.

- If you want to focus on the amount of organizational bureaucracy, don't add permission tokens for requests from direct stakeholders such as customers, users, or people who otherwise invest significant money or time in your product.
- The experiment "Break the Rules!" elsewhere in this chapter is great to test where asking for permission matters, and where it just gets in the way of doing the right thing.

Find Actions That Boost Both Integration and Autonomy

Organizations with self-managing Scrum Teams face the difficult challenge of balancing their autonomy while keeping their work integrated with the rest of the organization. Because both of these aspects are equally desirable, and we can't simply make an either-or decision, we are faced with what is called a "wicked question." Instead of letting the pendulum swing entirely to one side, this experiment is about finding ways of supporting both sides. With this approach, you help groups move from "either-or" to "yes-and" thinking. This experiment and its corresponding worksheet (see Figure 12.2) are based on the Liberating Structure "Integrated~Autonomy."[1]

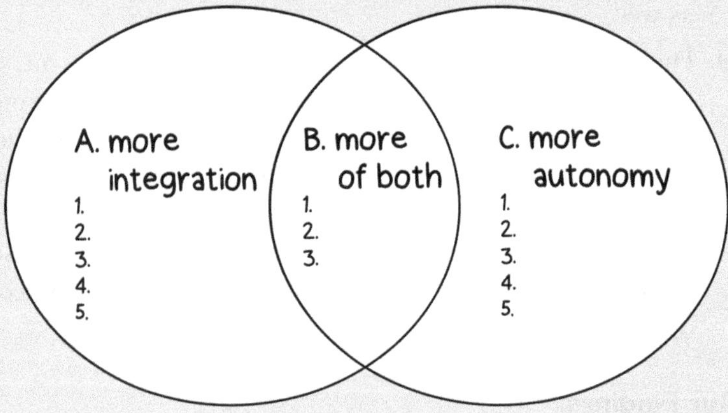

Figure 12.2 A simple worksheet for Integrated~Autonomy[2]

1. Lipmanowicz, H., and K. McCandless. 2014. *The Surprising Power of Liberating Structures: Simple Rules to Unleash a Culture of Innovation*. Liberating Structures Press. ASN: 978-0615975306.
2. Source: Lipmanowicz and McCandless, *The Surprising Power of Liberating Structures*.

Effort/Impact Ratio

Effort	★★★★☆	This experiment greatly benefits from tight facilitation and asking powerful questions to help the group move out of deadlocks.
Impact on survival	★★★★☆	As people start seeing that autonomy and integration are not opposed, more of both will be possible.

Steps

To try this experiment, do the following:

1. Invite people who have a stake in either increasing the autonomy of Scrum Teams or keeping them integrated with work done elsewhere. This includes the Scrum Teams themselves, departments they depend on (and vice versa), and management.
2. Begin by helping people make tensions between autonomy and integration tangible. Ask "For the Scrum Teams, where in their work is there tension between the desire for autonomy and the desire for integration?" Start with a minute of silent thinking (one minute), then invite people to share their ideas in pairs (two minutes). Capture salient examples from the whole group (five minutes). For example, there can be tension between the autonomy that Scrum Teams have over their Sprint Backlog and the need to be able to pick up urgent issues from people outside the team that emerge during a Sprint. There can be tension between the autonomy of a Product Owner to order the Product Backlog and keeping that ordering aligned with corporate strategy. Or between allowing Scrum Teams to pick their own tools and having mandated tools that are safe for corporate environments.
3. The next step is to explore actions that promote integration. For this step, the participants work with the Integrated~Autonomy worksheet shown in Figure 12.2. It shows three columns with space for writing down ideas that lead to either more integration (A), more autonomy (C), or both (B). The group will focus on column A first. Ask "What actions boost integration of the Scrum Teams' activities with what is happening

elsewhere?" Start with a minute of silent thinking (one minute), then invite people to share their ideas in groups of four (five minutes). Capture the most salient actions from the small groups on the left side of the worksheet (ten minutes).

4. As a follow-up, explore actions that promote autonomy. Ask "What actions boost the autonomy of Scrum Teams?" Capture them in the right column of the worksheet. Start with a minute of silent thinking (one minute), then invite people to share their ideas in groups of four (five minutes). Capture the most salient actions from the small groups on the right side of the worksheet (ten minutes).
5. Now that you have actions that each address one side of the wicked question, help the group move into yes-and thinking. Ask "Which actions boost both integration and autonomy?" Capture them on the worksheet in the middle. Start with a minute of silent thinking (one minute), then invite people to share their ideas in groups of four (five minutes). Capture the most salient actions from the small groups on the middle of the worksheet (ten minutes).
6. Now that people have experience identifying actions that serve both sides, investigate earlier actions to see if they can be shifted to the middle. Ask "Which actions on the left or the right of the worksheet can be creatively modified to boost both integration and autonomy?" Start with a minute of silent thinking (one minute), then invite people to share their ideas in groups of four (five minutes). Capture the most salient actions from the small groups on the middle of the worksheet (ten minutes).
7. Order actions by their ability to promote both integration and autonomy and identify 15% Solutions for the most impactful ones (see Chapter 10).

Our Findings

- Coming up with specific and tangible actions can be difficult. Keep asking "How would you do that for us?" or "What would that look like here?" in order to move groups beyond abstract ideas and platitudes (such as "more communication").
- If you have a large group, you can make each group of four responsible for one of the actions you identified during step 2. Let them fill in the entire worksheet in their small group from the perspective of that action.

- You can replace the sides—integration and autonomy—with other wicked challenges. For example, there is also tension between responding to change as quickly as possible and preventing huge mistakes. Or the tension between standardization on the one hand and customization on the other. Work with whatever wicked challenge makes the most sense!

Break the Rules!

Organizations create rules for a good reason. Usually they are intended to protect the company and the people working there from harm by preventing mistakes. But some mistakes are not as bad as the rule that exists to prevent them. Many Scrum Teams are unable to self-organize and act in the best interest of the company because rules get in their way. This experiment is about testing which rules matter. It might sound risky in a big company, but we will help you prepare.

Effort/Impact Ratio

Effort	★★★★★	This experiment requires you to be daring and careful at the same time. Going too far can have consequences.
Impact on survival	★★★★☆	If you pull this off, this experiment has the potential to set positive examples and trigger a wave of change.

Steps

To try this experiment, do the following:

1. Gather your entire Scrum Team. Identify an action that you are prohibited from taking but that has a clear benefit to your organization or your stakeholders, or would make your team more effective. For example, fixing a bug in the code base of another team or approving a change without asking for permission from a designated manager first might enable your team to fix a problem immediately when you encounter it rather than having to hand it off to someone else. The experiment "Make the Cost of Low Autonomy Transparent with Permission Tokens" elsewhere in this chapter is a great way to find more rules.

2. Discuss what would happen if you broke that rule. What would the consequences be? Does the result justify the means? What would happen to the organization if other teams disregarded this rule as well?
3. Make a plan for what you can do if you break the rule and get into trouble. How would you justify your actions? Is there a way to soften the blow in advance, such as sending a nice email or a box of chocolates?
4. When you are sure that your actions are in the best interest of the organization and the risk is acceptable, break the rule. Don't break the rule if you're not sure.
5. If you are successful, gather the team and discuss whether and how it would be possible to permanently change the rule. You can use your actions as an example of why the rule is obsolete. Experiments such as "Share an Impediment Newsletter throughout the Organization" and "Use Formal and Informal Networks to Drive Change" from Chapter 10 can help you get started.

Our Findings

- The goal of this experiment is not to create rebellious teams that disrupt everyone's work and cause harm, but to challenge obsolete rules that impede success. Don't choose actions that benefit only your team and not the organization.
- Don't cause lasting harm to individuals or the organization; choose a gentler way to question the rule than to simply break it.

EXPERIMENTS TO ENCOURAGE SELF-ORGANIZATION

Self-organization happens when the people who are doing the work develop their own rules and ways of working to deal with local challenges. These local solutions are more attuned to the challenges that teams face and more likely to work than solutions that are invented by others or copied from elsewhere. But teams often struggle to come up with high-quality local solutions until they become confident in their ability to make decisions for themselves. The following experiments help build that confidence.

FIND A MINIMUM SET OF RULES FOR SELF-ORGANIZATION

As we explored in Chapter 11, self-organization is the process by which rules spontaneously emerge when self-managing teams work together. A very small number of highly essential rules is better than having many inessential rules. You can facilitate the process of identifying these essential rules with the following experiment. It is based on the Liberating Structure "Min Specs."[3]

Effort/Impact Ratio

Effort	★★★★☆	This experiment requires tight facilitation and some effort to draw in everyone who is involved with the work done by the Scrum Teams.
Impact on survival	★★★★★	Just as swarms of birds can create beautiful shapes in the air by following a few rules, the same applies to Scrum Teams and how they work together.

Steps

To try this experiment, do the following:

1. Invite all Scrum Teams that are working on a specific product. Also include people that the teams depend on or people who benefit from the work done by the teams, such as stakeholders, management, and related departments. The purpose of the gathering is to clarify the rules that must be followed in order to be successful with Scrum.
2. A time box of two hours should be sufficient. Set the stage by clarifying the challenge: "What rules are absolutely essential for us to work together to deliver one integrated and Done Increment every Sprint?"
3. Invite everyone to take a few minutes for themselves and write down the rules—both large and small—that are necessary to achieve the challenge. Write rules as "We must . . ." or "We must not . . ." (two minutes). Then ask people to form small groups (three to five people) and combine their lists into one longer list (fifteen minutes). These are the "Max Specs." With the whole group, ask for some examples to spread ideas (five minutes).

3. Lipmanowicz and McCandless, *The Surprising Power of Liberating Structures.*

4. Reiterate the challenge so that it's fresh in everyone's mind.
5. Ask people to take a look at the list created in their small groups. In silence, let them test each item against the challenge (two minutes). Is it possible to achieve the challenge if that rule is broken or ignored? After a few minutes, encourage people to move their thinking into their small groups and work together to reduce the list to the smallest number (fifteen minutes). Remove rules where breaking or ignoring them doesn't prevent the group from achieving the challenge. Also remove or reformulate rules that are not clear about what they require in terms of behavior (e.g., "We must communicate more" or "We must work in a trusting environment"). Collect the remaining "Min Specs" and debrief them together.
6. You can run another reduction round on the collected "Min Specs" when you or the group feels that it can be trimmed down further. In that case, ask the small groups to consider the list of collected "Min Specs" and repeat the same steps.
7. Capture the resulting "Min Specs" as a set of essential rules for collaboration. Repeat this experiment periodically to update the rules. You can follow up with the experiment "Express Clear Requests for Help" elsewhere in this chapter to clearly express needs from the people involved in maintaining the rule.

Our Findings

- Teams are often tempted to come up with many rules. Their goal should be to identify the smallest possible number, which is more challenging than it sounds. We find that formulating three to five rules is a good goal for this exercise. The essential rules should be so important and specific that people will spring into action immediately when they are violated.
- The Liberating Structure "Min Specs" is ideally suited for helping groups identify rules for collaboration. You can apply it to challenges such as "As management, what rules must we follow in order to support our Scrum Teams?" or "As a Scrum Team, what rules must we follow in order to successfully achieve our Sprint Goal every Sprint?"

Express Clear Requests for Help

It's easy to complain when you don't get what you need from others, but how clear was your request? How clear was the actual response? It isn't easy to clearly express what you need from others to be successful, and it isn't easy to give a clear response when you are the recipient of such a request.

Vague communication can easily lead to frustration and blaming, and that's unfortunate, because self-managing teams often need a lot from others to be successful. The following experiment gives teams the opportunity to clearly express requests for help and give an unambiguous answer to the requests that come their way. It establishes more effective communication patterns that make a lasting impact. It is based on the Liberating Structure "What I Need from You."[4]

Effort/Impact Ratio

Effort	★★★★☆	This experiment requires tight facilitation. You may experience tension as this experiment makes things real (in a good way).
Impact on survival	★★★★★	This experiment is helpful in the moment but can have a lasting impact on how people communicate within the organization.

Steps

To try this experiment, do the following:

1. Invite the Scrum Team(s) and the other functions that contribute directly or indirectly to releasing a Done Product Increment. This can include maintenance or infrastructure teams, human resources, marketing, or management. Explain that the goal is for each function to ask others for things they need in order to be successful. They will then receive a clear response to whether that request can be met or not.

4. Lipmanowicz and McCandless, *The Surprising Power of Liberating Structures.*

2. Ask the participants to form groups corresponding to the function in which they normally work. A Scrum Team is one group, human resources is another group, and so on.
3. Ask the participants to make a list of their top needs from each of the other functions in the room. Invite them to do this first individually (one minute), then mixed in pairs (two minutes), then in groups of four (four minutes). Finally, have people gather with others from their group or function and reduce their collective needs to only the two most important ones (ten minutes). These requests are written in the form of "What I need from you is . . ." and should address a specific other group. Give the groups additional time to discuss and refine their requests, about five to ten minutes depending on their size. Ask them to be clear and unambiguous.
4. Ask each function to select a spokesperson and invite them into a circle in the middle. Each spokesperson states their top two needs to the relevant spokespersons from other functions. When a need is addressed to a group, its spokesperson takes notes but doesn't answer. It's important that there is no discussion or clarification.
5. When every request has been made, the spokespersons return to their groups and discuss what their answer is to each request. Answers are purposefully limited to "Yes," "No," or "Huh? (We don't understand your request.)."
6. The spokespersons gather in the circle again. One by one, each of them repeats the requests that were made to them and their answer. Again, there is no discussion and no elaboration.
7. Depending on the situation, you can do additional rounds of making requests and giving answers. The goal is to make (painfully) clear how crucial it is to be specific when asking for help. That's why we usually stop after one round. However, there are moments when the group has understood the concept clearly and being able to make another request might help them make a big leap forward. In this case, the benefits of doing another round outweigh the need for discipline and rigor.

Our Findings

- The goal of this experiment is to practice making precise requests and giving unambiguous answers. This is not a place for discussion. If requests are unclear, it is a sign that the group needs to work on being clearer in their communication.

- Some tension during this experiment is natural as groups express clear requests and (finally) get clear answers. Recognize that tension and accept it when it happens.
- Encourage participants to continue communicating their needs outside of this gathering using the same format. If a request was not understood or denied, try asking differently.
- If you see members of a group complaining about and blaming other people, ask them what it is they need specifically and whether they have communicated this need adequately.

Observe What Is Happening

Inexperienced Scrum Masters often rush to solve problems, offer suggestions, and show the path forward. While this can be helpful, it can also impede a team's ability to learn and grow, and undermine their ability to self-organize. This experiment is designed for Scrum Masters to find a better balance between solving problems and enabling growth and autonomy.

Effort/Impact Ratio

Effort	★★★☆☆	The difficulty depends on your ability to sit on your hands. Most Scrum Masters are eager to help, and that makes this difficult.
Impact on survival	★★★★☆	Being able to observe the system of the Scrum Team is a great way to start seeing bigger impediments.

Steps

To try this experiment, do the following:

1. At the start of a Sprint, ask for permission from the team to step back from this Sprint. This is a good moment to talk about self-organization and how you can get in the way of that. As a Scrum Master, you still participate in the various events, but not actively. No facilitation, no

making suggestions or taking the lead. You remain available to answer questions or help when the team is stuck.

2. During the Sprint, observe what is happening as the team does its work. Use the list as described in the next section as inspiration. Whenever you observe something, don't jump to conclusions or interpretations. Instead, ask yourself what you are specifically seeing or hearing.
3. In the Sprint Retrospective, explore what it was like for your team to have you in a passive role. What became possible because of it? Where did they notice self-organization?
4. If the team is up for this, you can share your factual observations during the Sprint Retrospective. For example, say "I see that seven out of ten items are 'In Progress' on the first day of the Sprint" or "I noticed that the Daily Scrum usually starts five to eight minutes later as people have to wait for others to join." Give your team the first opportunity to recognize and make sense of the observations, then share your own observations in a constructive way. What has the team learned about their work together? Which impediments have you noticed?
5. Use other experiments in this book to analyze and resolve the impediments that you discover. Use your observations to drive the open questions you ask during the Sprint. A well-timed powerful question, built on observations, can create huge insights that would otherwise take months to discover. For example: "This Sprint, we never interacted with our stakeholders. How does this align with our goal to build a valuable product for them?"

Here are some things you can pay attention to in your observations:

- What do interactions on the team look like? Who is often talking? Who is not?
- What usually happens when someone on the team suggests something? Is it considered? Ignored? Criticized? Expanded on with additional ideas?
- What does the flow of work look like during a Sprint? How much work is in progress on a given day of the Sprint? What kind of items tend to remain in their column for a long time? Who notices this?

- What impact do dependencies have on the team? When do they happen? What do they look like? How long do they have to wait in order to continue?
- What is the atmosphere like during a Sprint? Are people laughing or smiling? Are there strong emotional responses? Do people work with others or mostly alone?
- What happens when the team runs into problems? Who takes the initiative to resolve them? Who is involved and who isn't? Is it always the same person taking the lead? Do they explore different options and then pick one, or do they go straight to a solution?
- How does the Development Team interact with the Product Owner? How often is the Product Owner present? What kind of questions does the Product Owner get? And what kind of answers are given? What considerations does a Product Owner use in deciding how to order the Product Backlog? Is the Development Team involved in this?
- How does the team organize and coordinate its work? What kinds of decisions are made during the Daily Scrum?
- How does the team interact with its environment? How often do they interact with other Scrum Teams? How often are they interrupted by people walking in with requests?

Our Findings

- The skill to observe what is happening is also one for the Development Team to learn. You can experiment with rotating the role. The "observer" still does their work but takes a passive role during gatherings.
- It can be hard to sit on your hands when you're used to taking the lead. Especially when you notice that the team is struggling. Trust in their ability to figure things out. The flip side is also true: don't sit on your hands all the time. Scrum Masters have a lot of work to do when they want to help entire organizations work empirically. Consider this experiment as taking a breather and using that time to inform your next steps.

- This experiment requires that the team trusts you as a Scrum Master. Otherwise, observation will feel like spying. Be very clear about the purpose of your observations and that you share them only with the team. If trust is low, start with other experiments to build that trust. Or practice the role of observer for a single Scrum Event first.

EXPERIMENTS TO PROMOTE SELF-ALIGNMENT

The work of teams usually takes place in a broader organizational environment. Some form of alignment with work done elsewhere is often needed. Instead of the traditional approaches that rely on centralized management and top-down control, self-organization benefits from a process of self-alignment. Here, teams and individuals align themselves based on valuable goals and what is happening in their environment. The following experiments make this more concrete.

CREATE BETTER SPRINT GOALS WITH POWERFUL QUESTIONS

A Sprint Goal helps Scrum Teams self-organize their collaboration. The Sprint Goal also clarifies the purpose and value of the work on this Sprint. It gives flexibility to the Scrum Team to change their Sprint Backlog as needed in response to sudden changes. But creating clear goals is something many teams struggle with, especially in Zombie Scrum environments. This experiment offers ten powerful questions to help your Scrum Team create clear Sprint Goals.

Effort/Impact Ratio

Effort	★★☆☆☆	All you need to do is ask the questions and see how the team answers them. Having the team actually do something with the outcome can take the most effort.
Impact on survival	★★★★☆	You can really boost self-organization with clear Sprint Goals.

Steps

To try this experiment, do the following:

1. Print the questions, as described next, on index cards and take them with you to the various Scrum Events.
2. Invite people to ask one of the questions, or ask one yourself as an example, when the Scrum Team is considering what to focus on for the coming Sprint. Some questions are helpful to start creating the Sprint Goal while others are helpful when the team has one in mind, but it isn't clear enough yet.
   - If we were paying for this Sprint with our own money, what work would give us the highest chance to get that money back?
   - When we achieve this Sprint Goal, what has clearly changed or improved from the perspective of stakeholders?
   - If we didn't have another Sprint after this one because we ran out of money or time, what would be the one thing we'd still have to do in order to deliver at least some value?
   - If we just canceled the next Sprint and went on vacation, what would be inevitably lost or become much harder later?
   - Which steps are required to achieve this Sprint Goal? Which are the least required or could we do without if we really had to?
   - If we suddenly had half the team available and we could only do half the work required for the Sprint Goal, what should absolutely be on our Sprint Backlog to still be okay with the outcome? What could we let go of for now and return to later?
   - If there's an "and" in the Sprint Goal (that is, if the goal consists of more than one thing to achieve): Which would you naturally do first if you had to choose? What is irrevocably lost if we do that thing first and the second thing in another Sprint?
   - What would need to happen while working on this Sprint Goal that would be cause for celebration?
   - What worry about our product is keeping you up at night? What can we build or test this Sprint to make you sleep a bit better?

- In terms of value and learning about what else is needed from us as a team, what is the worst way to spend the upcoming Sprint? What should we focus on this Sprint to prevent that?

You may discover that these questions won't immediately offer you an answer because of constraints in your environment. How do you answer them when you are working on multiple products at the same time? Or when your Product Owner has no say in what order to implement work? Or when your Scrum Team is unable to deliver working software within a single Sprint? You should not focus on how to craft Sprint Goals within those constraints, but explore the impact of those constraints on your ability to work empirically.

As it turns out, struggling to craft Sprint Goals is a clear sign that you may need to improve elsewhere. Sprint Goals help a Scrum Team to find the impediments that are truly getting in your way.

Our Findings

- Ask for permission from the Scrum Team to run this experiment. When possible, do it together. Learning to think about coming Sprints in the light of these questions is a vital skill for teams to acquire.
- Don't fall into the trap of postponing the use of Sprint Goals until you've removed all the constraints that are making it hard. Imperfect Sprint Goals are still better than no goals. Without Sprint Goals, the implicit goal usually becomes to just complete everything on the Sprint Backlog. That doesn't give any flexibility to the team nor does it clarify the purpose and value of the work. Instead, it implicitly signals to teams to put their blinders on and work as fast as possible. It undermines the ability of a team to self-organize their collaboration around a common goal.

Use a Physical Scrum Board

In Chapter 11, we explored how stigmergy is a form of self-organization where coordination happens spontaneously by the traces that people leave in their environment. This may sound abstract, but it is remarkably applicable to Scrum Teams. In this experiment, we offer a great way to encourage stigmergy on the team level (see Figure 12.3).

Effort/Impact Ratio

Effort	★★☆☆☆	All this experiment requires is to set up a physical Scrum Board, together. Encouraging people to give it a try can take some effort.
Impact on survival	★★★☆☆	This experiment boosts self-organization on your team.

Steps

To try this experiment, do the following:

1. Together with your team, pick an empty wall or window in your team room and create a physical Scrum Board based on your Sprint Backlog. Use your preferred approach to structure your Scrum Board. We like to start with a column that holds the items on the Sprint Backlog on large index cards. Each item in the first column essentially gets its own row. The second column contains smaller cards to hold the actions needed to complete an item in the first column. Further columns represent the steps in the workflow of your team, for example, "To Do," "Coding," "Testing," and "Done."
2. Add a set of visual markers to signal important information. We often use red magnets to mark items that are blocked. You can use green magnets to mark items in the first column that are Done. Another idea is to give everyone on the team one unique avatar marker to add to the item they are actively working on.
3. Add your Definition of Done next to your Scrum Board and the Sprint Goal as a banner above it.
4. Add other elements that help your team coordinate their work. You may be tempted to throw everything you have at the wall. But keep in mind that it needs to be maintained in order to work. Also, your wall is best used for traces that are updated frequently during a Sprint and are so clear that seeing them tells you what to do next. The workflow for doing a release and your team's vacation planning are better kept elsewhere.

5. Together, update the board throughout the Sprint. Help your team use the board by drawing attention to it when something happens (e.g., an item becomes blocked or is completed). Set the example by writing clear items and helping others do the same.
6. Use your Sprint Retrospective to reflect on how you are using the Scrum Board. Specifically, look for ways to improve the actionability of the items you make transparent on it.

Figure 12.3 Create a tailor-made physical Scrum Board together with your Scrum Team.

You can add other actionable traces to your team room, such as the following:

- The status of a build pipeline
- Process metrics that are frequently updated and inform decisions about what to work on next (e.g., "work in progress" or wait time on urgent issues)
- Status indicators for important services that your team maintains

Nothing beats a physical Scrum Board when it comes to stigmergy. There are no constraints on how or what you display on it. The mere act of getting up to move a card to another column is a stigmergic action as it signals that something is ready for the next step. If you don't want to waste paper with stickies, you can also use writable sticky-size magnets. If your team is adamant about a digital board, make sure to have a big, movable monitor in the room to display it on.

Our Findings

- Initially, people may struggle to see the benefit of a physical Scrum Board compared to a digital one. This is a good opportunity to talk about stigmergy with your team and how it promotes self-organization. Give this experiment a try for a couple of Sprints and then decide what works best for your team.
- The book *96 Visualization Examples: How Great Teams Visualize Their Work*[5] by Jimmy Janlén is a great source of other examples.

Find Local Solutions

Although self-organization happens on individual teams, it becomes progressively more powerful as the scale increases. Also, some of the challenges that teams face may be so difficult that they can't figure out a solution on their own. The following experiments create an environment for getting help and for devising local solutions together.

Organize Scrum Master Impediment Gatherings

Scrum Masters are there to help their team *and* the entire organization understand and work empirically. This is hard, especially in environments infected with Zombie Scrum. We always start by bringing together the Scrum Masters to see where they can help and support each other. This experiment helps you do that. It is based on the Liberating Structure "Wise Crowds."[6]

5. Janlén, J. 2015. *96 Visualization Examples: How Great Teams Visualize Their Work*. Leanpub.
6. Lipmanowicz and McCandless, *The Surprising Power of Liberating Structures*.

Effort/Impact Ratio

Effort	★★☆☆☆	Getting your Scrum Masters together at least once a Sprint—even virtually—shouldn't be too difficult.
Impact on survival	★★★★☆	When Scrum Masters start working together, self-organization tends to take off across the organization.

Steps

To try this experiment, do the following:

1. Invite all Scrum Masters in your organization for the first "Scrum Master Impediment Gathering." Schedule an hour, remotely or in person. Once per Sprint is a good starting point, preferably after the Sprint Retrospectives so that impediments are fresh in mind. Be clear that the purpose is to resolve tough impediments. Ask everyone to bring their most difficult impediments, preferably those that transcend a single team.
2. The first step is to identify the most important patterns on which to focus this gathering. Ask everyone to pair up with someone else and take a few minutes to share their most urgent impediments (two minutes). Repeat this two more times in changing pairs (four minutes). Afterwards, capture the most obvious patterns noticed by the group (five minutes).
3. Ask everyone to pull up a chair and sit in a (large) circle. In the next steps, pick two or three Scrum Masters who will be getting help with their impediments. Each round, one of them is the client and the other participants are the consultants. Pick impediments that correspond to the patterns you noticed as a group.
4. The client shares their impediment and request for help (two minutes). The consultants ask open-ended, clarifying questions (three minutes). Then ask the client to turn their back to the consultants. Or turn the webcam off in a remote call. While the client has their back turned, the consultants talk among themselves by asking questions, offering suggestions, and giving recommendations to help the client. In the meantime, the client gives their best impression of a statute and only takes notes (eight minutes). Then the client turns back to the consultants and shares what was useful (two minutes).

5. Move to the next client. You have time for two or three rounds. Other Scrum Masters and impediments can be the focus for a subsequent gathering.
6. Capture action steps with "Create 15% Solutions" (Chapter 10). Consultants usually also get a lot of inspiration for their own team. Action steps can also involve helping others.

Our Findings

- The experiments "Use Formal and Informal Networks to Drive Change," "Dig Deeper into Problems and Potential Solutions, Together," "Create 15% Solutions," and "Create Improvement Recipes" from Chapter 10 are very useful when you want to spend a gathering digging deeper into specific, recurring impediments.
- Even when it feels awkward, make sure that the client has their back fully turned to the consultants during the third step of each round (that's number 4 in the preceding list of steps). The slightest facial expression from the client can influence the consultants in the ideas they're offering.
- You can also use this experiment for developers, architects, managers, and other roles. Or mixed together. There is a smaller variation called "Troika Consulting,"[7] where groups of three give and get help. Here, one person is the client and others become consultants. In three rounds, each participant gets to be the client once.

Develop Local Solutions with Open Space Technology

Organizations that suffer from Zombie Scrum often rely on solutions and best practices that may have worked elsewhere but are not tuned to the local challenges and environments. You can spur the development of localized solutions by providing people with space and time to work on overcoming shared challenges together.

7. Lipmanowicz and McCandless, *The Surprising Power of Liberating Structures.*

Open Space Technology[8] is a great way to do this. The agenda is created by the participants. People go where they feel they can contribute the most. Its self-organizing nature makes Open Space Technology a great way to learn self-organization. In this experiment we outline an abbreviated version and give options to make it more effective.

Effort/Impact Ratio

Effort	★★★☆☆	Open Space Technology works best when as many people as possible participate. This constitutes a considerable investment of time.
Impact on survival	★★★★☆	Frequent Open Spaces can transform an organization.

Steps

To try this experiment, do the following:

1. Invite the entire organization or a subset to an Open Space session that lasts anywhere from a couple of hours to several days. The invitation for an Open Space should always be on an opt-in basis. Open Spaces work best in large spaces or venues with a lot of smaller rooms. Prepare by creating a grid for the marketplace and providing stickies, markers, flip charts, and chairs.
2. Introduce the concept and mechanics of Open Space. Participants are free to vote with their feet by joining the session that is most useful to them, or leaving one that they can't contribute to. This is called the "Law of Two Feet." Furthermore, four essential rules maximize self-organization: (1) Whoever comes are the right people, (2) whenever it starts is the right time, (3) whatever happens is the only thing that could have, and (4) when it's over, it's over.
3. Introduce the core topic for the Open Space. Broad topics such as "What are current challenges we need to work on?", "How can we increase the

8. Harrison, O. H. 2008. *Open Space Technology: A User's Guide*. Berrett-Koehler Publishers. ASN: 978-1576754764.

autonomy of our teams?" or "How do we make progress with our Zombie Scrum situation?" work better than narrow topics.

4. Open the marketplace. Participants are invited to propose challenges or topics they want to explore with others along with a time and location where the session is going to take place. Display the sessions on a prominent timetable. Session proposers are also the ones initiating it, but they don't need to have experience with the topic.
5. Sessions take place at the scheduled time and at the specified place.
6. If it makes sense, you can ask the participants of each session to give a brief overview of the results or to publish them in a virtual space.

Our Findings

- You can support session proposers by having a group of volunteers ready to facilitate the session. This is especially helpful in sessions with marked power imbalances between participants. These imbalances often manifest between hierarchical layers, for example, and can drastically affect the discussion.
- A common pitfall of Open Spaces is that sessions devolve into unstructured group conversations where loud voices dominate. Or the session proposer takes the entire time slot to "broadcast information" without tapping into the knowledge and experience of those present. You can overcome this by making use of Liberating Structures such as "What, So What, Now What?", "Discovery and Action Dialogue," "1-2-4-All," and "15% Solutions." Make sure that every session has materials to capture people's insights (e.g., flips, stickies, and so on).

Now What?

In this chapter, we explored experiments that help your teams increase their autonomy and take responsibility for their own way of working. It is the final piece of the puzzle in this *Zombie Scrum Survival Guide*. Self-organization is a great catalyst that helps you build what stakeholders need, ship it fast, and improve continuously. When you create space for it to occur, the local solutions that emerge can drive lifelessness away and speed up your progress towards full recovery.

"Looking for more experiments, recruit? There is an extensive arsenal available at ***zombiescrum.org****. You can also help expand our arsenal by suggesting what worked well for you."*

13 The Road to Recovery

Everything's going to be okay.

—Carl Grimes,
The Walking Dead

In This Chapter

- Finalize your traineeship for the Zombie Scrum Resistance.
- Discover more resources that help on your road to recovery.
- Find others, work together, and overcome Zombie Scrum.

You've reached the end of the *Zombie Scrum Survival Guide*. Throughout the book, we've covered the most common symptoms and causes of Zombie Scrum. By now, you should have a clear understanding of how Zombie Scrum and healthy Scrum may seem similar on the surface but are wholly different upon closer inspection. This knowledge will help you focus your actions on areas where your efforts produce the greatest results, such as actually involving stakeholders, shipping faster, and helping your teams to manage their own work. It also shows you where and how transparency can help you to build urgency for change, such as showing how long cycle times make it hard for teams to respond to urgent changes. But while knowledge helps you understand what to change, you must convert that knowledge into decisive action to improve performance. We've offered lots of things to think about, and many experiments to try. In this final chapter, we give you one last push on your team's road to recovery.

"Congratulations, Recruit! You've made it to the end of your training. But the adventure really starts when you put everything into practice."

A Global Movement

Congratulations! You are now a full-fledged member of the Zombie Scrum Resistance. We are a global movement that aims to support teams and organizations on their road of recovery. You are not alone in your journey. Here are some tips to benefit from the movement and to contribute to it:

- Start an internal "Zombie Scrum Meetup." Read this book with people in your organization who share your belief that more is possible with the Scrum Framework. You can use the experiment "Start a Book Club" (available on the **zombiescrum.org** website) as inspiration for how to do this.
- Start a regional Zombie Scrum Resistance meetup to bring people from different organizations together. Work together to try different experiments from this book, refine them, and develop more. A meetup is a great place to support each other.
- Share your experiences with Zombie Scrum online. In particular, share what you tried, what worked, and what didn't. Honest stories are sources of inspiration for others. You can share your experiences on social media, with a video, or with a blog post.

What If Nothing Helps?

You have to be realistic. Not every organization is able or willing to recover from Zombie Scrum. In the group of people that make up your organization, persistent beliefs, existing structures, and power imbalances may make it hard to change anything outside of your team, or even on your own team. Especially when you are unable to find enough like-minded people. What can you do if nothing helps? What if you find yourself increasingly frustrated with your inability to effect even small, local changes?

We, too, have been part of organizations in which every hard-won forward step was met with fierce resistance. In the end, there's only so much you can do on your own. When you've reached the peak of what you can feasibly do, and you still can't change anything, you can easily slide into cynicism and negativity. This is what often happens when people who are excited about the possibilities of the Scrum Framework don't see their excitement reflected in others.

Take it from us: after trying many times and in many different ways, at some point, defeat is inevitable. There's no shame in that. And acceptance is also healthier for your state of mind. What this looks like depends on your situation. In some cases, we abandoned the Scrum Framework and reverted to the organization's prior status quo. Though far from ideal, we worked on areas in which we still exercised control—such as technical quality. In other cases, we resumed our efforts when we found a new ally in a colleague with a different style. And yes, in some cases we left for organizations that were more aligned with our ideas.

Your vision for your team or organization may not always be shared. Sometimes the best you can do is to work hard and try many different approaches to help people see possibilities. Something you can always do is join the Zombie Scrum Resistance. There's a large, passionate, and enthusiastic community eager to give you support and guidance. Join the community and fight Zombie Scrum, together!

MORE RESOURCES

If you're eager to start your journey after this book, the following resources are helpful:

- We've created a free digital Zombie Scrum First Aid Kit. It contains helpful materials for some of the experiments in this book, as well as other useful exercises. Download it at **zombiescrum.org/firstaidkit**. You can also order a physical copy there.
- The survey at **survey.zombiescrum.org** is available to diagnose your team or organization for Zombie Scrum. The survey is free and can be used as anonymously as you want. Both the survey and the feedback you receive afterward are continuously refined as we learn more from the analysis of the data. We are working with universities to develop this research and publish results in peer-reviewed journals.
- Our website **zombiescrum.org** is the central hub for the Zombie Scrum Resistance. Here you can find many more experiments, a listing of regional meetups, and guides for starting one yourself. We also share experiences from the field.
- The website **scrumguides.org** has the most up-to-date version of the official Scrum Guide available. The Scrum Guide is periodically inspected and adapted by its founders, Ken Schwaber and Jeff Sutherland, together with the global community of Scrum practitioners.
- **Scrum.org** (that's the web address too) is an established authority for developing your understanding of the Scrum Framework further. Scrum.org was founded by Ken Schwaber, one of the creators of the Scrum Framework.

CLOSING WORDS

We started this book with a serious message: Zombie Scrum has spread on a global scale and threatens the existence of many large and small organizations. For every team that successfully uses the Scrum Framework, two others struggle to make it work. And it's easy to see why. The purpose of the Scrum

Framework can be broken down into four interlocking areas: build what stakeholders need, ship results fast, improve continuously based on what you learn, and self-organize around impediments. This is the single best way to reduce the risk of complex work *and* become more responsive to your stakeholders. That is what agility is about.

Yet these areas are different from how work is often organized. This disconnect causes friction and impediments to the ability of teams to respond quickly to change. We've seen many examples of these problems throughout this book. The Scrum Framework helps overcome impediments by asking teams to follow one single rule: Create a releasable Done Increment every Sprint. If no effort is spared to help teams do this, all impediments to agility *will* eventually dissolve.

Zombie Scrum rears its ugly head when teams are consistently unable to follow this rule and nobody tries to improve. As a result, any change remains superficial. It looks like Scrum from a distance, but it doesn't create agility of any kind.

Our aim with this book was to use the perspective of Zombie Scrum to build a deep understanding of the purpose of the Scrum Framework. We also shared more than forty practical, hands-on experiments to start recovering from Zombie Scrum.

As a full member of the Zombie Scrum Resistance, it's now up to you to put what you've learned into practice (see Figure 13.1). Find others, work together, and overcome Zombie Scrum. We know you can!

Figure 13.1 All the best on your journey towards recovery. Although it may seem lonely and difficult at times, you are not alone in your desire to create better workplaces.

Index

N

O

P

Q

R

S

U-V

W

X-Y-Z